Advanced Android 4 Games

Vladimir Silva

Apress®

Advanced Android 4 Games

Copyright © 2012 by Vladimir Silva

ISBN-13 (pbk): 978-1-4302-4059-4

ISBN-13 (electronic): 978-1-4302-4060-0

Trademarked names, logos, and images may appear in this book. Rather than use a trademark symbol with every occurrence of a trademarked name, logo, or image we use the names, logos, and images only in an editorial fashion and to the benefit of the trademark owner, with no intention of infringement of the trademark.

The images of the Android Robot (01 / Android Robot) are reproduced from work created and shared by Google and used according to terms described in the Creative Commons 3.0 Attribution License. Android and all Android and Google-based marks are trademarks or registered trademarks of Google, Inc., in the U.S. and other countries. Apress Media, L.L.C. is not affiliated with Google, Inc., and this book was written without endorsement from Google, Inc.

The use in this publication of trade names, trademarks, service marks, and similar terms, even if they are not identified as such, is not to be taken as an expression of opinion as to whether or not they are subject to proprietary rights.

President and Publisher: Paul Manning
Lead Editor: Steve Anglin
Development Editor: James Markham
Technical Reviewer: Jim Graham and Vikram Goyal
Editorial Board: Steve Anglin, Mark Beckner, Ewan Buckingham, Gary Cornell,
    Morgan Engel, Jonathan Gennick, Jonathan Hassell, Robert Hutchinson,
    Michelle Lowman, James Markham, Matthew Moodie, Jeff Olson, Jeffrey Pepper,
    Douglas Pundick, Ben Renow-Clarke, Dominic Shakeshaft, Gwenan Spearing,
    Matt Wade, Tom Welsh
Coordinating Editor: Jessica Belanger
Copy Editor: Kimberly Burton
Compositor: MacPS, LLC
Cover Designer: Anna Ishchenko

Distributed to the book trade worldwide by Springer Science+Business Media, LLC., 233 Spring Street, 6th Floor, New York, NY 10013. Phone 1-800-SPRINGER, fax (201) 348-4505, e-mail orders-ny@springer-sbm.com, or visit www.springeronline.com.

For information on translations, please e-mail rights@apress.com, or visit www.apress.com.

Apress and friends of ED books may be purchased in bulk for academic, corporate, or promotional use. eBook versions and licenses are also available for most titles. For more information, reference our Special Bulk Sales–eBook Licensing web page at www.apress.com/bulk-sales.

Any source code or other supplementary materials referenced by the author in this text is available to readers at www.apress.com. For detailed information about how to locate your book's source code, go to http://www.apress.com/source-code/.

To all Android developers out there. The future of the platform is in your hands.

Contents at a Glance

Contents.. v

About the Author...xxi

About the Technical Reviewers xxii

Acknowledgment.. xiii

Introduction xiii

■Chapter 1: Welcome to the World of the Little Green Robot 1

■Chapter 2: Gaming Tricks for Phones or Tablets................................... 19

■Chapter 3: More Gaming Tricks with OpenGL and JNI............................ 59

■Chapter 4: Efficient Graphics with OpenGL ES 2.0............................. 113

■Chapter 5: 3D Shooters for Doom 145

■Chapter 6: 3D Shooters for Quake 193

■Chapter 7: 3D Shooters for Quake II.. 233

■Appendix: Deployment and Compilation Tips 261

Index.. 271

Contents

Contents at a Glance iv

About the Author xxi

About the Technical Reviewers xxii

Acknowledgment xxiii

Introduction xxiii

▓ Chapter 1: Welcome to the World of the Little Green Robot 1

Setting Up Your Machine 1

Download and Install the SDK 2

Configure your Eclipse 2

Installing the Native Development Kit 9

    NDK Install 10

    Install Cygwin 10

Creating an Android Emulator 10

    Creating an AVD 11

Configuring a Real Device 15

Summary 17

Gaming Tricks for Phones or Tablets 19

Compiling Native Code in Android 19

    Creating the Android Project with Native Support 21

    Application Architecture 23

Compiling the Shared Library 34

Testing the App on a Device 35

Java Wrappers for C/C++ Event Handling 38

    Handling Audio Independently 38

    Cascading Video Events 43

Multitouch Tricks 48

    MultiTouchGesture 48

    MultiTouchScreen 50

    TestActivity 52

Bluetooth Controllers (Zeemote) 53

Summary 58

More Gaming Tricks with OpenGL and JNI 59

The Power of Mobile Devices..60
OpenGL the Java Way 61
    Creating a Project 62
    Java Main Activity..67
    Surface View 68
    GL Thread 71
    Cube Renderer 74
    Cube Class 77
OpenGL the Native Way 80
    Main Activity 82
    Native Interface Class 84
    Changes to the Original Sample 85
    Native Cube Renderer 87
    Native Cube..93
    Compiling and Running the Sample 94
Scaling Video Buffers with Hybrid OpenGL ES 99
    Why Use Hybrid Scaling? 99
    Initializing the Surface 102
    Drawing into the Texture 103
    What Happens when the Image is not a Power of Two 106
Summary 111

Efficient Graphics with OpenGL ES 2.0 113

OpenGL ES 2.0 and Android 113
    Shaders..114
    GLSL...115
    Anatomy of a Shader 117
Invoking OpenGL ES 2.0 in Android...120
Project Icosahedron 121
    Reviewing the Shape 121
    Tackling the Project 123
    Native Icosahedron 133
Adding Swipe and Multi-Touch Pinch for Zooming..139
Compiling and Running..143
Summary 144

3D Shooters for Doom.. 145

The Sky Is the Limit with the Java/C Power Combo 146
Bringing Doom to a Mobile Device...147
Game Architecture for Doom 149
Java Main Activity...151
    Creation Handler 152
    Game Layout 152
    Menu and Selection Handlers 155
    Key and Touch Event Handlers 157
    Native Callback Handlers...158
    Navigation Controls...162
Handling Audio Independently of the Format..164

Native Interface Class 165
    Callback Listener 165
    Native Methods 166
    C to Java Callbacks 167
Native Layer 169
    Native Method Implementations 170
    Original Game Changes...181
Compiling Doom with the NDK 187
Testing Doom in the Emulator 189
Summary 192

3D Shooters for Quake... **193**
A Little About the Quake Jargon 193
The Power of Code Reuse: Quake in Less Than 500 Lines of New Code............................195
    OpenGL Is Not the Same as OpenGL ES 195
Is the Software Renderer a Possible Solution?...197
    NanoGL: The Live Saver 197
Quake for Android Architecture 202
    Java OpenGL Renderer Architecture 202
    Handling Audio Independently of the Format...207
    Handling Keyboard Events 210
    Handling Touch Events 212
    Game Startup Activity 214
Changes Required to the Native Quake Engine 216
    Video Handler Changes 216
    Handling Pitch and Yaw 219
    Handling Forward and Side Movement..220
    Audio Handler Changes..220
    Fixing the Game Loop 223
Running on a Device 225
Summary 232

3D Shooters for Quake II **233**
Reviewing the Code 233
Escaping the Shackles of the Java Heap 234
Taming the Mighty Quake II Engine 235
    Code Reusability 236
    What to Do When Fatal Errors Occur 245
    OpenGL Immediate Mode Issues 248
    Video Handlers...248
Building Quake II with the NDK 252
Running on the Device or Emulator 255
Quake II Performance on Multiple Devices 258
Summary 260

Deployment and Compilation Tips **261**
Signing Your Application..261
    Creating a Key Store 262
    Signing the Application 262
JNI Cheat Sheet 267

JNI Method Syntax 268

Loading a Java Class as Global Reference 268

Converting a Java Array to a C array 268

Invoking Java Within C (Callbacks) 269

Final Thoughts 269

Index 271

About the Author

Vladimir Silva was born in Quito, Ecuador. He received a system's analyst degree from Ecuador's Army Polytechnic Institute in 1994. The same year, he came to the United States as an exchange student pursuing a master's degree in computer science at Middle Tennessee State University. After graduation, he joined the IBM WebAhead technology think tank. His interests include grid computing, neural networks, and artificial intelligence. He also holds numerous IT certifications, including Oracle Certified Professional (OCP), Microsoft Certified Solution Developer (MCSD), and Microsoft Certified Professional (MCP). He has written many technical articles on security and grid computing for IBM developerWorks.

About the Technical Reviewers

Vikram Goyal is the author of several Apress books and works from home on several web sites. He currently lives in Brisbane, Australia.

James Graham was born in Alabama and grew up in Fort Walton Beach, Florida, and San Antonio, Texas. He received a BS in electronics with a specialty in telecommunications from Texas A&M University in 1988. He has been an associate network engineer for the Network Design group at Amoco Corporation and an intelligence systems analyst for the US Air Force Special Operations Command. In addition to being an Android developer, he is the author of the highly-rated freeware hurricane tracking program, JStrack.

Acknowledgment

We would like to thank the people at Apress for all their help in making this book possible.

Introduction

Welcome to *Advanced Android 4 Games*. This book will help you create great games for the Android platform. There are plenty of books out there that tackle this subject, but only this book gives you a unique perspective by showing you how easy it is to bring native PC games to the platform with minimum effort. This is done using real-world examples and source code in each chapter. Keep in mind that before you dig into this book, you will need a solid foundation in Java and ANSI C. I have tried to clearly and simply explain the most complicated concepts with a combination of graphics and sample code. The source code provided for each chapter will help you understand the concepts in detail and make the most of your time as a mobile game developer.

The Green Robot Has Taken Off

It is hard to believe that is has been just two years since Android came onto the smartphone scene; and it has taken off with a vengeance. Take a look at the US smartphone platform market share, shown in Figure 1, according to a survey by Nielsen.[1] In May 2011, Android commanded 36 percent of the smartphone market in the United States—not too shabby for a two-year-old OS. And the stats just keep getting better and better. Distimo, an analytics company specializing in app stores, forecasted that Android Market would surpass Apple's App Store in size by August 2011.[2] This opens a new frontier for developers looking to capitalize from the rocketing smartphone segment. *Advanced Android 4 Games* is just what you need to get running quickly in building cutting-edge games for the platform.

---

[1] "Android Leads in U.S. Smartphone Market Share and Data Usage," Nielsen Wire, http://blog.nielsen.com/nielsenwire/?p=27793.

[2] "Android to Surpass Apple's App Store In Size By August 2011," a report by Distimo available at http://techcrunch.com/2011/05/05/android-to-surpass-apples-app-store-in-size-in-august-2011-report-exclusive/.

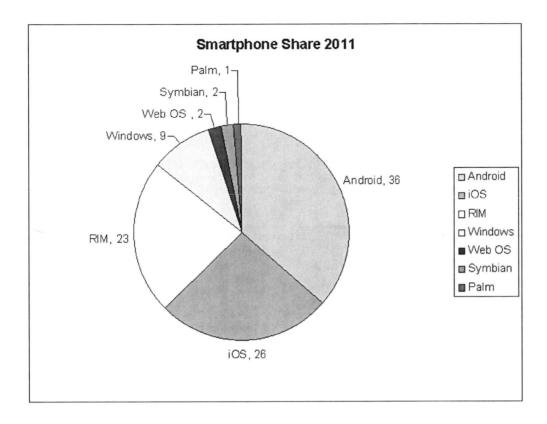

Figure F–1. Smartphone market share, April 2011, Nielsen

Who's the Target Audience?

This book targets seasoned game developers, not only in Java, but also in C. Performance is critical in game development. Other audiences include:

- *Business apps developers.* If you work on native applications, this book can be a valuable tool.

- *Scientific developers.* In the science world, raw performance matters. The chapters dealing with JNI and OpenGL can help you achieve your goals.

- *Computer science students* learning new mobile platforms. Android is open and fairly portable, thus this book can help students in many platforms, including iPhone, Blackberry, and Meego.

- *Anybody interested in Android development.* Android has taken over the mobile market space at a furious pace. You've got to expand your skill set to include games and graphics, or you may be left behind.

Skills Needed to Make the Most of This Book

The required skill set for Pro Android games includes C/C++ and Java, plus some basic LINUX shell scripting. Java provides elegant object-oriented capabilities, but only C gives you the power boost that game development requires. All in all, you must have the skill set described in the following sections.

A Solid Foundation of Android

This book assumes that you already know the basics of Android development; for example, you need to know what activities, views, and layouts are. If you understand what the following fragment does just by looking at it, then you are in good shape.

```
public class MainActivity extends Activity
{
    public void onCreate(Bundle savedInstanceState) {
        super.onCreate(savedInstanceState);
        setContentView(R.layout.main);
    }
}
```

This fragment defines the main activity or class that controls the life cycle of the application. The onCreate method will be called once when the application starts, and its job is to set the content layout or GUI for the application.

You should also have a basic understanding of how GUIs are created using XML. Take a look at the next fragment. Can you tell what it does?

```
<?xml version="1.0" encoding="utf-8"?>
<RelativeLayout
    xmlns:android="http://schemas.android.com/apk/res/android"
    android:layout_width="fill_parent"
    android:layout_height="fill_parent">

<ImageView android:id="@+id/doom_iv"
    android:layout_width="fill_parent"
    android:layout_height="fill_parent"
    android:background="@drawable/doom"
    android:focusableInTouchMode="true" android:focusable="true"/>

  <ImageButton android:id="@+id/btn_upleft"
        android:layout_width="wrap_content"
        android:layout_height="wrap_content"
        android:layout_alignParentBottom="true"
        android:layout_alignParentLeft="true"
        android:src="@drawable/img1" />
</RelativeLayout>
```

This code defines a relative layout. In a relative layout, widgets are placed relative to each other (sometimes overlapping). In this case, there is an image view that fills the entire screen. This image will display as the background the file called doom.png, stored in the res/drawable folder of the project, and receive key and touch events. In the lower left of the screen, overlapping the image view, an image button with the ID btn_upleft will be displayed.

```
┌─────────────────────────────────────────────────────────────────────┐
│                      NEED AN ANDROID TUTORIAL?                         │
└─────────────────────────────────────────────────────────────────────┘
```

There are a lot of concepts related to Android development and it is impossible to remember every detail about activities, views, and layouts. A handy place to access this information quickly is the Android tutorial:

http://developer.android.com/

The ultimate guide for Android developers—the latest releases, downloads, SDK Quick Start, version notes, native development tools, and previous releases—can be found at:

`http://developer.android.com/sdk/1.6_r1/index.html`

Throughout this book (especially in the chapters dealing with native code), I make extensive use of the Android Software Development Kit (SDK) command tools (for system administrator tasks). Thus, you should have a clear understanding of these tools, especially the Android Debug Bridge (adb). You should know how to do the following:

- *Create an Android Virtual Device* (AVD). An AVD encapsulates settings for a specific device configuration, such as firmware version and SD card path. Creating an AVD is really simple and can be done from the integrated development environment (IDE) by using the AVD Manager (accessed by clicking the black phone icon in the toolbar).
- *Create an SD card file*. Some of the games in later chapters have big files (5 MB or more). To save space, the code stores all game files in the device SD card, and you should know how to create one. For example, to create a 100 MB SD card file called sdcard.iso in your home directory, use the following command:

```
$ mksdcard 100M $HOME/sdcard.iso
```

- *Connect to the emulator*. You need to do this for miscellaneous system administration, such as library extraction. To open a shell to the device, use the following command:

```
$ adb shell
```

- *Upload and pull files from the emulator*. These tasks are helpful for storing and extracting game files to and from the device. Use the following commands:

```
$ adb push <LOCAL_FILE> <DEVICE_FILE>
$ adb pull <DEVICE_FILE> <LOCAL_FILE>
```

> **NOTE:** Make sure the SDK_HOME/tools directory is added to your system PATH variable before running the commands to create an SD card file, connect to the emulator, or upload and pull files.

A Basic Knowledge of Linux and Shell Scripting

For the chapters dealing with the hybrid games, you will do the work within Ubuntu Linux, so dust off all those old Unix skills.

You should know the basic shell commands, such as those for listing files, installing software components (this can be tricky, depending on your Linux distribution), and basic system administration.

There are a few very simple shell scripts in this book. A basic knowledge of the bash shell is always helpful.

> **TIP:** If you need a refresher on your Linux and shell scripting, check out the following tutorial by Ashley J.S Mills:
>
> http://supportweb.cs.bham.ac.uk/documentation/tutorials/docsystem/build/tutorials/ unixscripting/unixscripting.html.

What Hardware/Software Will You Need?

To make the most of this book, you will need the tools mentioned in this section.

A Windows or Linux PC with a Java SDK Properly Installed

I guess this is kind of obvious, as most development for Android is done in Java. Note that I mentioned a Java SDK, not JRE. The SDK is required because of the JNI header files and command line tools used throughout the latter chapters.

Eclipse IDE and Android SDK Properly Installed

Eclipse is the de facto IDE for Android development. I have used Eclipse Galileo to create the workspace for the book; nevertheless, Eclipse Ganymede should work as well.

NEED A DEVELOPMENT IDE?

Even though Eclipse Helios has been used to create the code workspace, you can use your favorite IDE; of course, that will require a bit of extra setup. You can get Eclipse from www.eclipse.org/.

For instructions on how to set up the Android SDK with other IDEs, such as IntelliJ or a basic editor, see http://developer.android.com/guide/developing/other-ide.html.

To have the Android SDK properly installed you need to do the following:

1. Install the Android SDK plug-ins for Eclipse:

    *   From the IDE main menu, click **Help ➤ Install New Software**.

    *   Click the Add button to add a new Site and enter:

        A name: Android SDK

A location: https://dl-ssl.google.com/android/eclipse/. Click OK.

- Select the Android SK from the Available Software dialog and follow the easy installation instructions from the wizard.

2. Install the Android SDK. It can be downloaded from the Android site mentioned earlier. Keep in mind that Eclipse must be told about the location of the Android SDK. From the main IDE menu, click **Window ➤ Preferences**. On the left navigation menu, select Android and enter the SDK location (see Figure 2). I used SDK 3.1 because that was the latest available at the time of this writing. Nevertheless, the code in this book has been tested with SDK 2.3 and 3.1 (see the SDK compatibility section for details).

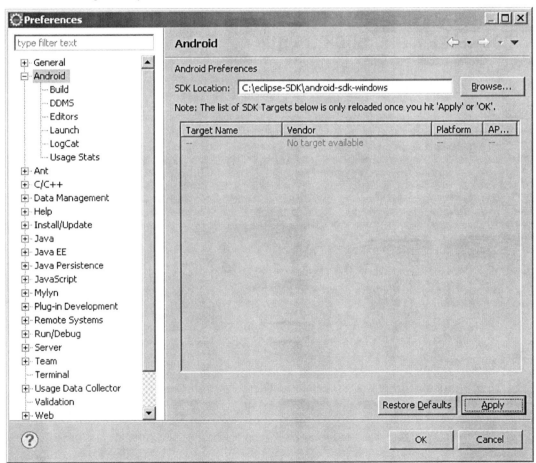

Figure F-2. Android SDK configuration dialog in Eclipse Galileo

Native Development Kit (NDK)

The NDK is the essential tool for any serious game developer out there. It provides the compiler chain, header files, and documentation required to bring your cutting-edge games to the mobile landscape. By using the NDK, developers can escape the shackles of the Java memory heap and unleash their creativity in building the most powerful C/C++ engines, limited only by what the hardware can provide. In this book you will use the NDK extensively, thus a solid foundation of C programming is required to fully understand the concepts presented in each chapter.

Chapter Source

This is an optional tool, but it will help you greatly to understand the concepts as you move along. I have made my best effort to describe each chapter as simply as possible; nevertheless, some of the games (especially *Wolf 3D* and *Doom*) have very large core engines written in C (100 K lines for *Doom*), which are poorly commented and very hard to understand. All in all, you will see how easy these great languages (Java and C) can be combined with minimal effort. Get the companion source for the book at www.apress.com. It was built using the latest Eclipse SDK.

What Makes This Book Unique?

I think it is important for the reader to understand my goal with this manuscript and what I believe sets this book apart. Even though Java is the primary development language for Android, Google has realized the need for hybrid Java/C development if Android is to succeed as a gaming platform; so much so that they released the Native Development Kit (NDK). I think that Google has been wise to support C development; otherwise, it would be left behind by the overwhelming number of native games written for other mobile platforms, like the iPhone.
PC games have been around for decades (mostly written in C), and by using a simple ARM C compiler, you could potentially bring thousands of PC games to the Android platform. This is what makes this book unique. Why translate 100 K lines of painfully complicated code from C to Java if you can just combine both languages in an elegant manner—and save yourself lots of time and money in the process? This is my goal and what makes this book stand out. Although, the book does include chapters with pure Java games, presented in a well-balanced layout to satisfy both the Java purist and the C lover in you.

What's Changed Since the Last Edition?

With the relentless pace of Android updates, many things have changed since the last iteration of this book, *Pro Android Games*. These changes include the following:

- *Updates to the latest versions* of the Android SDK, the Native Development Kit (NKD), and the Eclipse IDE.

- *Greater focus on tablets*. People are hungry for bigger screens and higher resolutions. Tablets are growing, my friends, and we must watch out for ever-changing device resolutions and hardware specs.

- *Greater focus on the native side*. I think is fair to say that Java has fallen from grace with the 3D game developers, especially the powerful ones. Java's memory constraints and lack of performance are the main culprits. Therefore, Pro Android Games puts greater emphasis on native game development and hardware-accelerated graphics.

- *Bigger and better real-world engines*. My goal is not to simply offer you some tricks to develop games, but to provide you real, powerful, bigger-than-life samples. This book will show you how powerful PC-caliber game engines such as *Quake I* and *II* can be brought to your mobile device with almost no changes whatsoever. It will also include Doom, an oldie from the previous edition.

Android SDK Compatibility

As a developer, you may ask yourself about the SDK compatibility of the code in this book. This is an important question as new versions of the Android SDK come out frequently. At the time of this writing, Google released Android SDK version 3.2. The code in this chapter has been fully tested with Android SDK versions 4.0 and 3.1.

The bottom line is that the code in this book will run in any version of the SDK and that was my intention all along.

This book has a well-balanced layout of very powerful hybrid games, divided by chapter.

Chapter 1

This chapter provides the first step to set up a Linux system for hybrid game compilation, including fetching the Android source, extracting device system libraries, setting up a custom compilation tool chain, custom compilation scripts, and details on setting up the Eclipse IDE for use throughout the rest of the book.

Chapter 2

In Chapter 2 you will learn how to combine Java and C code in an elegant manner by building a simple Java application on top of a native library. You will learn exciting concepts about the Java Native Interface (JNI) and the API used to combine Java and C in a single unit, including how to load native libraries, how to use the native keyword, how to generate the JNI headers, as well as method signatures, Java arrays vs. C arrays, invoking Java methods, compiling and packing the product, and more.

Chapter 3

This chapter deals with 3D graphics with OpenGL. It presents a neat trick that allows for mixing OpenGL API calls in both Java and C. This concept is illustrated by using the 3D cubes sample provided by Google to demonstrate OpenGL in pure Java and hybrid modes. This trick could open a new frontier of 3D development for Android, with the potential to bring a large number of 3D PC games to the platform with enormous savings in development costs and time.

Chapter 4

Chapter 4 tackles efficient graphics with OpenGL ES 2.0. It starts with a brief description of the most important features that OpenGL ES 2 can offer, including Shaders, GLSL, and how they affect the Android platform. Then, it takes a deeper look into GLSL by creating a neat Android project to render an icosahedron using OpenGL ES 2.0. As a bonus, it will show you how you can use single and multi-touch functionality to alter the rotation speed of the icosahedron, plus pinch for zooming in or out.

Chapter 5

Chapter 5 takes things to the next level with *Doom*, the ground-breaking game for the PC. *Doom* is arguably the greatest 3D game ever created, opening new frontiers in 3D graphics. The ultimate goal of this chapter is not to describe the game itself, but to show you how easy it is to bring a complex PC game like *Doom* to the Android platform. The proof? *Doom* has more than 100 K lines of C code—and is brought to Android with less than 200 lines of extra JNI API calls, plus the Java code required to build the mobile UI. This chapter shows that you don't have to translate 100 K lines of C into Java, but simply marry these two powerful languages in an elegant application. Consider the potential savings in development time and costs! This chapter is a must read.

Chapter 6

This is where things start to get really exiting. Chapter 6 brings you a first person shooter (FPS) gem: *Quake*. You will learn how a powerful PC engine of this caliber can be brought to the Android platform with minimum effort. So much so that 95 percent of the original C code is kept intact, with an extra 500–1,000 lines of new, very simple Java wrapper code. Start playing *Quake* in all its glory on your smartphone now!

Chapter 7

This chapter builds upon Chapter 6 to deliver the *Quake II* engine to your fingertips. You will be introduced to a wonderful tool called NanoGL, which allows developers to translate the complexity of the OpenGL immediate mode drawing into OpenGL ES, transparently keeping your original code intact. You will also learn how to make the *Quake II* engine behave properly in Android by creating custom audio and video handlers, which also demonstrates the great reusability features of the Java language. All in all, 99 percent of the original *Quake II* C code will be kept intact, plus the thin Java wrappers from Chapter 6 will be reused without change. Chapter 7 will show you how a simple combo of very powerful tools can tame the mighty *Quake II* OpenGL renderer. Check it out!

## Chapter 1

Welcome to the World of the Little Green Robot

This chapter kicks things off by explaining how to set up your environment to compile hybrid (C/Java) games. This includes the latest versions of the development IDE (Eclipse) and the Android SDK, plus the Native Devlopment Kit (NDK)which are the tools required to build powerful Android games. This information is critical if you wish to learn how to combine the elegant object-oriented features of Java with the raw power of C for maximum performance, and it is required when to build all the native game engines featured in later chapters.

The following software is assumed to be already installed on your desktop:

- *Eclipse:* This is the development IDE used to create your projects. At the time of this writing Eclipse Indigo version 3.7 is the latest. However Version 3.6 (Helios) or 3.5 (Galileo) will work as well.

- *Android SDK, properly configured*: At the time of this writing, the latest version of the SDK is 4.0.

- *Java JDK* : This is required to run Eclipse and the Android SDK itself. Any version of Java after 5.0 should work just fine.

In the next section we'll go through the process of setting up your machine step by step.

Setting Up Your Machine

There are a few steps to be completed before we can get to the nitty-gritty stuff of building games for Android. I summarize the steps as follows:

1. The very first and most basic thing we need is a current Java SDK/JRE (5.0 or later will do). Make sure you have the proper version installed before proceeding. The steps here assume that you already do.

2. Download and Install the Android SDK: The SDK contains the core resources to develop for Android.

3. Configure Your Eclipse: You need to install the Eclipse plugin for Android before you can build anything at all.

4. Install the Native Development Kit (NDK) if you don't have it: This is a critical component for any kind of game that uses native APIS such as OpenGL. By the time of this writing the latest version is r6b. All in all, keep in mind that Android 4 is binary compatible with older NDK versions. This means that if you have an old NDK it will work just fine. Nevertheless, it is always good to use the latest version, as it may provide a performance boost to your native code.

5. Create an Emulator: This is an optional step that will help you with testing your games in many API versions and screen sizes.

6. Configure a Real device: I prefer to work in a real device because it so much faster than using an emulator and is the best way to work if you use OpenGL.

Download and Install the SDK

Download the Android SDK Starter Package (r14) for windows from `http://developer.android.com/sdk/index.html` and unzip it to a working folder such as `C:\eclipse-SDK`.

> **TIP:** Try to keep the SDK, NDK, and Eclipse in the same work folder such as C:\eclipse-SDK. I find this helpful when working on multiple projects at the same time. Thus my development folder C:\eclipse-SDK contains the subfolders: android-sdk-windows (for the SDK), android-ndk-r6b (for the NDK), and eclipse (for Eclipse 3.7). Now let's configure our Eclipse environment.

Configure your Eclipse

You are ready to get your IDE up and running with the Android development kit. Let's go through the installation of the Android 4 SDK (available from `http://developer.android.com/sdk/index.html`) over Eclipse 3.7 (Indigo, available from `http://www.eclipse.org`).

1. Start Eclipse and select Help ➤ Check for Updates, as shown in Figure 1–1.

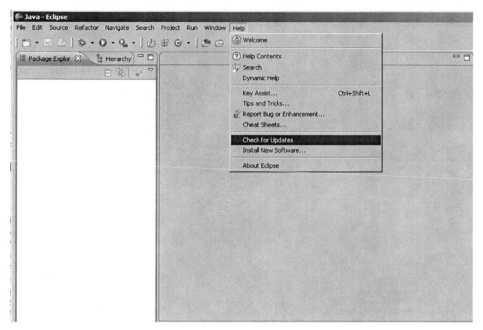

Figure 1–1. *Choosing Check for Updates from the Eclipse 3.7 workbench's Help menu*

2. In the Available Software window, shown in Figure 1–2, click the Add button to install new software.

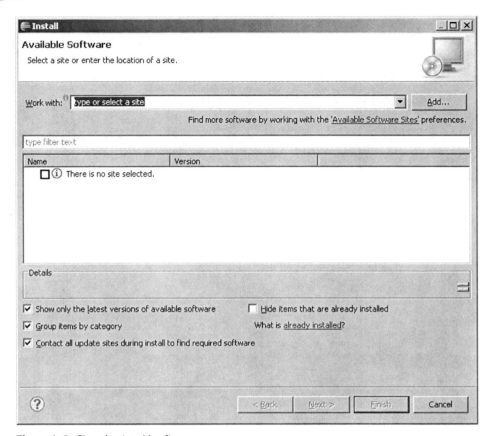

Figure 1–2. *Choosing to add software*

3. In the Add Site dialog box, enter **Android** for the name and `https://dl-ssl.`
`google.com/android/eclipse` for the location, as shown in Figure 1–3.

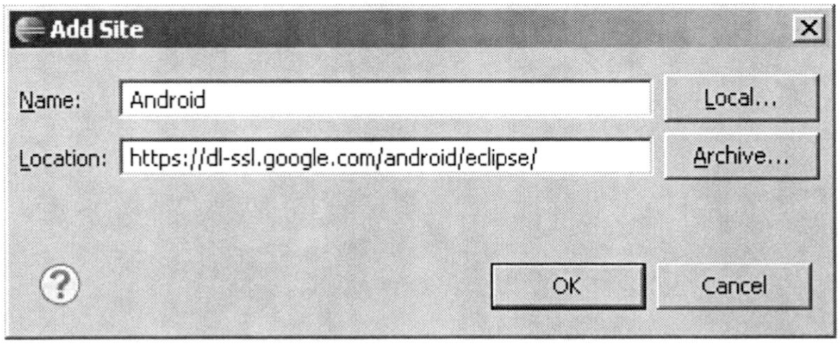

Figure 1–3. *Adding the Android site*

4.   From the Available Software window (Figure 1–2), select the Android site you just added from the Work with combo box. If the name is not shown in the list, click the Available Software Sites preferences link, and then click Add to insert the site into the list (see Figure 1–4).

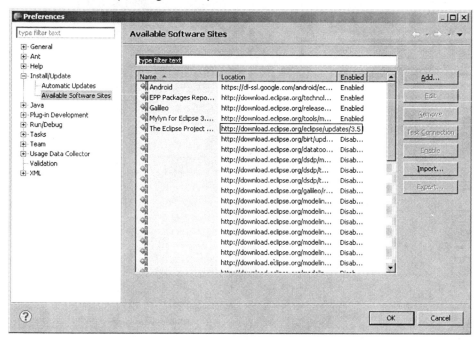

Figure 1–4. *The Available Software Sites Preferences window shows the recently added Android site.*

5.   Check the Developer Tools check box in the details section, as shown in Figure 1–5, and then click Next.

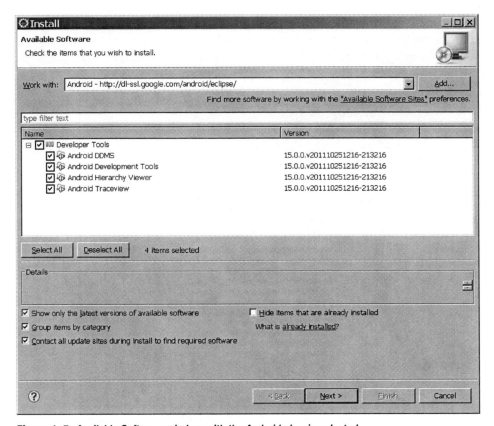

Figure 1–5. *Available Software window with the Android plug-in selected*

6. Follow the wizard installation instructions, accept the license agreement, as shown in Figure 1–6, and then complete the installation. At the end, the workbench should ask for a restart.

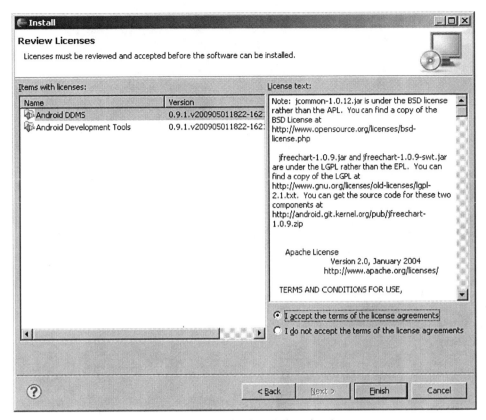

Figure 1–6. *Software license agreement from the installation wizard*

7. After the workbench restarts, select **Window ➤ Preferences** to open the workbench Preferences window, and select the Android option from the left navigation tree. In the Preferences section, set the location of your SDK, as shown in Figure 1–7. Make sure all the build targets are shown. Then click Apply.

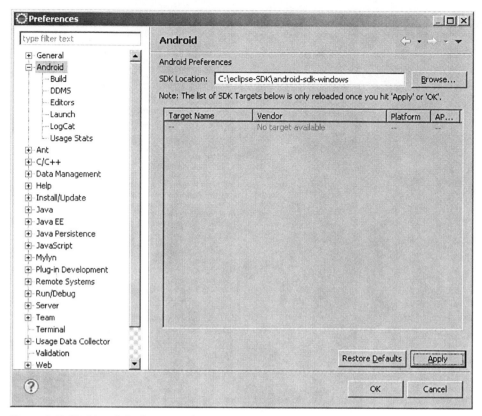

Figure 1–7. *Workbench Preferences window showing Android options*

8. Click OK, and then open the New Project wizard to make sure the Android plug-in has been successfully installed. If so, you should see a folder to create an Android project, as shown in Figure 1–8.

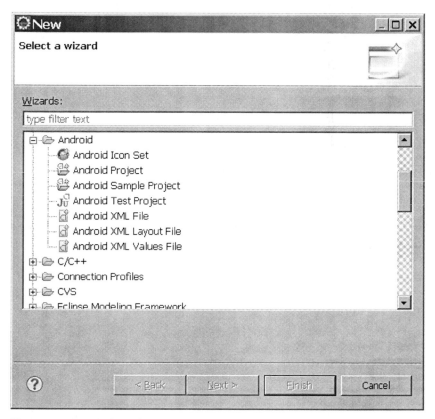

Figure 1-8. *New Project wizard showing the Android options after final configuration*

Our Eclipse is ready for use. Now we must install the NDK.

Installing the Native Development Kit

The NDK is the critical component to create OpenGL games. It provides all the tools (compilers, libraries, and header files) to build apps that access the device natively.

> **NOTE:** The NDK site is a very helpful resource to find step-by-step instructions, API descriptions, changes, and all things related to native development. It is a must for all C/C++ developers.
> `http://developer.android.com/sdk/ndk/index.html`

The NDK installation requires two simple steps: downloading the NDK and installing Cygwin.

NDK Install

Download and unzip the latest NDK from
http://developer.android.com/sdk/ndk/index.html into your work folder (in my case
C:\eclipse-SDK).

Install Cygwin

Android is built on top of Linux which mixes with windows just like oil and water. Cygwin
(version 1.7.9-1) is a tool that provides a Linux look and feel environment for Windows. It
is necessary to run the NDK compilation scripts, and it is required if you are doing any
type of native development in Windows.

> **NOTE:** Cygwin is not required for native development in Linux.

To Install Cywin, download and run the installer (setup.exe) from the Cywin site available
at http://www.cygwin.com/. Follow the wizard instructions. After the installer completes
you should see the Cygwin icon in your desktop. Double click it and test by changing to
your work folder (type cd /cygdrive/c/eclipse-SDK, see Figure 1–9).

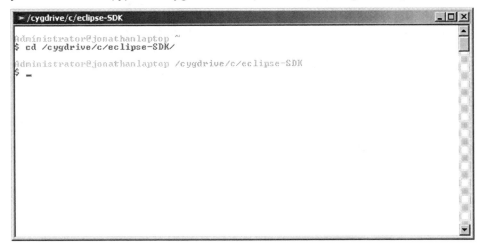

Figure 1–9. *Cygwin console*

Creating an Android Emulator

The first step in creating our native app is to create an Android Virtual Device (AVD) we
can use to test it. However, if you have a real device such as a phone or tablet you can
skip this section and jump to Configure a Real Device.

> **NOTE:** I would encourage you to test all of your code in a real device. For performance reasons it is the best way to do it. AVDs are notoriously slow and lack many advanced features such as a robust implementation of OpenGL. I work in a laptop and running an OpenGL app in the emulator is painfully slow and full of missing API calls.

Creating an AVD

With version 1.5 and later of the SDK, Google introduced the concept of virtual devices (AVDs). An AVD is simply a set of configuration attributes applied to an emulator image that allows the developer to target a specific version of the SDK. Let's take a look at the Android toolbar in Eclipse (see Figure 1–10).

Figure 1–10. *Android toolbar in Eclipse*

Press the green robot icon with the white down arrow (see Figure 1–10) to start the AVD Manager shown in Figure 1–11.

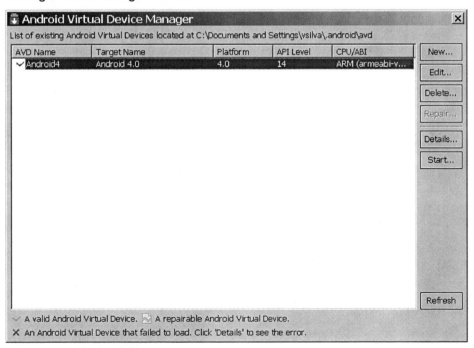

Figure 1–11. *The AVD manager*

The AVD manager provides everything you need to create:

- Virtual devices (emulators)
- Install/ remove SDK documentation
- Manage other Android APIS such as maps, in-App purchases, Android licensing, and more.

Figure 1–11 shows that we have not created any AVDs. Simply press the New button and let's create a device to target Android 4.0 (for tablets, see Figure 1–12).

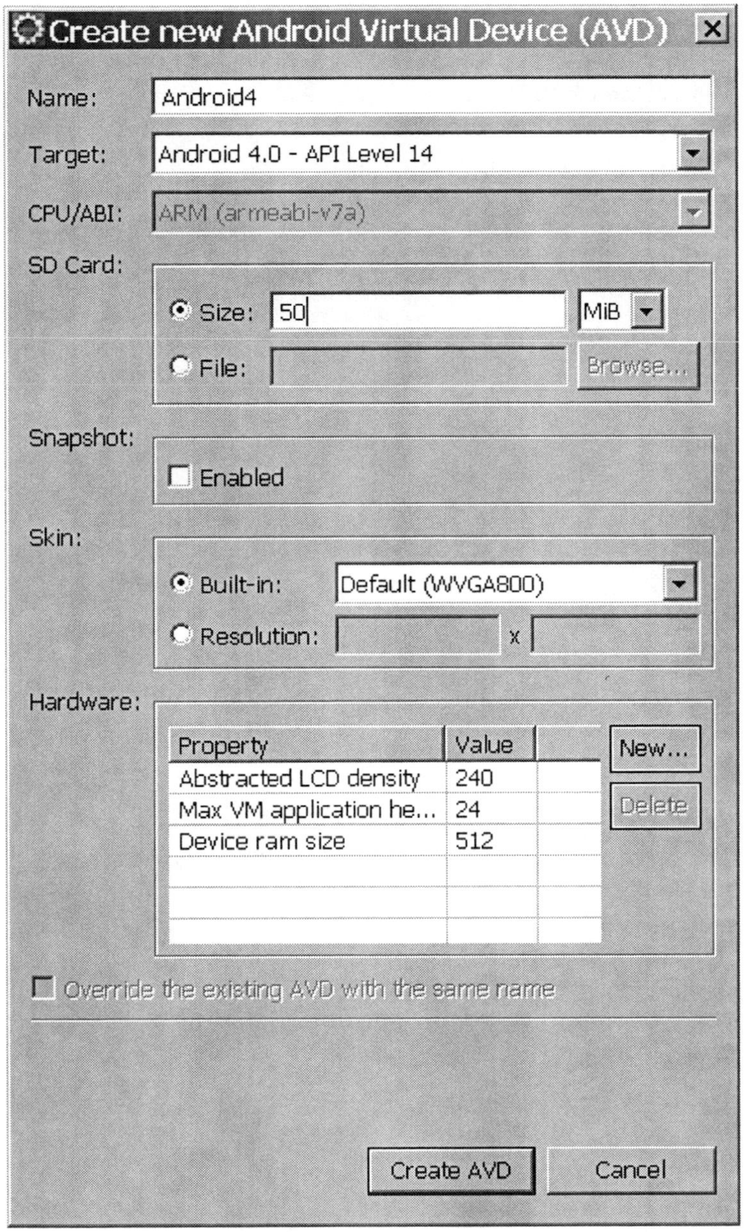

Figure 1–12. *The new AVD dialog*

In the new device dialog enter the device name. In the target box select the latest API level 12 (tablets). The next step is important. Create an SD Card that can be used to store game data and other assets (I chose a size of 200 MB but you can enter the value that best fits your needs). Then press Create AVD.

> **TIP:** You can create as many devices in as many versions or resolutions as you wish. This is helpful for testing in multiple API versions or screen sizes.

The device is now ready for use, as seen in Figure 1–13.

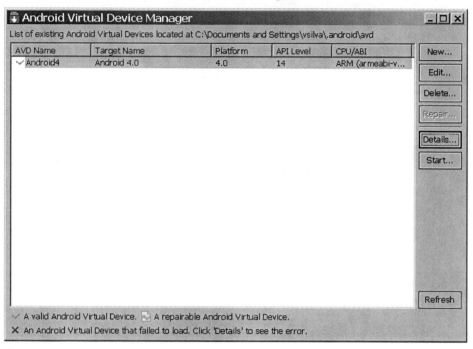

Figure 1–13. *AVD manager with brand new tablet device*

Our tablet emulator is ready for use. Select the device in the dialog from Figure 1–13 and press Start. The emulator should boot up and after a while you will be able to start playing with your tablet (see Figure 1–14).

Figure 1–14. *Tablet emulator (API level 14)*

Configuring a Real Device

Personally, I think this is the best way to develop games and apps that use OpenGL. A real device gives many advantages the emulator doesn't, namely, Speed and API reliability. The only caveat is that the emulator gives you the chance to test multiple screen sizes and API versions. Before Eclipse can recognize your device, you need to install a USB driver required for communications.

MORE ON THE USB DRIVER

The USB driver from Google is only compatible with the following devices:
   ADP1 / T-Mobile G1*
   ADP2 / Google Ion / T-Mobile myTouch 3G*
   Verizon Droid*
   Nexus One
   Nexus S
If you have other devices you'll need to contact your vendor. A list of OEMs and more details on the USB driver for windows are available at:
`http://developer.android.com/sdk/win-usb.html`

To install the driver in your windows host:

1. Connect your device to your computer's USB port. Windows will detect the device and launch the Hardware Update Wizard.

2. Select Install from a list or specific location and click Next.

3. Select Search for the best driver in these locations; un-check Search removable media; and check Include this location in the search.

4. Click Browse and locate the USB driver folder. (`c:\eclipse-SDK\android-sdk-windows\extras\google\usb_driver\.`)

5. Click Next to install the driver.

> **TIP:** The USB driver can be downloaded or upgraded from the Android AVD Manager: Select
> Available Packages ➤ Google Inc ➤ Google USB Driver and press Install Selected as shown in
> Figure 1–15.

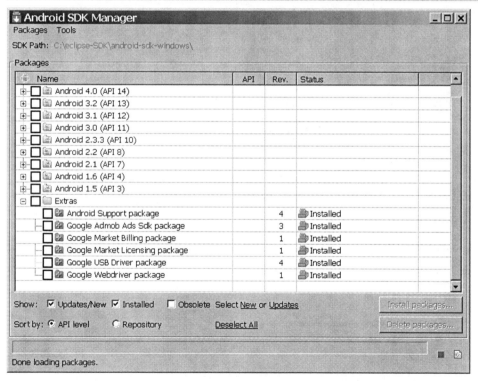

Figure 1–15. *Installing the USB driver from the AVD Manager*

At this point, your environment should be configured and ready for development.

Summary

Congratulations! You have taken the first step toward your mastery of Android game development. In this chapter, you learned how to set up your system to compile hybrid games, which included the following tasks:

- Installing the SDK and NDK
- Setting up your Eclipse ID
- Creating emulators or real devices

This chapter provided the foundation to compile the games described throughout this book. In Chapter 2, you will learn how to write and compile a basic native program—a simple shared library—and call the shared library within a Java application.

## Chapter 2

Gaming Tricks for Phones or Tablets

This chapter contains a lot of goodies to get your feet wet with native development in Android.

We begin by showing you how easy it is to build a simple Android app that loads a native library and executes methods written in C within Java. But it also shows how you can call back Java methods within C, so the communication goes both ways between the languages.

Next we look at how we can cascade Audio, Video, Key, and Touch events from Java to C by using thin Java wrappers that simply pass event information to the native library.

And then we tackle multitouch, which is a useful subject for advanced games such as shooters and others. Multitouch can be a tricky subject so check it out.

Finally we end up with Bluetooth controllers. Some games that require complex and precision movement can be frustrating to play on a touch screen. Here is where a Bluetooth controller such as a Zeemote comes handy. You will learn how to enable this neat joystick device in your game. The beauty of this is that everything contained within this chapter is fully compatible with Android 4.

Compiling Native Code in Android

For the pure Java developer, writing apps that talk to C code can be daunting in the beginning. I felt that way the first time I tried to write a Java/C hybrid (with painful success I may add). It turns out to be surprisingly simple if you understand the way these languages interface together. My goal in this section is to show you how simple it can be to call a C function from Java.

> **TIP:** Java/C Communication goes both ways. Which means you can call C functions from Java or you can call Java Classes, methods, or Exceptions from C.

Consider the arbitrary Java class MyApp in Listing 2–1. For the sake of simplicity let's say we wish to call a native game startup function (GameMain) written in C from this class. All we need are a Java class and a C file implementation. Let's take a closer look at MyApp:

Listing 2–1. *Java class to call a native function*

```
package myapp;
public class MyApp {
    // load C lib
    System.loadLibrary("myapp");

    // C function
    native void GameMain(String[] args);

    static void main(Sttring args[] ) {
      MyApp app = new MyApp();
      app.GameMain(args);
  }
}
```

In Listing 2–1, the first thing we need to do is to load the native library containing the function GameMain by calling System.loadLibrary. Note that the name of the library is important (myapp). Behind the scenes, this name gets translated to libmyapp.so in Android/Linux (in windows it would be myapp.dll but that's another story). Next we tell Java the native library has a function GameMain that takes an array of strings as arguments. The native keyword in Java is used to declare native functions. Finally we simply call the native function from the Java main subroutine.

> **NOTE:** libmyapp.so must be in the system class path; otherwise the System.loadLibray call will throw an UnsatisfiedLinkError which can be very annoying. This is done by running the program with the java.library.path VM argument such as: java –Djava.library.path=[PATH_TO_THE_LIB] myapp.MyApp.

Now, for the native side implementation of GameMain. Be careful with the syntax of the function in C. We can't just write a C function called GameMain. It must follow a strict JNI syntax. Thus the C implementation file is shown in Listing 2–2:

Listing 2–2. *Native implementation for the native code in Listing 2–1*

```
// myapp.c
#include<stdio.h>
#include <jni.h>

JNIEXPORT void JNICALL Java_myapp_GameMain
  (JNIEnv * env, jclass class, jobjectArray jargv)
{
```

```
    // extract string args
    // call main (int argc, const char ** argv)
}
```

Note in Listing 2–2 that the native implementation name is not GameMain but Java_myapp_GameMain. The syntax must follow the convention:

```
    Java_{package_name}_{function_name}(JNI arguments);
```

If the package name has multiple namespaces such as com.acme.myapp, dots must be replaced by underscores. Also, notice the syntax of the arguments:

- JNIEnv * env: This is a reference to the JNI environment, which is very helpful in doing lots of things, such as extracting the real string arguments from the object array jargv.

- jclass class: This is a reference to the Java class that called the native function. It could be used to call back a Java method or to throw an Exception if something happens.

- jobjectArray jargv: This is a reference to the array of strings sent as arguments from the Java side packed as a JNI jobjectArray. We need to massage this reference to extract the real strings and send them to the native main function.

So far so good; it looks very simple but the tricky part comes when you need to extract complex arguments, such as strings or objects, from the JNI arguments. In the next section you will put these concepts to the test by creating an Android native app step by step. Let's continue.

Creating the Android Project with Native Support

Here we will create a simple Android project to apply the concepts we learned in the previous section. The project will consist of the following components:

- An Android activity: This is the main entry point for the application. Its job is to load a native library and call a C function within sending an array of strings as arguments.

- A native library: This library implements a simple C log function to extract a string argument from the Java activity and print the message to the Android log console.

Now, let's create the project for this section, as follows:

1. In Eclipse, click the New Android Project icon on the main toolbar or press CTRL-N and select **Android ➤ Android project**. This opens the New Android Project dialog box.

2. In the dialog box, enter a project name (ch02.Project in this example).

3. Enter an application name (Ch02.Project in this example).

4. Enter a package name (ch02.project in this example).

5. Enter an activity name (Ch02.ProjectActivity in this example).

6. Specify a minimum SDK version 4 API 14 in this example. Figure 2–1 shows the completed New Android Project dialog box for this example.

7. Click Finish.

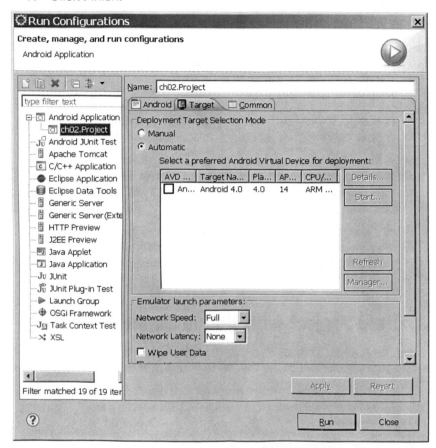

Figure 2–1. *New Android Project dialog box for this chapter's example*

Now that we have our project skeleton let's look at how this application is architected. We'll start with a basic layout (architecture) of the components of the app including the Java main activity, a native interface (also written in Java), and the C implementation. Next we'll see how to compile the native code, and finally we'll test on the emulator. Let's get started.

Application Architecture

Let's consider what we wish to accomplish with this application:

- We want to create the basic Android application. When run in the emulator, the app will create a default view with the text "Hello Chapter2!".

- Within the project, we will create a native folder with files to accomplish the following:

    - Create a native library with a main subroutine that will be called from the Android main activity using JNI.

    - The main library subroutine will invoke a Java method (using JNI) within the Android project, sending a text message back to the Android Java layer.

- The library will be loaded at runtime within Java using a System.load(path).

Figure 2–2 shows the file system layout of the project.

> **TIP:** It would be helpful to import the project source (ch02.Project) into your workspace to go along with this chapter.

The following Java files describe the project:

- ch02.project.MainActivity.java: This file is created by the wizard and should already exist in the project.

- jni.Natives.java: This is a new file that contains native methods to be invoked within the native library and callbacks that the C library will perform within Java.

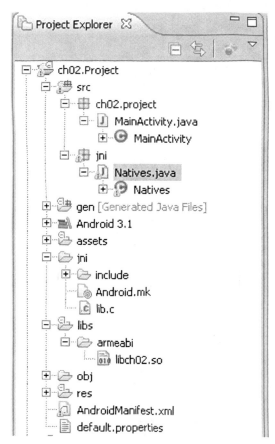

Figure 2–2. *Project layout*

The jni folder contains the native code including (see Figure 2–2):

- lib.c: This is the main library code. It contains all the necessary JNI system calls to cascade information back and forth between Android and C.

- *Android.mk*: This is the Android makefile used to build the native library which will be stored in libs/armeabi/libch02.so.

Let's look at the files in more detail to understand what they do. We'll start from the top with the Java main activity and its companion native interface. These two work together with the native library. Finally we will glue all the pieces at compilation time. Let's carry on.

Main Activity

The file ch02.project.MainActivity.java is created by the wizard, and it is the entry point to the phone application. Listing 2–3 shows the code for this file. There are some remarkable things to note about this file.

As you should know, when the application starts, the method onCreate(Bundle savedInstanceState) will be invoked by Android. This method performs these critical steps:

- It loads the native library using System.loadLibrary(name).

- It runs the main library sub by invoking the native method Natives.LibMain(String[] argv).

Listing 2–3 shows the implementation of the Activity.

Listing 2–3. *Main Activity for This Chapter's Example*

```
package ch02.project;

import java.io.IOException;
import java.io.InputStream;
import java.io.OutputStream;

import jni.Natives;

import android.app.Activity;
import android.os.Bundle;

public class MainActivity extends Activity {
    {
      // load lib
      System.loadLibrary("ch02");
    }

    /** Called when the activity is first created. */
    @Override
    public void onCreate(Bundle savedInstanceState) {
        super.onCreate(savedInstanceState);
        setContentView(R.layout.main);

        try {
            // Run native method
            String[] argv = { "MyLib", "arg1", "arg2" };

            Natives.LibMain(argv);

        } catch (Exception e) {
            e.printStackTrace();
        }
    }
}
```

The main activity is the first piece of our puzzle. Note that listing 2–3 makes a call to Natives.LibMain. This is what I call a native interface (the second piece). Natives.LibMain is defined in the class Natives.java described in the next section.

Native Interface

The native interface defined in jni.Natives.java has two important methods that deal with the C library (see Listing 2–4):

- static native int LibMain(String[] argv): This is the native library main subroutine. It will be called within the Android main activity with an array of strings as arguments. Notice the keyword native, which tells the Java compiler it is implemented natively.

- private static void OnMessage(String text, int level): This method is meant to be called from the C library, with a string message and integer value (level). This method will simply print the message to the console.

> **NOTE:** As you should know, with JNI, you can invoke subroutines both ways: from Java to C (using the native keyword) or from C to Java, as you'll see once we get to the native stuff.

Listing 2–4. *Native Interface Class*

```
package jni;

public class Natives
{
    /**
     * Native Main Loop
     *
     * @param argv
     * @return
     */
    public static native int LibMain(String[] argv);

    /**
     * This fires on messages from the C layer
     *
     * @param text
     */
    @SuppressWarnings("unused")
    private static void OnMessage(String text, int level) {
        System.out.println("OnMessage text:" + text + " level=" + level);
    }

}
```

Thus the native interface effectively defines a two-way pipeline between Java and C. In one hand, LibMain sends information to the C library. On the other hand, OnMessage receives information from it, and simply prints the message to standard output. Now let's take a look at the final piece: the native library.

Native Library

Here is where all the work takes place. The implementation is provided in lib.c (see Listing 2–5). This file lives under the jni folder within the project.

> **NOTE:** Native libraries in Linux (also known as shared objects) are the equivalents of dynamic link libraries (DLLs) in Windows. By convention, shared objects are named as lib<NAME><VERSION>.so.

Listing 2–5. *Native Library Implementation (lib.c)*

```
#include <stdio.h>
#include <stdlib.h>

/* JNI Includes */
#include <jni.h>

#include "include/jni_Natives.h"

#define CB_CLASS "jni/Natives"

/**
 * OnMessage callback
 */
#define CB_CLASS_MSG_CB   "OnMessage"
#define CB_CLASS_MSG_SIG  "(Ljava/lang/String;I)V"

// prototypes

// Lib main Sub
int lib_main(int argc, char **argv) ;

// Used to get the len of a Java Array
const int getArrayLen(JNIEnv * env, jobjectArray jarray);

// printf str messages back to java
void jni_printf(char *format, ...);

// Global env ref (for callbacks)
static JavaVM *g_VM;

// Global Reference to the native Java class jni.Natives.java
static jclass jNativesCls;

/*
 * Class:     jni_Natives
 * Method:    LibMain
 * Signature: ([Ljava/lang/String;)V
 */
JNIEXPORT jint JNICALL Java_jni_Natives_LibMain
```

```
    (JNIEnv * env, jclass class, jobjectArray jargv)
{
    // Obtain a global ref to the caller jclass
    (*env)->GetJavaVM(env, &g_VM);

    // Extract char ** args from Java array
    jsize clen = getArrayLen(env, jargv);

    char * args[(int)clen];

    int i;
    jstring jrow;
    for (i = 0; i < clen; i++)
    {
        // Get C string from Java String[i]
        jrow = (jstring)(*env)->GetObjectArrayElement(env, jargv, i);
        const char *row  = (*env)->GetStringUTFChars(env, jrow, 0);

        args[i] = malloc( strlen(row) + 1);
        strcpy (args[i], row);

        // Print args
        jni_printf("Main argv[%d]=%s", i, args[i]);

        // Free Java string jrow
        (*env)->ReleaseStringUTFChars(env, jrow, row);
    }

    /*
     * Load the jni.Natives class
     */
    jNativesCls = (*env)->FindClass(env, CB_CLASS);

    if ( jNativesCls == 0 ) {
        jni_printf("Unable to find class: %s", CB_CLASS);
        return -1;
    }

    // Invoke the Lib main sub.
    // Program args come from Java
    lib_main (clen, args);
    return 0;
}


/**
 * Send a string back to Java
 */
jmethodID mSendStr;

static void jni_send_str( const char * text, int level) {
    JNIEnv *env;

    if ( !g_VM) {
        printf("I_JNI-NOVM: %s\n", text);
        return;
    }
```

```c
    (*g_VM)->AttachCurrentThread (g_VM, (void **) &env, NULL);

    // Load jni.Natives if missing
    if ( !jNativesCls ) {
        jNativesCls = (*env)->FindClass(env, CB_CLASS);

        if ( jNativesCls == 0 ) {
                printf("Unable to find class: %s", CB_CLASS);
                return;
        }
    }

    // Call jni.Natives.OnMessage(String, int)
    if (! mSendStr ) {
        // Get  aref to the static method: jni.Natives.OnMessage
        mSendStr = (*env)->GetStaticMethodID(env, jNativesCls
            , CB_CLASS_MSG_CB
            , CB_CLASS_MSG_SIG);
    }
    if (mSendStr) {
        // Call method
        (*env)->CallStaticVoidMethod(env, jNativesCls
                , mSendStr
                , (*env)->NewStringUTF(env, text)
                , (jint) level );
    }
    else {
        printf("Unable to find method: %s, signature: %s\n"
                , CB_CLASS_MSG_CB, CB_CLASS_MSG_SIG );
    }
}

/**
 * Printf into the Java layer
 * does a varargs printf into a temp buffer
 * and calls jni_sebd_str
 */
void jni_printf(char *format, ...)
{
    va_list         argptr;
    static char             string[1024];

    va_start (argptr, format);
    vsprintf (string, format,argptr);
    va_end (argptr);

    jni_send_str (string, 0);
}

/**
 * Get Java array length
 */
const int getArrayLen(JNIEnv * env, jobjectArray jarray)
{
    return (*env)->GetArrayLength(env, jarray);
}
```

```
/**
 * Library main sub
 */
int lib_main(int argc, char **argv)
{
    int i;

    jni_printf("Entering LIB MAIN");

    for ( i = 0 ; i < argc ; i++ ) {
        jni_printf("Lib Main argv[%d]=%s", i, argv[i]);
    }
    return 0;
}
```

Let's dissect this file to understand what it does. Any C/C++ program that does JNI calls must include the header file:

```
#include <jni.h>
```

This header file has the prototypes for all the JNI system calls to be used by your library. It can be found in your system's Java home under JAVA_HOME/include, with extra Linux dependencies under JAVA_HOME/include/linux. At compile time, Android will take care of finding this file for us. Next, it includes the jni_Natives header file:

```
#include "include/jni_Natives.h"
```

This file contains the user-defined JNI prototypes for all native methods defined in the jni.Natives class. It is machine-generated and must not be edited by the user. To generate this file manually, the following command can be used:

```
javah -cp ../bin -d include jni.Natives
```

Here, javah is the Java Virtual Machine (JVM) command to generate native header files from Java classes, -cp defines the class path search path, -d include tells javah to save the file in the include folder (creating it if required), and jni.Natives is the Java class name from which you wish to extract the headers. Next, the following constants are defined:

```
#define CB_CLASS "jni/Natives"
#define CB_CLASS_MSG_CB  "OnMessage"
#define CB_CLASS_MSG_SIG  "(Ljava/lang/String;I)V"
```

CB_CLASS is the name of the Java class that will be invoked within C (note that the period separating path names is replaced by /). CB_CLASS_MSG_CB is the name of the Java method (OnMessage) that will be invoked (see Listing 2–2). CB_CLASS_MSG_SIG is a critical constant that defines the Java signature of the OnMessage Java method. Let's take a closer look at this signature:

```
(Ljava/lang/String;I)V
```

A Java method signature has the format `(ARGUMENTS)RETURN_TYPE`, where the arguments can be encoded as follows:

> `I` = Integer
>
> `B` = Byte
>
> `S` = Short
>
> `C` = Char
>
> `LJava_Class;` = For Java classes enclosed by : `L` and `;`

In our case, the first argument is a Java string (`Ljava/lang/String;`), and the second is an integer (`I`). Note that all arguments are defined by a single character (except for classes that are enclosed by `L;`), and there are no separators between them. Finally, `V` is the return type defined as void.

CAUTION: Method signatures are a major pain when coding in JNI. Any mistake in this string, and the library will not be able to find the method at runtime.

Next, the file defines the prototypes for the functions within the library:

- `int lib_main(int argc, char **argv)`: This is the entry point to the library. It receives the number of arguments (`argc`) and a list of arguments (`argv`), similar to the standard C `main()` function.

- `int getArrayLen(JNIEnv * env, jobjectArray jarray)`: This function is used to get the length of a Java array, which will be translated into a C array for use by the library.

- `void jni_printf(char *format, ...)`: This function is used by the library to send a text message back to Java. Note that `...` indicates that the function will receive a vector of arguments.

Finally, we need two global references:

```
static JavaVM *g_VM;
static jclass jNativesCls;
```

`g_VM` is a reference to the JVM, and it will be used make JNI system calls. `jNativesCls` is a reference to the `jni.Natives` Java class used to invoke the Java method `OnMessage`. Note that the `static` keyword tells the compiler that these variables should be visible only within code in `lib.c`. Now let's look at some of the functions defined in Listing 2–5. In the next sections I describe some of the key tasks performed by these functions including:

- Converting a Java array of strings into a C array, performed by Java_jni_Natives_LibMain (the native implementation of Java's LibMain). This function also illustrates how to get the size of a Java Array within C.

- Invoking a Java static void method: This technique is illustrated by the jni_send_str function, and shows how you can efficiently call back a Java method from C.

- If you are a core C developer at heart you will appreciate how to define a variable-arguments function (defined in jni_printf). It can be a life-saver when logging text.

Converting a Java Array of Strings into a C Array

Converting a Java string array to a C char array is a very useful tool to send arguments to a native library. As you can see from Listing 2–6, this can be a tricky situation. The following are the key steps:

- Get the size of the Java array, and for each element of the array:

  - Get the Java String[i] element using GetObjectArrayElement(JNIEnv * env, jobjectArray jarray, int pos).

  - Convert the retrieved element into a C string (char *) using GetStringUTFChars(JNIEnv * env, jstring jrow, 0).

- Allocate space for the C array using malloc(length of string + 1). Note that an extra space is allocated for the terminator character.

- Copy the characters using strcpy (char ** target , char * source).

- Release Java String[i] using ReleaseStringUTFChars(JNIEnv * env, jstring jrow, char * row).

Listing 2–6. *Converting a Java String Array into a C Char Array*

```
// Extract char ** args from Java array
jsize clen =  getArrayLen(env, jargv);

char * args[(int)clen];

int i;
jstring jrow;

// Loop thru Java array
for (i = 0; i < clen; i++)
{
    // Get String[i]
    jrow = (jstring)(*env)->GetObjectArrayElement(env, jargv, i);

    // Convert String[i] to char *
    const char *row  = (*env)->GetStringUTFChars(env, jrow, 0);

    // Allocate space
    args[i] = malloc( strlen(row) + 1);
```

```
    // Copy
    strcpy (args[i], row);

    // Free java string jrow
    (*env)->ReleaseStringUTFChars(env, jrow, row);
}
```

Getting the Size of a Java Array

To get the size of a Java array, use the JNI function (*env)->GetArrayLength(env, jobjectArray jarray), where env is a pointer to the JNI environment, and jarray is a reference to the Java array. For example, to get the size of the array jargs using environment env, use the following:

(*env)->GetArrayLength(env, jargs)

Invoking a Java Static Void Method

To invoke the static void jni.Natives.OnMessage method, you must perform the following steps:

1. Load the jni.Natives class with the following:

(*env)->FindClass(env, "jni/Natives")

2. Get the ID of the method to be invoked using a reference to the jni.Natives class, the name of the method (OnMessage), and the signature (Ljava/lang/String;I)V.

```
jmethodID mSendStr = (*env)->GetStaticMethodID(env
            , jNativesCls
            , "OnMessage"
            , "(Ljava/lang/String;I)V");
```

3. Call the static void method, passing the class, method ID, and the method arguments: a Java string and integer in this case.

```
(*env)->CallStaticVoidMethod(env, jNativesCls
            , mSendStr
            , (*env)->NewStringUTF(env, text)
            , (jint) level );
```

Defining a Variable-Arguments Function in C

The final piece of the puzzle is a function to perform the actual invocation of the Java method described in the previous section, as shown in Listing 2–7. This function is meant to be called anywhere within the library after jni.Natives.LibMain() is invoked. It is called jni_printf and works pretty much as printf does, using the very useful variable-arguments technique.

Listing 2–7. *Sending a String to Java Using Variable Arguments*

```
void jni_printf(char *format, ...)
{
    va_list        argptr;
    static char    string[1024];

    va_start (argptr, format);
    vsprintf (string, format, argptr);
    va_end (argptr);
    jni_send_str (string, 0);
}
```

`va_list`, `va_start`, and `va_end` are used to build an output string using a C string format and a sequence of arguments. This allows the developer to mimic a `printf`-style function for a specific need. Thus, for example, to print an arbitrary message to the Java console within the library, use the following command:

```
jni_printf("This is a message %d, %p, %x, %s", 10, somePointer, 0xFF, "Hello Java")
```

`"This is a message %d, %p, %x, %s"` is called a character format. The rest are variable arguments sent to the function. Also note that you should add the header `#include <stdarg.h>` to use variable arguments. We have described the native library and the key tasks that perform within the app. Now we can finally compile it and see how all the pieces fit together by running our project in the emulator as seen in the following section.

Compiling the Shared Library

Before we can run our native Android app we need to compile the native library. For that, the file Android.mk must be created in the jni folder of the project (see figure 2–2). This file describes the module name and the source files of the library as shown in Listing 2–8.

Listing 2–8. *Compilation file for the project's native library*

```
LOCAL_PATH := $(call my-dir)

include $(CLEAR_VARS)

LOCAL_MODULE    := ch02

LOCAL_CFLAGS := -O2

LOCAL_SRC_FILES := lib.c

include $(BUILD_SHARED_LIBRARY)
```

To build the library, open your cygwin console and change to the folder containing the project files:

```
$cd [PATH_TO]/ch02.Project
```

Then call the helpful NDK build script ndk-build (see Figure 2–3):

```
$ ndk-build
```

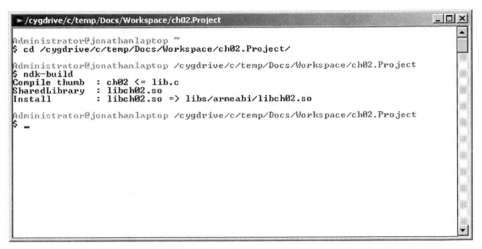

Figure 2–3. *Native library compilation with cygwin*

NOTE: The path to the NDK install directory must be included in you system Path variable; otherwise cygwin won't be able to locate the ndk-build command.

Now, start your emulator and let's test the library.

Testing the App on a Device

To run our app on the device we must create a Run configuration and fire up the emulator. Here is how:

1. Select Run Configurations from the main menu.

2. In the Run Configurations dialog box, right-click Android Application in the left tree and choose New.

3. Enter a configuration name (ch02.Project) and select a project (ch02.Project), as shown in Figure 2–4. Then click Run.

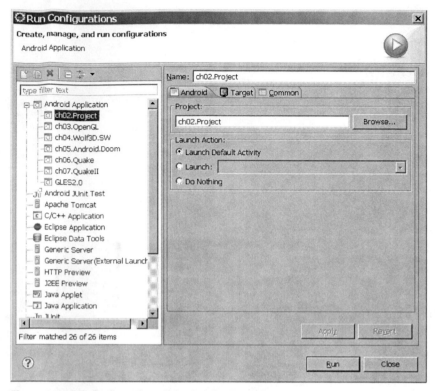

Figure 2–4. *Run Configurations dialog box for the project*

The application will run in the emulator and display the text "Hello Chapter2!". There is nothing out of the ordinary here. We must look at the logcat view to see the messages from the native layer. Figure 2–5 shows the output of the device log.

```
 Console    LogCat ⊠                                    Ⓥ Ⓓ Ⓘ Ⓦ


Message
Debugger has detached; object registry had 1 entries

VM cleaning up

Start proc ch02.project for activity ch02.project/.MainActivity: pid=954 uid=10018

LinearAlloc 0x0 used 639228 of 4194304 (15%)

received file descriptor 20 from ADB

Installing LIB: libch02.so

Trying to load lib /data/data/ch02.project/files/libch02.so 0x43733e98

Added shared lib /data/data/ch02.project/files/libch02.so 0x43733e98

No JNI_OnLoad found in /data/data/ch02.project/files/libch02.so 0x43733e98

+++ not scanning '/system/lib/libwebcore.so' for 'LibMain' (wrong CL)

+++ not scanning '/system/lib/libmedia_jni.so' for 'LibMain' (wrong CL)

OnMessage text:Main argv[0]=MyLib level=0

OnMessage text:Main argv[1]=arg1 level=0

OnMessage text:Main argv[2]=arg2 level=0

OnMessage text:Entering LIB MAIN level=0

OnMessage text:Lib Main argv[0]=MyLib level=0

OnMessage text:Lib Main argv[1]=arg1 level=0

OnMessage text:Lib Main argv[2]=arg2 level=0

Displayed activity ch02.project/.MainActivity: 3436 ms
```

Figure 2–5. *logcat output for the project*

In the output, notice the following lines:

```
Trying to load lib /data/data/ch02.project/files/libch02.so ...
Added shared lib /data/data/ch02.project/files/libch02.so ...
```

These are JNI messages that tell us the library loaded successfully and the native methods can now be invoked within Java. The lines in **green** represent the callbacks performed by the native library calling the jni.Natives.OnMessage() method. Success!

We have got our feet wet with this section but there is so much more we can do with native apps. We have learned the basics of Java/C interaction which serve as the foundation to the next section, where we build upon previous knowledge to learn more advanced techniques such as how to cascade audio, video, and other types of events into the native side. We'll start with the concept of thin Java Wrappers and how they can help with efficient event handling. Audio is the simplest and therefore our starting point. Next, things get tough with video events where you'll learn about software, hybrid, and hardware renderers. Then we finish with input events via keyboard or touch screen. Let's get started.

Java Wrappers for C/C++ Event Handling

As a game developer in your organization you probably have to build your code to support multiple platforms. Java is an elegant object-oriented language but when it comes to max performance it simply stinks. Many people would disagree with this statement, claiming that the Just in Time (JIT) a.k.a dynamic compilation nature of the Java language puts it at par with C performance wise. That is simply not true. Any game developer that has worked in both languages and is concerned with squeezing every single bit of speed in to a device will tell you that Java code is at least six times slower than raw native C. Specially if you work in advanced OpenGL graphics. As a matter of fact if you take a look at the underpinnings of the Android source you'll find out that most of the Java APIs are simply JNI wrappers to a bunch of C libraries, especially when it comes to Audio/Video. All in all, because of the multiplatform nature of today's mobile landscape: iPhone, Android, Blackberry, Symbian, and others, most game developers build their engines in portable C. Then they simply build wrappers to target a specific platform: be that Objective-C for the iPhone or Java in Android. Keeping that in mind, in this section you will learn how to cascade the most important events for gaming: Audio, Video, Key, and Touch by using thin Java wrappers. We'll start with audio.

Handling Audio Independently

Google has made it difficult in Android to handle audio directly on the native side. Before version 2.x of the SDK it was simply not worth it to try to implement audio handling natively. Google used a very obscure audio implementation in the early days (Enhanced Audio System – EAS). Although, slowly but surely they have been turning into open standards such as OpenAL (Audio Library). Nevertheless, I still find it simpler just to read the native audio buffer and play it using the standard Android AudioTrack API.

> **TIP:** The MediaTrack API gives you the power of handling audio independent of the format. Behind the scenes, the API will detect the binary format and call the apropriate audio driver for any format supported by the platform: WAV, MP3, OGG, etc.

The process of handling audio directly on the native side can be summarized as follows:

1. The game engine loads audio assets typically from game files. Audio assets are simply audio files such as waves (wav) and Ogg Vorbis (ogg).

2. The game engine will typically initialize the audio hardware and define the overall audio properties such as frequency (in Hz), audio resolution (16 vs. 32 bit), and number of channels (2 for stereo 1 for mono).

3. Whenever an audio event occurs in the game, such as the player fires a gun or jumps, the engine will play the specific raw audio assets by writing an audio buffer to the device hardware.

> **WARNING:** Handling Audio in the native side only via OpenAL is not supported in Android versions prior to 3. Nevertheless it is the most efficient way of doing it. On the other hand, using a thin Java wrapper will work in all Android versions. It will be a bit slower however.

By using a thin Java wrapper to the Mediatrack API, we can work around Android's lack of support of popular audio standards such as OpenAL and others. With a wrapper we can read the audio buffer from the native library and render it using the AudioTrack API. Thus the steps above get slightly modified as follows:

1. The native game engine loads audio assets. This step remains unchanged.

2. The game engine initializes the audio hardware. This step can be used not to initialize the audio hardware but to tell the Android Java code that audio has been initialized with a specific frequency, resolution, and number of channels.

3. The thin Java wrapper will use a thread to read bytes from the native audio buffer and render them to the hardware using an AudioTrack.

This may not be the best way of doing things but it works quite well, as you'll see in the chapters dealing with the 3D Quake engines later on in this book. To illustrate the steps above, let's consider a Java class dubbed NativeAudio (see Listing 2–9) which performs the following tasks:

- It defines a native audio painter PaintAudio(ByteBuffer buf) which reads the audio buffer from the native library.

- It implements the following methods for audio playback:

  - start(freq, channels, bits, bufferSize): Here is where the good stuff happens. This method starts a thread that reads the audio buffer from the native engine (by calling PaitnAudio). The thread will loop continuously until it is told to stop using a boolean flag. The arguments to this sub are: Sound frequency in Hertz, the number of channels (1 for mono, 2 for stereo), sound resolution in bits, and the size of the buffer.

  - stop(): This subroutine is used to stop the audio thread from Java.

  - OnInitAudio(freq, channels, bits): This is one of a series of magic subs called from C that tell the Java code it is time to start playing. This function will be called whenever the native library initializes the audio. It receives the frequency, number of channels, and resolution. It then calls the start method with those arguments.

▪ OnLockAudio()/OnUnlockAudio(): These methods are used to lock/unlock the audio when the user pauses the game for example. They simply tell the main thread when to read data.

▪ OnCloseAudio(): This function is fired from the native side to close the audio and cleanup resources.

Listing 2–9. *A Java class to read audio data from a native library*

```java
public class NativeAudio {
    private static boolean mDone = false;
    private static boolean mAudioLocked = false;
    private static boolean mAudioRuning = false;
    private static boolean mNativeAudioInitialized = false;

    // Native audio painter
    native int PaintAudio(ByteBuffer buf);

    // Audio will start from C
    private static void start(final int freq, final int channels,
            final int bits, final int bufferSize) {
        if (isRunning()) {
            Log.w(TAG, "WARNING: Java Audio thread alredy runing!!");
            return;
        }

        // Must be direct for JNI to work!
        // Native BUFFERS MUST BE DIRECT!!! ByteBuffer
        final ByteBuffer audioBuffer = ByteBuffer.allocateDirect(bufferSize);
        final byte[] audioData8 = new byte[bufferSize];

        Thread t = new Thread(new Runnable() {
            public void run() {
                AudioTrack mTrack = new AudioTrack(
                        android.media.AudioManager.STREAM_MUSIC,
                         freq,              // frequency in Hz
                        channels == 1 ? AudioFormat.CHANNEL_CONFIGURATION_MONO
                                : AudioFormat.CHANNEL_CONFIGURATION_STEREO,
                        bits == 16 ? AudioFormat.ENCODING_PCM_16BIT
                                : AudioFormat.ENCODING_PCM_8BIT,
                        4 * (freq / 5),
                        AudioTrack.MODE_STREAM);

                Log.d(TAG, "Audio thread start. Freq=" + freq + " Channels="
                        + channels + " Bits=" + bits + " Buf Size="
                        + bufferSize);

                mDone = false;
                mAudioRuning = true;

                try {
                    mTrack.play();
                } catch (Exception e) {
                    Log.e(TAG, e.toString());
                    mDone = true;
                }
```

```
            while (!mDone) {
                if (!mAudioLocked) {
                    // Read audio buffer from C
                    PaintAudio(audioBuffer);

                    // set the buffer position
                    audioBuffer.position(0);

                    // get bytes
                    audioBuffer.get(audioData8);

                    // Write the byte array to the track
                    mTrack.write(audioData8, 0, audioData8.length);
                } else {
                    // sleep for a while if au locked
                    sleep(50);
                }
            }

            // Audio thread loop done.
            mAudioRuning = false;
        }
    });
    // start thread
    t.start();
}

public static void stop() {
    // signal stop
    mDone = true;

    // wait until au thread quits
    while (mAudioRuning) {
        Log.d(TAG, "Waiting for audio thread...");
        sleep(200);
    }
}

public static boolean isRunning() {
    return mAudioRuning;
}

/***************************************************************
 * C - CALLBACKS - Entry points
 ***************************************************************/
private static void OnInitAudio(int freq, int channels, int bits) {
    Log.d(TAG, "NATIVE THREAD::OnInitAudio Au Start -> freq:" + freq
            + " channels:" + channels + " bits:" + bits);
    // start audio
    start(freq, channels, bits);
}

private static void OnLockAudio() {
    mAudioLocked = true;
}

private static void OnUnLockAudio() {
```

```
        mAudioLocked = false;
    }

    private static void OnCloseAudio() {
        stop();
    }
}
```

Now we need a C implementation of PaintAudio (see Listing 2–10). Notice the third argument: jobject buf which encapsulates a reference to the ByteBuffer used to store the audio data. We can access a Java bByteBuffer memory address and capacity directly from C by calling the JNI functions: **GetDirectBufferAddress** and **GetDirectBufferCapacity** respectively. The prototype paint_audio defines the C function that writes the audio data into the game audio buffer. PaintAudio calls this subroutine to fill the Java ByteBuffer with data from the native audio buffer. The final result is a Java thread that receives a sequence of audio bytes which in turn are sent to the Android AudioTrack for playback.

Listing 2–10. *C companion for NativeAudio.java*

```
// engine audio renderer
extern int paint_audio (void *unused, void * stream, int len);

JNIEXPORT jint JNICALL Java_ NativeAudio_PaintAudio
 ( JNIEnv* env, jobject thiz, jobject buf )
{
    void *stream;
    int len;

    stream = (*env)->GetDirectBufferAddress(env,  buf);
    len = (*env)->GetDirectBufferCapacity (env, buf);

    return paint_audio ( NULL, stream, len );
}

// Init audio
void jni_init_audio(int freq, int channels, int bits)
{
    JNIEnv *env;

    (*g_VM)->AttachCurrentThread ( g_VM, &env, NULL);

    jmethodID mid  = (*env)->GetStaticMethodID(env
        , jNativesCls
        , "OnInitAudio", "(III)V");

    if ( mid ) {
        (*env)->CallStaticVoidMethod(env, jNativesCls, mid , freq, channels, bits);
    }
}
```

Listing 2–10 also shows how we can call a Java method within C to initialize the audio. The function jni_init_audio will be called by the engine on audio startup which in turn will call the Java method OnInitAudio with three arguments: frequency, number of channels, and audio resolution. Note that this function is called from a separate thread (the game thread), therefore it must attach to the current (Java) thread by calling:

```
(*g_VM)->AttachCurrentThread ( g_VM, &env, NULL);
```

Here g_VM is a global reference to the Java virtual machine which must be saved the first time you call JNI (when we call the game main function for example). jNativesCls is a class reference that points to the NativeAudio Java class obtained by doing a JNI class lookup with FindClass and NewGlobalRef in the same spot:

```
jclass clazz = (*env)->FindClass(env, "NativeAudio");
jNativesCls = (jclass)(*env)->NewGlobalRef(env, clazz);
```

Finally, jni_init_audio calls OnInitAudio in NativeAudio.java using JNI's CallStaticVoidMethod with the three arguments: frequency, channels, and bits. We have effectively created a C to Java callback:

```
(*env)->CallStaticVoidMethod(env, jNativesCls, mid , freq, channels, bits);
```

This is the technique used to play audio in the Quake and Quake II engines demonstrated in this book. More details will be explained in those chapters. Now, let's tackle video buffers.

Cascading Video Events

When it comes to handling video, game engine designers typically will decouple the rendering process from the actual drawing. This keeps the engine modularized and makes it easy to port to multiple platforms. For example, low-end devices may not support a Graphics Processing Unit (GPU) thus decoupling the drawing and rendering will allow developers to use a software renderer. On the other hand, if a device does have a GPU, a hardware renderer could be used, all these while keeping the drawing pipeline intact. With that in mind video handling could be classified in three groups, as described in the following sections.

Pure Software Renderer

Pure Software Renderer is good for low-end devices with poor quality or no GPUs. This renderer is typical on simple games that don't require a lot of horse power. The Wolfestein 3D chapter in this book used a software renderer. The process is simple; at the end of every interaction of the game loop, an image buffer is drawn with all the sprites for that state in the game. The image buffer is then sent to the Android activity which will render it in a specific view (see Figure 2–6).

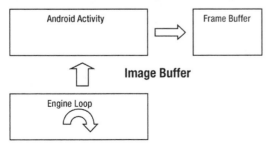

Figure 2–6. *Pure software renderer*

The drawback of this technique is that it is the slowest and can consume more memory of the three.

Mixed or Hybrid Renderer

In a mixed renderer, the drawing of the sprites is performed in software, but the actual rendering is performed in hardware (typically by using OpenGL ES). Figure 2–7 shows the component interactions of this technique. The benefits? It is faster than the previous one (by orders of magnitude). The caveats? It requires a GPU to implement an OpenGL ES renderer.

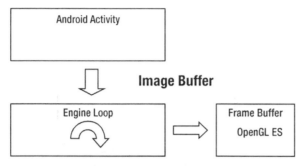

Figure 2–7. *Mixed renderer*

Figure 2–7 shows that the native engine is in charge of drawing the image buffer into the hardware. Depending on how OpenGL ES is initialized the engine may have to tell the Android activity it is time to draw. Usually the Android activity will take care of initializing the OpenGL context and obtaining a display surface; in this case the engine must tell Android it is time to draw (swap buffers) whenever an image frame is rendered. This renderer is used in the chapter dealing with Doom for Android.

Pure Hardware

This is the fastest and most powerful of them all, but requires a device with a GPU. It can be painful to program for Android where there is a lot of hardware fragmentation. Many people had made a lot of fuss about version fragmentation but the real problem (for game developers at least) resides in all the different types of GPUs in today's Android devices. I can attest of these pains trying to deal with the big three GPU OEMs:

- PowerVR: By experience I can tell you this is a hell of a GPU. The best and most powerful one out there (the iPhone uses this type of GPU; there's no wonder why). Devices that use this GPU are the Motorola Droid & Samsung Galaxy S family.

- Qualcomm: Commonly used by HTC smartphones. This is probably the worst GPU I had to deal with. It really is substandard compared with PowerVR. Very limited when there are a lot of polygons and textures in your game.

■ Tegra: The new kid in the block. Certainly powerful and fast.

Figure 2–8 shows the components of this renderer. The chapters dealing with the Quake I/II engines in this book use this type of rendering.

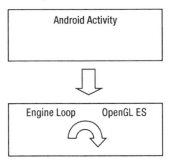

Figure 2–8. *Pure hardware renderer*

So you can have an idea of the difference in performance for these rendering techniques I have created a chart of the number of frames per second (FPS) rendered by the Doom engine running in a Motorola Droid 1 for each renderer (see Figure 2–9).

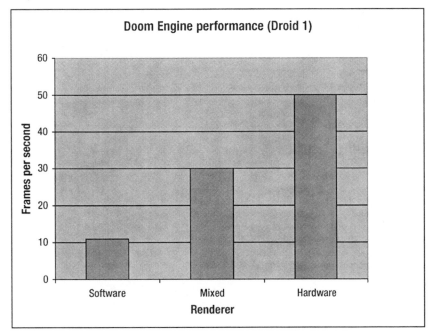

Figure 2–9. *Renderer performance for the Doom engine*

As you can see from Figure 2–9, the hardware renderer is orders of magnitude faster than the software or hybrid. Next we tackle key events. Let's continue.

Cascading Key Events

Cascading key events from Android to a native engine involves the following steps:

1. Listening for key presses or releases from the Android activity.

2. Translating the android keys to ASCII (or whatever format the engine uses to encode keys).

3. Calling the native methods keyPress or keyrelease for presses and releases respectively.

Note that Android uses its own format to encode key values; thus the tricky part is to translate the Android key codes to a format understood by the engine (ASCII is the format for most portable engines). Listing 2–11 shows a simple way of doing this. We start by defining two Java native methods: keyPress and keyRelease in the Android activity. Both of these take an ASCII code as the argument. When the user presses/releases a key on the device Android will fire the events onKeyDown and onKeyUp respectively. These events receive an Android key value and a KeyEvent containing detailed information about the event. We then use the Android built-in function queueEvent to queue a runnable to be run on the GL rendering thread. This can be used to communicate with the Renderer on the rendering thread in the game engine. The function keyCodeToASCIICode is used to translate the Android key code to a portable ASCII code. Finally the native engine must implement the Java methods keyPress/keyRelease as Java _keyPress and Java _keyPress respectively. These methods will receive the ASCII code and push it to the event queue (in this case the event queue for the Quake engine).

Listing 2–11. *Cascading keys from Java to C*

```
// In Java
public static native int keyPress(int key);
public static native int keyRelease(int key);

public boolean onKeyDown(final int keyCode, final KeyEvent event)
{
    queueEvent(new Runnable() {
        public void run() {
            keyPress(keyCodeToASCIICode(keyCode));
        }
    });

    return true;
}

public boolean onKeyUp(final int keyCode, final KeyEvent event)
{
    queueEvent(new Runnable() {
        public void run() {
            keyRelease(keyCodeToASCIICode(keyCode));
        }
    });
    return true;
```

```
}

// In C
// Push key to the event queue in Quake
extern void Key_Event (int key, qboolean down);

/*
 * C Implementation of Java native int keyPress(int key);
 */
JNIEXPORT jint JNICALL Java _keyPress
  (JNIEnv * env, jclass cls, jint key)
{
    Key_Event((int)key, 1);
    return key;
}

/*
 * C Implementation of Java native int keyRelese(int key);
 */
JNIEXPORT jint JNICALL Java _keyRelease
  (JNIEnv * env, jclass cls, jint key)
{
    Key_Event((int)key, 0);
    return key;
}
```

Cascading Touch Events

Touch events work in a similar way as key events. When the user touches the device screen, the Java activity overrides onTouchEvent which receives a MotionEvent. The event contains the coordinates of the pointer where the top-left corner of the device represents the origin (0,0). The type of event: ACTION_DOWN, ACTION_UP or ACTION_MOVE can be obtained by calling event.getAction(). Based on this value, we save the start XY coordinates. Finally, when we drag a finger, the XY increments (dx, dy) are calculated and sent to the native layer for consumption. When the finger goes up, the start XY coordinates are reset as shown in Listing 2–12. The final effect is a sequence of delta XY increments which the native engine can use to either move a character in 3D space or look around the surroundings. This is how Quake handles movement.

Listing 2–12. *Cascading touch events between Java and C*

```
// Java: Natives to be implemented in C
public static native int mouseLook(int deltaX, int deltaY);
public static native int mouseMove(int deltaX, int deltaY);

// down corrdinaes
float startX = -1, startY = -1;

public boolean onTouchEvent(MotionEvent event)
{
    int action = event.getAction();
    if ( action == MotionEvent.ACTION_DOWN ) {
        startX = event.x;
        startY = event.y;
    }
    else if ( action == MotionEvent.ACTION_UP ) {
```

```
        startX = startY = 0;
    }
    else if ( action == MotionEvent.ACTION_MOVE)
    {
        final float dx = event.x - startX;
        final float dy = event.y - startY;

        // decide to move or look
        mouseLook(dx , dy );
        //mouseMove (dx, dy);
    }
    return true;
}

// C implementation of int mouseLook(int deltaX, int deltaY)
JNIEXPORT jint JNICALL Java_Natives_mouseMove
  (JNIEnv * env, jclass cls, jint dx, jint dy)
{
    LOGD("Mouse Move %d, %d", dx, dy);
}

// C implementation of int mouseLook(int deltaX, int deltaY)
JNIEXPORT jint JNICALL Java_Natives_mouseLook
  (JNIEnv * env, jclass cls, jint dx, jint dy)
{
    LOGD("Mouse Look %d, %d", dx, dy);
}
```

In the previous section we looked at single touch events which may not be adequate for some types of games such as first-person shooters where the player needs to move and aim at the same time. The next section can help. Multitouch is a technique that expands on the touch API to provide more fingers you can use around your game for more complex interactions.

Multitouch Tricks

The multitouch capabilities of Android are an extension of MotionEvent. It has all the information you need to implement a multitouch scheme. For example, let's assume that we have a game where sweeping a finger on the left side will move a character forward or sideways in 3D space, and sweeping on the right side will look around. Using the Android MotionEvent, we can easily implement such a scheme. Consider three sample classes: MultiTouchGesture, MultiTouchScreen, and TestActivity from Listings 2–13, 2–14, and 2–15 respectively, all of which are discussed in the following sections.

MultiTouchGesture

This is a class that encapsulates a gesture type such as a character move or look (Listing 2–13). It also defines the bounds on the screen where this gesture is valid (by using the Rect Android class). When the gesture is valid it will execute some action (sending the move or look increments to the native engine for example).

Listing 2–13. *Multitouch gesture*

```java
package com.touch;

import android.graphics.Point;
import android.graphics.Rect;
import android.view.MotionEvent;

public class MultiTouchGesture {
  public enum eGestureType {  MOVE, LOOK };

  Rect bounds;
  eGestureType type;

  public MultiTouchGesture(eGestureType type, Rect bounds) {
    this.type = type;
    this.bounds = bounds;
  }

  /**
   * Execute gesture
   * @param action
   *            {@link MotionEvent} action: ACTION_UP, ACTION_MOVE,...
   * @param p
   *            Finger point XY coordinates
   */
  public boolean execute(int action, Point p) {
    switch (type) {
    case MOVE:
      doMove(action, p);
      break;

    case LOOK:
      doLook(action, p);
      break;

    default:
      break;
    }
    return true;
  }

  public void reset() {
    switch (type) {
    case MOVE:

      break;
    case LOOK:
      break;

    default:
      break;
    }
  }

  private void doMove(int action, Point p) {
    // Tell the native engine to move
  }
```

```
      private void doLook(int action, Point p) {
        // Tell native engine to look
      }
    }
```

MultiTouchGesture will execute by checking its type (in this case MOVE or LOOK). Depending on the type, a native method could be fired to send the XY coordinates to the game engine. The action argument tells the gesture what kind of MotionEvent has fired. It can be one of the following:

```
MotionEvent.ACTION_DOWN (first finger)
MotionEvent.ACTION_UP (first finger)
MotionEvent.ACTION_MOVE (first finger)
ACTION_POINTER_1_DOWN (second)
ACTION_POINTER_1_UP (second)
ACTION_POINTER_2_DOWN (third)
ACTION_POINTER_2_UP (third)
ACTION_POINTER_3_DOWN (fourth)
ACTION_POINTER_3_UP (fourth)
```

> **TIP:** Android supports up to 4 simultaneous pointers/fingers on screen.

MultiTouchScreen

This class is in charge of storing a list of gestures, checking their bounds and interacting with the main activity (Listing 2–14).

Listing 2–14. *MultiTouchScreen*

```
package com.touch;

import java.util.ArrayList;
import android.graphics.Point;
import android.view.MotionEvent;

public class MultiTouchScreen {

  private ArrayList<MultiTouchGesture> mGestures;

  /**
   * Constructor
   * @param gestures
   */
  public MultiTouchScreen(ArrayList<MultiTouchGesture> gestures) {
    mGestures = gestures;
  }

  /**
   * Touch Event. Events with bogus pressure pop up when using 1 finger
   * @param e
   */
  public void onTouchEvent(MotionEvent e) {
    final int action = e.getAction();
    int count = e.getPointerCount();
```

```
    Point[] points = new Point[count];

    // for each finger extract coords
    for (int i = 0; i < points.length; i++) {
      points[i] = new Point((int) e.getX(i), (int) e.getY(i));
    }

    // for each gesture
    for (MultiTouchGesture g : mGestures) {
      // for each finger (pointer)
      for (int j = 0; j < count; j++) {
        if (g.bounds.contains(points[j].x, points[j].y)) {
          g.execute(action, points[j]);
        }
      }
    }

    // reset when finger goes up
    if (action == MotionEvent.ACTION_UP) {
      for (MultiTouchGesture g : mGestures) {
        g.reset();
      }
    }
  }
}
```

The class MultiTouchScreen receives the MotionEvent from the main activity and checks each gesture to see if the XY coordinates of the finger fall within the bounds of the gesture. If so, then the gesture is executed. You can get the number of pointers from the MotionEvent by calling:

```
int count = e.getPointerCount();
```

Then, the coordinates for each pointer can be obtained by looping through the number of pointers and extracting their XY coordinates:

```
    Point[] points = new Point[count];

    // for each finger extract coords
    for (int i = 0; i < points.length; i++) {
      points[i] = new Point((int) e.getX(i), (int) e.getY(i));
    }
```

Finally we can check if the pointer falls within the gesture bounds by looping through each gesture and checking if each pointer XY coordinates falls within the gesture bounding rectangle.

```
    for (MultiTouchGesture g : mGestures) {
      // for each finger (pointer)
      for (int j = 0; j < count; j++) {
        if (g.bounds.contains(points[j].x, points[j].y)) {
          g.execute(action, points[j]);
        }
      }
    }
```

TestActivity

Last thing we need is an Activity that will initialize the multitouch screen, the gesture bounds, and listen for touch events (see Listing 2–15).

Listing 2–15. *test Activity for the MultiTouchScreen class*

```
public class TestActivity extends Activity {

  MultiTouchScreen mtScreen;

  @Override
  public void onCreate(Bundle savedInstanceState) {
    super.onCreate(savedInstanceState);
    setContentView(R.layout.main);

    // init multi touch screen
    ArrayList<MultiTouchGesture> gestures = new ArrayList<MultiTouchGesture>();

    int w = getWindow().getWindowManager().getDefaultDisplay().getWidth();
    int h = getWindow().getWindowManager().getDefaultDisplay().getHeight();

    // move: left half of the screen
    gestures.add(
     new MultiTouchGesture(eGestureType.MOVE, new Rect(0, 0, w / 2, h)));

    // look right halsf
    gestures.add(
        new MultiTouchGesture(eGestureType.LOOK, new Rect(w / 2, 0, w, h)));

    mtScreen = new MultiTouchScreen(gestures);
  }

  @Override
  public boolean onTouchEvent(MotionEvent event) {
    mtScreen.onTouchEvent(event);
    return true;
  }
}
```

TestActivity initializes the gestures coordinates by obtaining the display width and height (using getWindow().getWindowManager().getDefaultDisplay()). It then initializes two types of gestures: MOVE with bounds on the left half of the screen, and LOOK with bounds on the right half. The gestures are passed to the MultiTouchScreen constructor. Finally when a single or multitouch event fires, onTouchEvent in the main activity will be called and the event relayed to MultiTouchScreen for consumption. This will allow our game character to move and look simultaneously in 3D space. This technique will be put to the test in the Quake I & II chapters of this book.

A WORD OF CAUTION ABOUT MULTITOUCH

Before you think about implementing complex multitouch schemes on your game you shoud be aware that the Android multitouch API is very buggy (full of bogus pointers and false coordinates) in old devices such as the Motorola Droid 1 and first generation phones. For example when you touch and slide two fingers across the screen and simply dump the MotionEvent coordinates on screen, you will get a ton of false coordinates and bogus pointers which can be very frustrating especially for 3D shooters such as Quake. Perhaps this is the reason 3D shooters have not been able to make in the Android market. It is unclear what the reasons for those bugs are. Perhaps cheap hardware or buggy kernel drivers. Although I am happy to report that in second- and third-generation devices such as the Droid 3 things have improved dramatically. In the latest Android SDK multitouch drivers have improved even further to the point that if you have a device with decent hardware, chances are that you will not encounter this type of multitouch issue. However beware of cheap hardware and old Android versions.

We have seen some neat tricks for handling audio, video, and input using keyboard, single and multitouch. But if you are a hardcore gamer you will always hear complaints about how difficult is to play hardcore games (shooters for example) with a touch interface or a tiny keyboard. Try playing doom with a touch screen versus a controller. You will get frustrated very quickly with the touch screen. Some games simply require a controller. This is the reason for the next section: Bluetooth controllers. I am sure your customers will be happy that you provide Bluetooth controller support in your game.

Bluetooth Controllers (Zeemote)

Zeemote is a Bluetooth joystick controller very popular in Nokia phones. With the rising in popularity of other smartphones, its creators released an SDK for other platforms such as Android and iPhone. The Zeemote consists of a joystick and four buttons (A, B, C, and D - see Figure 2–10).

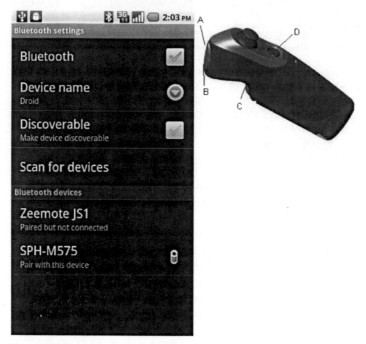

Figure 2–10. *Bluetooth settings and Zemmote joystick*

Before you can start using a Zeemote you need to turn it on, enable Bluetooth and pair the controller. Put two AAA batteries in the controller, press the D button for 3 seconds to turn it on, then enable Bluetooth as seen in Figure 2–10. Press scan for devices, Android should show the controller in the device list. Press Zeemote JS1 and select Pair Device. You don't need to connect, pairing is enough.

> **TIP:** Pairing stores the Zeemote message authentication code (MAC) address in your phone. This is sort of a device ID used to communicate between both devices. You need to pair a Bluetooth device only once.

Now we can start writing code that connects to our Zeemote but first we need to download the SDK with the libraries required to enable it in our app. The latest Zeemote SDK is available online at http://www.zeemote.com or in the Book's source under ch02.Project/libs (see Figure 2–11).

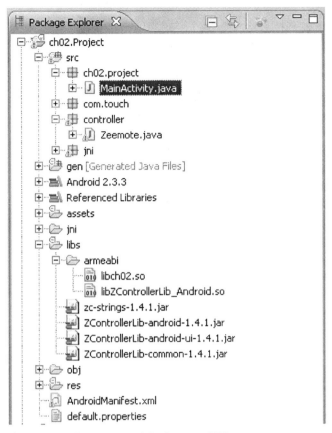

Figure 2–11. *Components of the Zeemote SDK*

Figure 2–11 shows the required JARs for the Zeemote SDK 1.4: ZControllerLib-android-1.4.1.jar, ZControllerLib-android-ui-1.4.1.jar, ZControllerLib-common-1.4.1.jar, zc-strings-1.4.1.jar, and the native libZControllerLib_Android.so. You will need to include all these files in the app you wish to enable the Zeemote.

Listing 2–16 shows the simple class Zeemote that connects to a controller and listens for status, button, and joystick events. The steps can be summarized as follows:

1. Create an instance of Controller by calling new `Controller(Controller.CONTROLLER_1)`. This object is used to interface with the device.

2. Listen for controller events by implementing any of the API interfaces:

- IStatusListener: This interface fires the events batteryUpdate(BatteryEvent) which gives information bout power levels; connected(ControllerEvent) which fires when the controller is successfully connected; and disconnected(DisconnectEvent) which fires when a disconnection occurs.

- IButtonListener: This interface fires the events buttonPressed(ButtonEvent) or buttonPressed(ButtonEvent) whenever any of the 4 buttons is presses and released.

- IJoystickListener: This interface fires the event joystickMoved(JoystickEvent) which gives the scaled XY coordinated of the joystick.

3.   Handle the above events accordingly.

Listing 2–16. Class to connect a Zeemote

```
public class Zeemote implements IStatusListener, IJoystickListener,
    IButtonListener
{
  private static final String TAG = "Zeemote";
  private Controller mZeeController;
  private Context mContext;

  public Zeemote(Context context) {
    mContext = context;
    mZeeController = new Controller(Controller.CONTROLLER_1);

    mZeeController.addStatusListener(this);
    mZeeController.addJoystickListener(this);
    mZeeController.addButtonListener(this);
  }

  public void  connect() {
    ControllerAndroidUi controllerUi = new ControllerAndroidUi(mContext,
        mZeeController);
    controllerUi.startConnectionProcess();
  }

  /**********************************************
   * ZEEMOTE EVENTS
   **********************************************/
  public void batteryUpdate(BatteryEvent event) {
    int id = event.getController().getId();
    int max = event.getMaximumLevel();
    int min = event.getMinimumLevel();
    int warn = event.getWarningLevel();
    int cur = event.getCurrentLevel();
    int pctLeft = (int) (((float) (cur - min) / (float) (max - min)) * 100);

    Log.d(TAG, "Battery Update: Controller ID=" + id + " cur=" + cur + ", max="
        + max + ", min=" + min + ", warn=" + warn + " %left=" + pctLeft);

    /* battery low? */
```

```java
    if (cur <= warn) {
      // do somthing
    }
  }

  public void connected(ControllerEvent event) {
    com.zeemote.zc.Configuration config = event.getController()
        .getConfiguration();

    Log.d(TAG, "Connected to controller:");
    Log.d(TAG, "Num Buttons=" + config.getButtonCount());
    Log.d(TAG, "Num Joysticks=" + config.getJoystickCount());

  }

  public void disconnected(DisconnectEvent event) {
    Log.d(TAG, "Disconnected from controller: "
        + (event.isUnexpected() ? "unexpected" : "expected"));

    if (mZeeController != null) {
      Log.d(TAG, "Removing Zee listeners.");

      mZeeController.removeStatusListener(this);
      mZeeController.removeJoystickListener(this);
      mZeeController.removeButtonListener(this);
    }
  }

  /**********************************************
   * ZEEMOTE BUTTON EVENTS
   **********************************************/
  public void buttonPressed(ButtonEvent event) {
    int b = event.getButtonID();
    String label = event.getController().getConfiguration().getButtonLabel(b);

  }

  public void buttonReleased(ButtonEvent event) {
    String buttonName = event.getController().getConfiguration()
        .getButtonLabel(event.getButtonID());
  }

  /**********************************************
   * ZEEMOTE JOYSTIC EVEN
   **********************************************/
  public void joystickMoved(JoystickEvent e) {
    // A joystick moved. Scale the values between -100 and 100
    int x = e.getScaledX(-100, 100);
    int y = e.getScaledY(-100, 100);

    Log.d(TAG, "X=" + x + ",Y=" + y);
  }
}
```

To connect to the Zeemote from your app activity call the connect method of the Zeemote class:

```
Zeemote zee = new Zeemote(this);
zee.connect();
```

When the connect method fires the Zeemote connection UI will take over and allow you to connect (if the controller is on and close to the phone). As a bonus you can check programmatically if Bluetooth is enabled using BluetoothAdapter.getDefaultAdapter(), and if not enabled use the built-in Android UI to do it (see Listing 2–17).

Listing 2–17. *Enabling the Bluetooth adapter*

```
BluetoothAdapter mBluetoothAdapter = BluetoothAdapter.getDefaultAdapter();

if (mBluetoothAdapter == null) {
  // Device does not support Bluetooth
}
// Enable it
if (!mBluetoothAdapter.isEnabled()) {
  Intent enableBtIntent = new Intent(BluetoothAdapter.ACTION_REQUEST_ENABLE);
  ctx.startActivityForResult(enableBtIntent, REQUEST_ENABLE_BT);
}
```

Summary

In this chapter, you have taken the first steps for building a hybrid game using JNI by learning how to create the main Java activity and loading a native library within it. Next, you learned about Java native methods using the native keyword plus the C header file required to implement them. You also learned some useful C tricks, such as converting Java arrays to C arrays, getting the size of a Java array, and invoking Java methods within C.

You then learned how to cascade Audio, Video, Key, and Touch events from Java to C by using thin Java wrappers that simply pass event information to the native library. You learned about Multitouch, and how you can track multiple pointers across the screen reacting accordingly. Finally, you saw how to enable the slick Zeemote Bluetooth controller in you app.

This and the previous chapter provide the basic foundation if you are planning to port a game that has significant Linux C code to the Android platform. In Chapter 3 we tackle native OpenGL in more detail.

## Chapter 3

More Gaming Tricks with OpenGL and JNI

Chapter 2 provided a great introduction to some basic gaming techniques for Android, including handling Audio/Video, I/O Events, and Bluetooth controllers. Now it's time to ramp things up a notch.

In this chapter, you will learn a neat trick to mix OpenGL code in Java and C. This is a key step in reusing large portions of OpenGL C code along with Java code, thus using the best features of each language for maximum savings in time and costs.

Any game developer knows that OpenGL is the holy grail of advanced game development. You won't find any powerful games that are not written with this API, because it takes advantage of hardware acceleration, which is infinitely superior to any kind of software renderer.

OpenGL can be a scary subject to the newcomer due to its complexity. But you don't have to be an OpenGL guru to understand what it does and how to draw elements with this API. All you need is the desire to learn a powerful and exciting tool for gaming.

The goal of this chapter is not to teach you OpenGL (a whole book wouldn't be enough for that), but to show you how you can take the Android OpenGL sample provided by Google and modify it in a completely different way by mixing OpenGL API calls in both Java and native C for maximum reusability.

Some may say this is simply another OpenGL chapter for a mobile device (dime a dozen, right?). Well, it is not. This chapter presents a technique for OpenGL in Android that is unique, and at the time of this writing, not available anywhere in the Android sphere (on the Web). This is a technique I stumbled on by accident when thinking about porting the game Quake to Android. In a nutshell, the technique consists of creating the OpenGL context, display, and surface objects in Java, and performing all drawing operations natively in C. At the end of the rendering cycle, a JNI callback is used by the C engine to tell the Java side to swap the buffers (render the image). The cycle then repeats itself. This technique is extremely useful when you have a 200,000-line code game like Quake, and rewriting this code in Java is simply not feasible (an introduction to this method is given in the section OpenGL the Native Way and explained thoroughly in the later chapter Doom for Android).

The chapter starts by examining the OpenGL tumbling cubes sample to expose how OpenGL works in Java. Next, we will look at how sections of the rendering process can be implemented in the native layer, and how everything is bound by JNI. The final section discusses some of the limitations of the OpenGL Embedded System when it comes to advanced 3D games. And, as is the previous chapter, all material discussed within this one is Android 4 compatible.

Let's get started.

NEED AN OPENGL REFRESHER?

For this chapter, you'll need a basic understanding of OpenGL. If your OpenGL is a bit rusty, I suggest referring to the best tutorials I have found on the Web:

■ Greg Sidelnikov's tutorial about the OpenGL coordinate system. It covers the basics such as perspectives, orthographic projections, 3D camera, graphics pipeline, variable and function naming conventions, and more. It is a good place to start:

http://www.falloutsoftware.com/tutorials/gl/glo.htm

■ If you are confused about OpenGL projections, MathWorld has some good information about all kinds of 3D projections used in OpenGL:

http://mathworld.wolfram.com/OrthographicProjection.html

■ NeHe Productions has compiled a comprehensive set of tutorials that cover pretty much everything you need to write an OpenGL application. These are very popular:

http://nehe.gamedev.net/

The Power of Mobile Devices

Mobile Android devices have become pretty powerful for graphics development. Check out the following hardware stats for the Samsung Galaxy S:

■ ARM processor running at 1 GHz

■ Graphics processing unit (GPU) with 256 KB of RAM

■ 320x480 pixel display

To make good use of the GPU, Google has included the OpenGL Embedded System (ES) within Android. OpenGL ES provides the software API to make high-performance, hardware-accelerated games possible. This is a Java API, which is good news for Java developers who wish to create 3D games from scratch, but bad news for C developers who wish to reuse 3D engines written in C. 3D game engines are very complex and large, and are mostly written in C. Rewriting these engines in Java would be a very difficult task, consuming significant development and time resources.

Consider how easy it is to reuse OpenGL code in C. Let's look at another powerful smartphone: Apple's iPhone. If you search the iPhone App Store (or the Web), you will find that dozens of OpenGL-based 3D games have already been ported to the platform, including some of the greatest 3D shooters for the PC: Wolfenstein 3D, Doom, and Quake I. Even Quake III Arena—a game that has extremely advanced 3D graphics for a mobile device—has been ported! What do all these games have in common? They are written in C. Furthermore, Apple provides a C toolchain that makes it easy to have the games running in the platform. Clearly, Android is at a big disadvantage in this field. Nevertheless, porting these games to Android is still possible.

Even though Android supports only Java development, the Android OS is built in a stripped version of GNU Linux featuring a C runtime. Using an ARM C toolchain, you can write and compile C code and bind it to Java using JNI.

A HEAD START: THE SOURCE CODE FOR THIS CHAPTER

In this chapter, we'll use the Android 3D cubes sample in its original Java language, but we will also move code to the native side. This sample is available from the Android site; however, the sample is composed of many resources, which are bundled as part of the overall Android samples pack. To make things simpler, I have packed the required files, plus the changes described throughout this chapter, in the chapter source code.

If you wish, you can import the project into your workspace. To do so, select File → Import. In the dialog box, select Existing Projects into Workspace. Next, navigate to the chapter source ch03.OpenGL. Optionally, check Copy project into workspace. When you click Finish, the automated build will load.

Try to familiarize yourself with the project layout, especially with the following folders:

- ▓ `src`: contains the Java classes used by the project.
- ▓ `jni`: contains the cube renderer and the cube-drawing subroutines.

OpenGL the Java Way

Let's look at how OpenGL graphics are done in Java. We'll start by creating a project for our sample application. Then we'll look at the classes that make up the project: The main activity used to launch the app, the surface view used to render graphics, the GL thread used to perform drawing operations in the background, the cube renderer used to draw the actual cube, and the cube class which has information such as dimensions, color, and others.

Creating a Project

For this exploration, let's create a project to hold the GL tumbling cubes application from the Android samples.

Here is how:

1. Click the New Android Project button.

2. In the New Android Project dialog box, enter a project name, such as ch03.OpenGL. Click Next.

3. Specify the build target (Android 4 in this case). Click next.

4. Enter an application name, such as Ch03.OpenGL.

5. Enter a package name, such as opengl.test.

6. Select Create Activity and enter JavaGLActivity.

7. Specify the minimum SDK version as 14 for Android 4. Figure 3–1 shows all the wizard dialogs for this example.

8. Click Finish.

> **NOTE:** The original sample code will be modified to fit the changes described throughout this chapter.

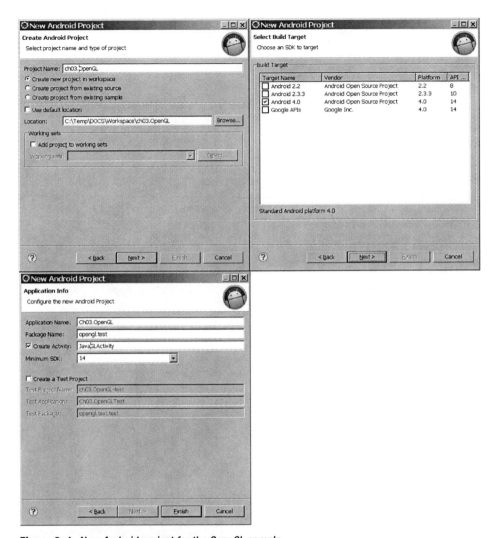

Figure 3–1. *New Android project for the OpenGL sample*

The Android cubes sample consists of the following Java classes (see Figure 3–2):

■ GLSurfaceView: This is an implementation of SurfaceView that uses a dedicated surface for displaying an OpenGL animation. The animation will run in a separate thread (GLThread).

■ GLThread: This is a generic thread with a loop for GL operations. Its job is to perform resource initialization. It also delegates rendering to an instance of the Renderer interface.

■ Renderer: This is a generic interface for rendering objects. In this case, we will be rendering two tumbling cubes.

- EglHelper: This is a GL helper class used to do the following:

  - Initialize the EGL context.

  - Create the GL surface.

  - Swap buffers (perform the actual drawing).

- CubeRenderer: This is an implementation of the Renderer interface to draw the cubes.

- Cube: This class encapsulates a GL cube, including vertices, colors, and indices for each face.

Because the sample needs to be slightly modified to illustrate the concepts of the chapter, the following classes have been added for this purpose:

- JavaGLActivity: This is the Android activity that will start the Java-only version of the application.

- NativeGLActivity: This activity will start the hybrid version of the sample (with Java/C/JNI code).

- Natives: This class defines the native methods used by this sample.

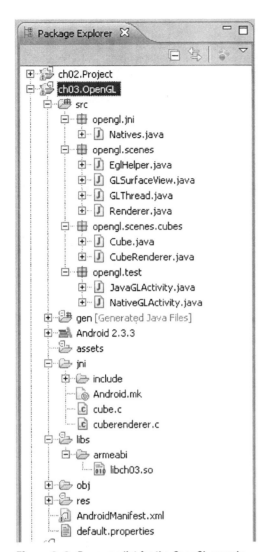

Figure 3–2. *Resource list for the OpenGL sample*

The Android manifest needs to be updated to include the new activities defined in the previous paragraph, as shown in bold in Listing 3–1.

Listing 3–1. *Manifest File for This Chapter's Example*

```xml
<?xml version="1.0" encoding="utf-8"?>
<manifest xmlns:android="http://schemas.android.com/apk/res/android"
     package="opengl.test"
     android:versionCode="1"
     android:versionName="1.0">
  <application android:icon="@drawable/icon"
     android:label="@string/app_name">
     <activity android:name=".JavaGLActivity"
```

```
                android:label="OpenGL Java">
            <intent-filter>
                <action android:name="android.intent.action.MAIN" />
                <category android:name="android.intent.category.LAUNCHER" />
            </intent-filter>
        </activity>
        <activity android:name=".NativeGLActivity"
                android:label="OpenGL Native">
            <intent-filter>
                <action android:name="android.intent.action.MAIN" />
                <category android:name="android.intent.category.LAUNCHER" />
            </intent-filter>
        </activity>
    </application>
    <uses-sdk android:minSdkVersion="3" />
</manifest>
```

The following lines tell Android to create two application launchers in the device launchpad, one for each of the activities OpenGL Java and OpenGL Native:

```
<action android:name="android.intent.action.MAIN" />
<category android:name="android.intent.category.LAUNCHER" />
```

Let's start with the Java-only implementation. Figure 3–3 defines the basic workflow of the OpenGL application. The figure shows the main activity (JavaGLActivity), which creates the rendering surface (GLSurfaceView). The surface creates a renderer (CubeRenderer) which contains a thread (GLThread). GLThread in turn contains the loop that invokes the renderer draw() method that draws the tumbling cubes seen on the device display.

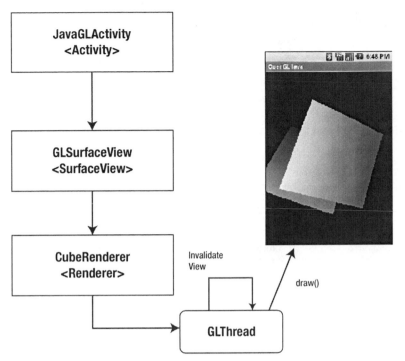

Figure 3–3. *Workflow of the Java-only cubes sample*

Java Main Activity

When the user starts the application, the JavaGLActivity.onCreate() method will be called (see Listing 3–2). Here is where the surface view (mGLSurfaceView) is initialized and set as the application content:

```
mGLSurfaceView = new GLSurfaceView(this);
mGLSurfaceView.setRenderer(new CubeRenderer(true));
setContentView(mGLSurfaceView);
```

Note that the GL surface view must use a renderer (CubeRenderer in this case), which implements the Renderer interface and takes a Boolean argument indicating if a translucent background should be used.

Listing 3–2. *Main Activity for the Java-Only Version of the GL Cubes Sample*

```
package opengl.test;

import opengl.scenes.GLSurfaceView;
import opengl.scenes.cubes.CubeRenderer;
import android.app.Activity;
import android.os.Bundle;

public class JavaGLActivity extends Activity
{
    private GLSurfaceView mGLSurfaceView;
```

```
/** Called when the activity is first created. */
@Override
public void onCreate(Bundle savedInstanceState) {
    super.onCreate(savedInstanceState);

    mGLSurfaceView = new GLSurfaceView(this);

    try {
        mGLSurfaceView.setRenderer(new CubeRenderer(true));
        setContentView(mGLSurfaceView);

    } catch (Exception e) {
        e.printStackTrace();
    }
}

@Override
protected void onPause() {
    // Ideally a game should implement onResume() and onPause()
    // to take appropriate action when the activity loses focus
    super.onPause();
    mGLSurfaceView.onPause();
}

@Override
protected void onResume() {
    super.onResume();
    mGLSurfaceView.onResume();
}
}
```

When the application loses focus or resumes, the onPause() or onResume() method will be called, respectively. These methods delegate to the surface view (GLSurfaceView) to take the appropriate action, such as saving application state or suspending/resuming the rendering process.

Surface View

The class GLSurfaceView (see Listing 3–3) defines the surface where the tumbling cubes animation will take place. The class constructor starts by initializing a callback to receive notifications when the surface is changed, created, or destroyed:

```
mHolder = getHolder();
mHolder.addCallback(this);
mHolder.setType(SurfaceHolder.SURFACE_TYPE_GPU);
```

By implementing SurfaceHolder.Callback and calling SurfaceHolder.addCallback(), the class will receive the events:

  ▪ surfaceCreated(SurfaceHolder holder): This is called immediately after the surface is first created. In this case, the surface delegates to the inner thread GLThread.surfaceCreated().

- surfaceDestroyed(SurfaceHolder holder): This method is called immediately before a surface is being destroyed. After returning from this call, the surface should not be accessed. In this case, the method delegates to the rendering thread GLThread.surfaceDestroyed().

- surfaceChanged(SurfaceHolder holder, int format, int w, int h): This method is called immediately after any structural changes (format or size) have been made to the surface. Here is where you tell the inner thread that the size has changed. This method is always called at least once, after surfaceCreated(). The second argument of this method (format) is the pixel format of the graphics defined in the PixelFormat class.

Listing 3–3. *Surface View for the GL Cubes Sample*

```
package opengl.scenes;

import opengl.jni.Natives;
import android.content.Context;
import android.util.AttributeSet;
import android.view.SurfaceHolder;
import android.view.SurfaceView;

/**
 * An implementation of SurfaceView that uses the dedicated surface for
 * displaying an OpenGL animation. This allows the animation to run in a
 * separate thread, without requiring that it be driven by the update
 * mechanism of the view hierarchy.
 *
 * The application-specific rendering code is delegated to a GLView.Renderer
 * instance.
 */
public class GLSurfaceView extends SurfaceView
  implements  SurfaceHolder.Callback
{
    public GLSurfaceView(Context context) {
        super(context);
        init();
    }

    public GLSurfaceView(Context context, AttributeSet attrs) {
        super(context, attrs);
        init();
    }

    private void init() {
        // Install a SurfaceHolder.Callback so we get notified when the
        // underlying surface is created and destroyed
        mHolder = getHolder();
        mHolder.addCallback(this);
        mHolder.setType(SurfaceHolder.SURFACE_TYPE_GPU);
    }

    public SurfaceHolder getSurfaceHolder() {
        return mHolder;
```

```java
    }

    public void setRenderer(Renderer renderer) {
        mGLThread = new GLThread(renderer, mHolder);
        mGLThread.start();
    }

    public void surfaceCreated(SurfaceHolder holder) {
        mGLThread.surfaceCreated();
    }

    public void surfaceDestroyed(SurfaceHolder holder) {
        // Surface will be destroyed when we return
        mGLThread.surfaceDestroyed();
    }

    public void surfaceChanged(SurfaceHolder holder, int format, int w,
            int h) {
        // Surface size or format has changed. This should not happen in
        // this example.
        mGLThread.onWindowResize(w, h);
    }

    /**
     * Inform the view that the activity is paused.
     */
    public void onPause() {
        mGLThread.onPause();
    }

    /**
     * Inform the view that the activity is resumed.
     */
    public void onResume() {
        mGLThread.onResume();
    }

    /**
     * Inform the view that the window focus has changed.
     */
    @Override
    public void onWindowFocusChanged(boolean hasFocus) {
        super.onWindowFocusChanged(hasFocus);
        mGLThread.onWindowFocusChanged(hasFocus);
    }
    /**
     * Queue an "event" to be run on the GL rendering thread.
     *
     * @param r
     *            the runnable to be run on the GL rendering thread.
     */
    public void queueEvent(Runnable r) {
        mGLThread.queueEvent(r);
    }

    @Override
    protected void onDetachedFromWindow() {
        super.onDetachedFromWindow();
```

```
    mGLThread.requestExitAndWait();
}

private SurfaceHolder mHolder;
private GLThread mGLThread;
```

}

Other important methods in the surface view include the following:

- setRenderer(): This method creates the inner thread that does all the work and starts it. The thread keeps a reference to the surface holder available by calling getHolder().

```
public void setRenderer(Renderer renderer) {
    mGLThread = new GLThread(renderer, mHolder);
    mGLThread.start();
}
```

- queueEvent(Runnable r): This method sends an event to be run by the inner thread.

- onDetachedFromWindow(): This method is called when the view is detached from a window. At this point, it no longer has a surface for drawing.

The surface view provides the drawing canvas for the next component: the GL thread. A thread is required to perform tasks in the background thus offloading processing time from the main application thread to make the application run seamlessly. Let's see what it does.

GL Thread

The main loop of the animation is performed by GLThread. When started, this thread performs the following steps:

1. It creates a semaphore:

```
sEglSemaphore.acquire();
guardedRun();   // Only 1 thread can access this code
sEglSemaphore.release();
```

2. It runs the critical animation loop. Within the loop, the actual drawing is delegated to the CubeRenderer.

3. When asked to quit, the loops terminates, and the OpenGL resources are released.

> **NOTE:** A *semaphore* is an object often used to restrict the number of threads that can access the OpenGL context. When the Android framework launches a second instance of an activity, the new instance's onCreate() method may be called before the first instance returns from onDestroy(). A semaphore ensures that only one instance at a time accesses the GL API. We must do this because OpenGL is a single-threaded API (which means that only one thread can access the GLContext at a time).

Listing 3–4 shows a fragment of the GLThread class taken from the GL cubes sample. When the thread starts, the run() method will be invoked, and a semaphore used to ensure that guardedRun() can be accessed by one thread only. guardedRun() performs other important steps, such as the following:

- Initialize the Embedded OpenGL (EGL) for a given configuration specification. The configuration specification defines information, such as pixel format and image depth.

- Create the OpenGL surface and tell the renderer about it.

- Check if the size of the surface has changed and tell the renderer about it.

- Queue and get events to be run on the GL rendering thread.

Listing 3–4. *Rendering Thread for the GL Cubes Sample*

```
package opengl.scenes;

// …

/**
 * A generic GL Thread. Takes care of initializing EGL and GL.
 * Delegates to a Renderer instance to do the actual drawing.
 */
public class GLThread extends Thread
{
    public GLThread(Renderer renderer, SurfaceHolder holder) {
        super();
        mDone = false;
        mWidth = 0;
        mHeight = 0;
        mRenderer = renderer;
        mHolder = holder;
        setName("GLThread");
    }

@Override
    public void run() {
        try {
            try {
                sEglSemaphore.acquire();
            } catch (InterruptedException e) {
                return;
```

```
            }
            guardedRun();
        } catch (Exception ex) {
            ex.printStackTrace();
        } finally {
            sEglSemaphore.release();
        }
    }

    private void guardedRun() throws InterruptedException {
        mEglHelper = new EglHelper();

        // Specify a configuration for our OpenGL session
        int[] configSpec = mRenderer.getConfigSpec();
        mEglHelper.start(configSpec);

        GL10 gl = null;
        boolean tellRendererSurfaceCreated = true;
        boolean tellRendererSurfaceChanged = true;

        // This is our main activity thread's loop,
        while (!mDone) {

            // Update the asynchronous state (window size)
            int w, h;
            boolean changed;
            boolean needStart = false;
            synchronized (this) {
                Runnable r;
                while ((r = getEvent()) != null) {
                    r.run();
                }
                if (mPaused) {
                    mEglHelper.finish();
                    needStart = true;
                }
                if (needToWait()) {
                    while (needToWait()) {
                        wait();
                    }
                }
                if (mDone) {
                    break;
                }
                changed = mSizeChanged;
                w = mWidth;
                h = mHeight;
                mSizeChanged = false;
            }
            if (needStart) {
                mEglHelper.start(configSpec);
                tellRendererSurfaceCreated = true;
                changed = true;
            }
            if (changed) {
                // Create the surface
                gl = (GL10) mEglHelper.createSurface(mHolder);
                tellRendererSurfaceChanged = true;
```

```
        }
        if (tellRendererSurfaceCreated) {
            mRenderer.surfaceCreated(gl);
            tellRendererSurfaceCreated = false;
        }
        if (tellRendererSurfaceChanged) {
            mRenderer.sizeChanged(gl, w, h);
            tellRendererSurfaceChanged = false;
        }
        if ((w > 0) && (h > 0)) {
            /* draw a frame here */
            mRenderer.drawFrame(gl);

            // Call swapBuffers() to instruct the system to display
            mEglHelper.swap();
        }
    }

    // Clean up...
    mEglHelper.finish();
}

// …
private static final Semaphore sEglSemaphore = new Semaphore(1);
private EglHelper mEglHelper;
}
```

The GL thread will make use of the next two sections: The cube renderer to perform drawing, rotation, and positioning operations on the cube, and the cube class which has information about the cube itself. Let's look at the renderer in more detail.

Cube Renderer

CubeRenderer is the class that renders the pair of tumbling cubes (see Listing 3–5). It implements the Renderer interface and does some very interesting things.

The void drawFrame(GL10 gl) method does the actual drawing and gets called many times per second. The method starts by setting the matrix mode to GL_MODELVIEW. This essentially says to render things in a 3D perspective (model view). Next, it clears all screen buffers by calling glLoadIdentity().

```
gl.glMatrixMode(GL10.GL_MODELVIEW);
gl.glLoadIdentity();
```

Next, the perspective is translated in the z axis by three units toward the eye viewpoint (also known as the camera):

```
gl.glTranslatef(0, 0, -3.0f);
```

The next two instructions tell the pipeline to rotate the perspective in the y and x axes by an angle given in radians (0-6.28, 0 meaning zero degrees, and 6.28, meaning 360 degrees).

```
gl.glRotatef(mAngle, 0, 1, 0);
gl.glRotatef(mAngle * 0.25f, 1, 0, 0);
```

Next, it requests that vertices and colors be rendered. These are defined within the Cube class:

```
gl.glEnableClientState(GL10.GL_VERTEX_ARRAY);
gl.glEnableClientState(GL10.GL_COLOR_ARRAY);
```

Then the cube is drawn:

```
mCube.draw(gl);
```

The perspective is rotated again in the y and z axes, and translated half a unit away from the eye:

```
gl.glRotatef(mAngle * 2.0f, 0, 1, 1);
gl.glTranslatef(0.5f, 0.5f, 0.5f);
```

The second cube is drawn, and the angle of rotation is increased for the next iteration.

```
mCube.draw(gl);
mAngle += 1.2f;
```

The int[] getConfigSpec() method initializes the pixel format and the depth of the display. The pixel format describes the size of the ARGB values used to describe a pixel. The depth indicates the maximum number of colors used. For example, the following integer array requests 32 bits per pixel (ARGB 32bpp) with a depth of 16 (2^{16} colors).

```
int[] configSpec = {
EGL10.EGL_RED_SIZE,      8,
EGL10.EGL_GREEN_SIZE,    8,
EGL10.EGL_BLUE_SIZE,     8,
EGL10.EGL_ALPHA_SIZE,    8,
EGL10.EGL_DEPTH_SIZE,    16,
EGL10.EGL_NONE
};
```

The following are two other interesting methods in the cube renderer:

- void sizeChanged(GL10 gl, int width, int height): This method fires when the size of the viewport changes. It scales the cubes by setting the ratio of the projection matrix and resizing the viewport.

- void surfaceCreated(GL10 gl): This method fires when the surface is created. Here, some initialization is performed, such as setting a translucent background (if requested) and miscellaneous OpenGL renderer tweaking.

When the code in drawFrame() is executed many times per second, the result is two tumbling cubes (see Figure 3–4).

Listing 3–5. *Cube Renderer for the Pair of Tumbling Cubes*

```
package opengl.scenes.cubes;

import javax.microedition.khronos.egl.EGL10;
import javax.microedition.khronos.opengles.GL10;

import opengl.jni.Natives;
import opengl.scenes.Renderer;
```

```java
/**
 * Render a pair of tumbling cubes.
 */
public class CubeRenderer implements Renderer {

    public CubeRenderer(boolean useTranslucentBackground) {
        mTranslucentBackground = useTranslucentBackground;
        mNativeDraw = nativeDraw;
        mCube = new Cube();
    }

    public void drawFrame(GL10 gl) {
        /*
         * Usually, the first thing one might want to do is to clear
         * the screen. The most efficient way of doing this is
         * to use glClear().
         */
        gl.glClear(GL10.GL_COLOR_BUFFER_BIT | GL10.GL_DEPTH_BUFFER_BIT);

        /*
         * Now we're ready to draw some 3D objects
         */
        gl.glMatrixMode(GL10.GL_MODELVIEW);
        gl.glLoadIdentity();
        gl.glTranslatef(0, 0, -3.0f);
        gl.glRotatef(mAngle, 0, 1, 0);
        gl.glRotatef(mAngle * 0.25f, 1, 0, 0);

        gl.glEnableClientState(GL10.GL_VERTEX_ARRAY);
        gl.glEnableClientState(GL10.GL_COLOR_ARRAY);

        mCube.draw(gl);

        gl.glRotatef(mAngle * 2.0f, 0, 1, 1);
        gl.glTranslatef(0.5f, 0.5f, 0.5f);

        mCube.draw(gl);

        mAngle += 1.2f;
    }

    public int[] getConfigSpec() {
        if (mTranslucentBackground) {
            // We want a depth buffer and an alpha buffer
            int[] configSpec = { EGL10.EGL_RED_SIZE, 8,
                    EGL10.EGL_GREEN_SIZE, 8, EGL10.EGL_BLUE_SIZE, 8,
                    EGL10.EGL_ALPHA_SIZE, 8, EGL10.EGL_DEPTH_SIZE, 16,
                    EGL10.EGL_NONE };
            return configSpec;
        } else {
            // We want a depth buffer, don't care about the
            // details of the color buffer.
            int[] configSpec = { EGL10.EGL_DEPTH_SIZE, 16,
                    EGL10.EGL_NONE };
            return configSpec;
        }
    }
```

```
    public void sizeChanged(GL10 gl, int width, int height) {
        gl.glViewport(0, 0, width, height);

        /*
         * Set our projection matrix. This doesn't have to be done each time we
         * draw, but usually a new projection needs to be set when the viewport
         * is resized.
         */
        float ratio = (float) width / height;
        gl.glMatrixMode(GL10.GL_PROJECTION);
        gl.glLoadIdentity();
        gl.glFrustumf(-ratio, ratio, -1, 1, 1, 10);
    }

    public void surfaceCreated(GL10 gl) {
        /*
         * By default, OpenGL enables features that improve quality but reduce
         * performance. One might want to tweak that especially on software
         * renderer.
         */
        gl.glDisable(GL10.GL_DITHER);

        /*
         * Some one-time OpenGL initialization can be made here probably based
         * on features of this particular context
         */
        gl.glHint(GL10.GL_PERSPECTIVE_CORRECTION_HINT
            , GL10.GL_FASTEST);
        if (mTranslucentBackground) {
            gl.glClearColor(0, 0, 0, 0.5f);
        } else {
            gl.glClearColor(1, 1, 1, 0.5f);
        }

        gl.glEnable(GL10.GL_CULL_FACE);
        gl.glShadeModel(GL10.GL_SMOOTH);
        gl.glEnable(GL10.GL_DEPTH_TEST);
    }

    private boolean mTranslucentBackground;
    private Cube mCube;
    private float mAngle;
}
```

The final piece of this puzzle is the cube itself which has information such as dimensions, colors, and others. It works in tandem with the previous two components. Let's see what the cube does.

Cube Class

CubeRenderer delegates drawing to the Cube class (see Listing 3–6). This class defines a 12-sided cube with 8 vertices (8 * x,y,z coordinates), 32 colors (8 vertices * 4 ARGB values), and 36 indices for the x,y,z coordinates of each side. The class consists of two methods:

- Cube(): This is the class constructor. It initializes arrays for the vertices, colors, and indices required to draw. It then uses direct Java buffers to place the data on the native heap, where the garbage collector cannot move them. This is required by the gl*Pointer() API functions that do the actual drawing.

- draw(): To draw the cube, we simply set the vertices and colors, and issue a call to glDrawElements using triangles (GL_TRIANGLES). Note that a cube has 6 faces, 8 vertices, and 12 sides:

```
gl.glVertexPointer(3, GL10.GL_FIXED, 0, mVertexBuffer);
gl.glColorPointer(4, GL10.GL_FIXED, 0, mColorBuffer);
gl.glDrawElements(GL10.GL_TRIANGLES, 36
      , GL10.GL_UNSIGNED_BYTE,  mIndexBuffer);
```

Listing 3–6. *Cube Class for the GL Cubes Sample*

```
package opengl.scenes.cubes;

import java.nio.ByteBuffer;
import java.nio.ByteOrder;
import java.nio.IntBuffer;
import javax.microedition.khronos.opengles.GL10;

/**
 * A vertex shaded cube.
 */
public class Cube {
    public Cube() {
        int one = 0x10000;
        // 8 vertices each with 3 xyz coordinates
        int vertices[] = { -one, -one, -one
                , one, -one, -one
                , one, one,  -one
                , -one, one, -one
                , -one, -one, one
                , one, -one, one
                , one, one, one
                , -one, one, one };

        // 8 colors each with  4 RGBA values
        int colors[] = { 0, 0, 0, one
                , one, 0, 0, one
                , one, one, 0, one
                , 0, one, 0, one
                , 0, 0, one, one
                , one, 0, one, one
                , one, one, one, one
                , 0, one, one, one};
        // 12 indices each with 3 xyz coordinates
        byte indices[] = { 0, 4, 5, 0, 5, 1, 1, 5, 6, 1, 6, 2, 2, 6, 7,
                2, 7, 3, 3, 7, 4, 3, 4, 0, 4, 7, 6, 4, 6, 5, 3, 0, 1,
                3, 1, 2 };

        ByteBuffer vbb = ByteBuffer.allocateDirect(vertices.length * 4);
        vbb.order(ByteOrder.nativeOrder());
```

```
            mVertexBuffer = vbb.asIntBuffer();
            mVertexBuffer.put(vertices);
            mVertexBuffer.position(0);

            ByteBuffer cbb = ByteBuffer.allocateDirect(colors.length * 4);
            cbb.order(ByteOrder.nativeOrder());
            mColorBuffer = cbb.asIntBuffer();
            mColorBuffer.put(colors);
            mColorBuffer.position(0);

            mIndexBuffer = ByteBuffer.allocateDirect(indices.length);
            mIndexBuffer.put(indices);
            mIndexBuffer.position(0);
        }

    public void draw(GL10 gl) {
        gl.glFrontFace(GL10.GL_CW);
        gl.glVertexPointer(3, GL10.GL_FIXED, 0, mVertexBuffer);
        gl.glColorPointer(4, GL10.GL_FIXED, 0, mColorBuffer);
        gl.glDrawElements(GL10.GL_TRIANGLES, 36, GL10.GL_UNSIGNED_BYTE,
                mIndexBuffer);
    }

    private IntBuffer mVertexBuffer;
    private IntBuffer mColorBuffer;
    private ByteBuffer mIndexBuffer;
}
```

Figure 3–4 shows the sample in action. In the next section, you'll see how portions of this code can be implemented natively.

Figure 3–4. *Tumbling cubes from the Java sample*

OpenGL the Native Way

In the previous section, you saw how a pure Java OpenGL application works from the ground up. This applies if you write an application from scratch in Java. However, if you already have a C OpenGL renderer and wish to interface with Android, you probably don't want to rewrite your application (especially if it has thousands of lines of code). This would consume significant time and resources, and more than likely, give you terrible headache. To understand how you can maximize the return on your investment, let's look at the general steps used to create an OpenGL application:

1. *Initialization*: OpenGL is a single-threaded system that requires a GLContext to be initialized. Only one thread can access this context at a time. In EGL, this step is subdivided as follows:

   a. Get an EGL instance. In Android, this can be done using the EGLContext class:

```
mEgl = EGLContext.getEGL();
```

   b. Get a default display. The display is required for the rendering process. In Android, use this call:

```
mEglDisplay = mEgl.eglGetDisplay(EGL10.EGL_DEFAULT_DISPLAY);
```

   c. Initialize the display, as follows:

```
int[] version = new int[2];
mEgl.eglInitialize(mEglDisplay, version);
```

   d. You must also specify the pixel format and image depth you wish
   to use. The following requests a 32bpp pixel format with an image
   depth of 16:

```
EGLConfig[] configs = new EGLConfig[1];
int[] num_config = new int[1];

int[] configSpec = {
  EGL10.EGL_RED_SIZE,       8,
  EGL10.EGL_GREEN_SIZE,     8,
  EGL10.EGL_BLUE_SIZE,      8,
  EGL10.EGL_ALPHA_SIZE,     8,
  EGL10.EGL_DEPTH_SIZE,    16,
  EGL10.EGL_NONE
};
mEgl.eglChooseConfig(mEglDisplay, configSpec, configs, 1, num_config);
```

   2. *Main loop*: This is usually a user-defined thread that performs or delegates
   drawing operations.

   3. *Drawing*: In the drawing process, a set of GL operations is performed for each
   iteration of the *loop*. At the end of each iteration, buffers must be swapped to
   display the rendered surface on the screen.

   4. *Cleanup*: In this step, the GLContext is destroyed and resources released back to
   the system.

All these steps can be performed in Java. So it happened that one day I wanted to port
an OpenGL-based game to Android written in C, and wondered if some steps could be
done in Java and some in C. I was very happy to discover that this is indeed possible.
For example, the following steps can be performed in Java within an Android activity:

   ■ *Initialization*: Get the EGL instance, initialize the default display, and
   set the pixel format and image depth.

   ■ *Main loop*: The main loop can be a combination of a Java thread that
   calls a native game loop. Here is where things get interesting.

> **NOTE:** OpenGL operations can be performed natively after the GLContext is initialized by an
> Android activity if, and only if, the native code is loaded by the activity as a shared library through
> JNI.

   ■ *Swap buffers*: This step can be performed in Java, provided that the
   native library issues a callback after all GL operations have been
   completed. This is simply using JNI callbacks and will result in a
   rendered surface on the screen.

This is great news. You don't need to rewrite large portions of an OpenGL game. You simply need to initialize the GLContext within your Java activity, load the shared library, do all the rendering operations natively, and issue a swap buffers callback to Java on each iteration of the game loop.

Let's apply this concept by rewriting portions of the GL cubes Java sample in C. The portion that will be rewritten is the rendering of the cubes. The rest—initialization, main loop, and swap buffers—will remain in Java. To accomplish this, you must make some simple changes to the sample classes and add a new native activity.

Main Activity

Let's create a new activity (with its own launcher) to load the native code (see Listing 3–7). This activity is almost identical to its Java counterpart, except for the following:

- A native library is loaded using System.loadLibrary("ch03").

- The Renderer constructor has been modified to accept a second Boolean argument (use native rendering): mGLSurfaceView.setRenderer(new CubeRenderer(true, true)). This tells the cube renderer to use a translucent background and native rendering.

Listing 3–7. *Native Cubes Activity*

```
package opengl.test;

import opengl.scenes.GLSurfaceView;
import opengl.scenes.cubes.CubeRenderer;
import android.app.Activity;
import android.os.Bundle;

public class NativeGLActivity extends Activity {
    private GLSurfaceView mGLSurfaceView;

    {
        System.loadLibrary("ch03");
    }

    /** Called when the activity is first created. */
    @Override
    public void onCreate(Bundle savedInstanceState) {
        super.onCreate(savedInstanceState);

        mGLSurfaceView = new GLSurfaceView(this);

        try {
            mGLSurfaceView.setRenderer(new CubeRenderer(true, true));
            setContentView(mGLSurfaceView);

        } catch (Exception e) {
            e.printStackTrace();
        }
    }
}
```

```
    @Override
    protected void onResume() {
        // Ideally a game should implement onResume() and onPause()
        // to take appropriate action when the activity loses focus
        super.onResume();
        mGLSurfaceView.onResume();
    }

    @Override
    protected void onPause() {
        // Ideally a game should implement onResume() and onPause()
        // to take appropriate action when the activity loses focus
        super.onPause();
        mGLSurfaceView.onPause();
    }
}
```

These new files will be added to the project and discussed in the following sections (see Figure 3–5):

- *Native activity*: This is the main entry point to the application. It can be run from its own launcher on the device.

- *Native interface class*: This is a new Java class that contains the native methods to be invoked within the renderer thread.

- *Native cube renderer* (cuberenderer.c): This is the C equivalent of CubeRenderer.java. It initializes the scene and draws a frame. It also contains all the JNI callbacks.

- *Native cube* (cube.c): This file is equivalent to Cube.java; it draws the cube.

TIP: The native files cube.c and cuberenerer.c are available in the project source under ch03.OpenGL/jni.

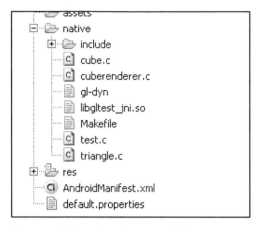

Figure 3–5. *GL native cubes sample file layout.*

The main activity is the first component of the native version of the tumbling cubes, but we also need a native interface class to provide a two-way communication pipeline with the native library loaded by the main activity. This new interface is described in the following section.

Native Interface Class

The native interface class defines native methods to be invoked within the application thread (see Listing 3–8). It includes one native method and one callback:

- `static native int NativeRender()`: This is the actual native method that will render the cube. It is implemented natively in C and executed through JNI.

- `static void GLSwapBuffers()`: This is a callback invoked within the native layer to request a buffer swap (render it). For this sample, this method will not be actually invoked (as the loop is defined in Java), but it could be useful in other situations (when the main loop is implemented natively).

> **TIP:** As you may know, using JNI, you can invoke C functions from Java. You may not know that you can also load classes and invoke Java methods within C.

Listing 3–8. *Native Interface for the GL Cubes Sample*

```
package opengl.jni;

public class Natives {

    private static EventListener listener;

    public static interface EventListener {
        void OnMessage(String text);
        void GLSwapBuffers();
    }

    public static void setListener(EventListener l) {
        listener = l;
    }

    /**
     * Native Render test
     *
     * @return
     */
    public static native int NativeRender();

    @SuppressWarnings("unused")
    private static void GLSwapBuffers() {
        if (listener != null)
            listener.GLSwapBuffers();
    }
}
```

This class needs a way to notify components (the activity, for example) that some message has been received from the native layer. You do this by creating the interface EventListener. In this way, a class that wants to receive messages must implement EventListener and issue a call to Natives.setListener(this).

Before we jump to the C code, let's take a look at the Java changes required to the classes CubeRenderer, GLSurfaceView, and GLThread for the sample.

Changes to the Original Sample

The class CubeRenderer has been modified to accept a Boolean argument in its constructor to request a native draw (see Listing 3–9).

Listing 3–9. *Changes for CubeRenderer Class (highlighted in bold)*

```
public class CubeRenderer implements Renderer
{
    private boolean mNativeDraw = false;

    public CubeRenderer(boolean useTranslucentBackground,
            boolean nativeDraw)
    {
        mTranslucentBackground = useTranslucentBackground;
        mNativeDraw = nativeDraw;
```

```
        mCube = new Cube();
    }

    public void drawFrame(GL10 gl) {
        if (mNativeDraw) {
            doNativeDraw();
                }
        else {
                doJavaDraw(gl);
                }
    }

    private void doJavaDraw(GL10 gl) {
        // Same as before
        // ...
    }

    public void doNativeDraw() {
        Natives.NativeRender();
    }

    // ...
}
```

When `drawFrame()` is invoked and `mNativeDraw` is true, the cube will be rendered from C (by calling `Natives.NativeRender()`). Otherwise, the Java implementation will be used.

When the surface is created, and a renderer is set for that surface using `GLSurfaceView.setRenderer(Renderer renderer)`, you must tell the native interface class (`Natives.java`) that you wish to listen for messages by sending a reference to the loop thread:

```
public void setRenderer(Renderer renderer) {
    mGLThread = new GLThread(renderer, mHolder);
    mGLThread.start();
    Natives.setListener(mGLThread);
}
```

Note that `GLThread` must implement `Natives.EventListener` for this to work.

Finally, the last class to be updated is `GLThread` (see Listing 3–10), which contains the main loop.

Listing 3–10. *Changes for GLThread.java*

```
public class GLThread extends Thread implements EventListener
{
    // ...
    @Override
    public void GLSwapBuffers() {
        if ( mEglHelper != null ) {
            mEglHelper.swap();
        }
    }
}
```

GLThread implements EventListener. This allows the C code to send text messages if something is wrong. The method GLSwapBuffers() will be invoked when the C code requests a buffer swap.

This takes care of the Java portion of the sample. Now let's look at the C files: cuberenderer.c and cube.c.

Native Cube Renderer

The native cube renderer (cuberenderer.c) is similar to the Java class CubeRenderer. This file performs the following tasks (see Listings 3–11 through 3–14):

- It initializes the scene. This function is almost identical to CubeRenderer.surfaceCreated().

- It draws a frame using the drawFrame() function. This function is similar in nature to CubeRenderer.drawFrame().

- It contains the Java callback jni_gl_swap_buffers () which will invoke a Java method to request a buffer swap within Java.

- It contains the native implementation of the native interface class opengl.jni.Natives.NativeRender (mapped in C as Java_opengl_jni_Natives_NativeRender). This function will be invoked every time a frame is rendered from the GLThread Java class.

These tasks are discussed in the following four sections.

Scene Initialization

Scene initialization is performed by the init_scene() function (see Listing 3–11). Its job is to perform trivial GL initialization calls, such as setting a perspective correction hint, background color, and shade model, and in this case, enabling face culling and depth tests.

init_scene() is meant to mirror the Java method CubeRenderer.surfaceCreated, which initializes the scene after the surface is created. Note that Java lines such as gl.glDisable(GL10.GL_DITHER) become glDisable(GL_DITHER). Because the context is already initialized in Java, you can simply make the GL commands you need in the equivalent C function.

> **TIP:** cuberenderer.c is located in the book source under ch03.OpenGL/jni.

Listing 3–11. *Scene Initialization from cuberenderer.c*

```c
#include <stdlib.h>
#include <stdio.h>
#include <stdarg.h>
#include <string.h>
#include <math.h>

#include <EGL/egl.h>
#include <GLES/gl.h>
#include <GLES/glext.h>

#include "include/opengl_jni_Natives.h"

#define ONE   1.0f
#define FIXED_ONE 0x10000

// Prototypes
void jni_printf(char *format, ...);
void jni_gl_swap_buffers ();

// Rotation Angle
static float mAngle = 0.0;

extern void Cube_draw();

static void init_scene(void)
{
        glDisable(GL_DITHER);

        /*
         * Some one-time OpenGL initialization can be made here
         * probably based on features of this particular context
         */
        glHint(GL_PERSPECTIVE_CORRECTION_HINT,GL_FASTEST);

        glClearColor(.5f, .5f, .5f, 1);

        glEnable(GL_CULL_FACE);
        glShadeModel(GL_SMOOTH);
        glEnable(GL_DEPTH_TEST);
}
```

Drawing Frames

Drawing the actual frames is performed by the drawFrame() function. This function performs the following steps:

- It clears the screen via glClear().

- It sets the framework to draw 3D objects via the glMatrixMode(GL_MODELVIEW) system call.

- It performs an initial translation—a rotation to be applied to the first cube.

- It draws the first cube by calling Cube_draw(). Note that vertices and colors must be enabled via glEnableClientState().

- It performs a second rotation/translation and draws a second cube by calling Cube_draw() again.

- It increases the angle for the next interaction.

drawFrame() is meant to mirror the Java method CubeRenderer.drawFrame(), which includes the code in the next fragment:

```
gl.glClear(GL10.GL_COLOR_BUFFER_BIT | GL10.GL_DEPTH_BUFFER_BIT);
gl.glMatrixMode(GL10.GL_MODELVIEW);
gl.glLoadIdentity();
gl.glTranslatef(0, 0, -3.0f);
gl.glRotatef(mAngle,        0, 1, 0);
gl.glRotatef(mAngle*0.25f,  1, 0, 0);

gl.glEnableClientState(GL10.GL_VERTEX_ARRAY);
gl.glEnableClientState(GL10.GL_COLOR_ARRAY);

mCube.draw(gl);

gl.glRotatef(mAngle*2.0f, 0, 1, 1);
gl.glTranslatef(0.5f, 0.5f, 0.5f);

mCube.draw(gl);

mAngle += 1.2f;
```

In C, the preceding code simply becomes the following:

```
glDisable(GL_DITHER);

glTexEnvx(GL_TEXTURE_ENV,
      GL_TEXTURE_ENV_MODE,GL_MODULATE);
glClear(GL_COLOR_BUFFER_BIT | GL_DEPTH_BUFFER_BIT);

glMatrixMode(GL_MODELVIEW);
glLoadIdentity();
```

```
glTranslatef(0, 0, -3.0f);
glRotatef(mAngle,        0, 0, 1.0f);
glRotatef(mAngle*0.25f,  1, 0, 0);

glEnableClientState(GL_VERTEX_ARRAY);
glEnableClientState(GL_COLOR_ARRAY);

Cube_draw();

glRotatef(mAngle*2.0f, 0, 1, 1);
glTranslatef(0.5f, 0.5f, 0.5f);

Cube_draw();

mAngle += 1.2f;
```

Note that drawFrame() is defined as static, which tells the compiler that this function will be visible only by functions within cuberenderer.c (a bit similar to the private keyword in Java). Furthermore, the function Cube_draw() is implemented in cube.c.

Listing 3–12. *Drawing Frames from cuberenderer.c*

```
static void drawFrame()
{
        /*
         * By default, OpenGL enables features that improve quality
         * but reduce performance. One might want to tweak that
         * especially on software renderer.
         */
        glDisable(GL_DITHER);
        glTexEnvx(GL_TEXTURE_ENV,
            GL_TEXTURE_ENV_MODE,GL_MODULATE);

        /*
         * Usually, the first thing one might want to do is to clear
         * the screen. The most efficient way of doing this is to use
         * glClear().
         */
        glClear(GL_COLOR_BUFFER_BIT | GL_DEPTH_BUFFER_BIT);

        /*
         * Now we're ready to draw some 3D objects
         */
        glMatrixMode(GL_MODELVIEW);
        glLoadIdentity();

        glTranslatef(0, 0, -3.0f);
        glRotatef(mAngle,        0, 0, 1.0f);
        glRotatef(mAngle*0.25f,  1, 0, 0);

        glEnableClientState(GL_VERTEX_ARRAY);
        glEnableClientState(GL_COLOR_ARRAY);

        Cube_draw();

        glRotatef(mAngle*2.0f, 0, 1, 1);
        glTranslatef(0.5f, 0.5f, 0.5f);
```

```
        Cube_draw();

        mAngle += 1.2f;
}
```

Java Callback

A Java callback is used to send messages from the native layer to the Java layer (see Listing 3–13). The cube renderer implements the callback: jni_gl_swap_buffers (). This callback tells Java that it is time to swap the OpenGL buffers. In OpenGL lingo, that means render the graphics. This step must be performed at the end of each frame of the rendering loop. The callback implementation is similar to the previous one. The main difference is that it invokes the Java method opengl.jni.Natives.GLSwapBuffers ().

Listing 3–13. *Java Callbacks from cuberenderer.c*

```c
// Java Natives class reference
static jclass jNativesCls;
static JavaVM *g_VM;

void jni_gl_swap_buffers () {
    JNIEnv *env;

    if ( !g_VM) {
        return;
    }

    (*g_VM)->AttachCurrentThread (g_VM, (void **) &env, NULL);


    if ( !jNativesCls ) {
        jNativesCls = (*env)->FindClass(env, "opengl/jni/Natives");

    }
    if ( jNativesCls == 0 ) {
            return;
    }

    // Call opengl.jni.Natives.GLSwapBuffers ()
    jmethodID mid = (*env)->GetStaticMethodID(env, jNativesCls
            , "GLSwapBuffers"
            , "()V");

    if (mid) {
        (*env)->CallStaticVoidMethod(env, jNativesCls
                , mid
                );
    }
}


/**
 * Printf into the java layer
 * does a varargs printf into a temp buffer
 * and calls jni_sebd_str
 */
```

```
void jni_printf(char *format, ...)
{
    va_list             argptr;
    static char                string[1024];

    va_start (argptr, format);
    vsprintf (string, format,argptr);
    va_end (argptr);

    LOGD("%s", string);
}
```

Let's take a closer look at the anatomy of a JNI Java callback. To start using JNI, a C program must include the system header:

```
#include <jni.h>
```

Now, if your function is called from a different place than the one that started Java_opengl_jni_Natives_NativeRender, you must attach to the current thread with the following:

```
(*g_VM)->AttachCurrentThread (g_VM, (void **) &env, NULL);
```

This is required if, for example, your program implements its own game loop, and then sends messages back to Java through JNI. This isn't the case in our example, but I've included it so the function can be invoked either way. g_VM is a global reference to the JVM, which must be saved within the very first call to Java_opengl_jni_Natives_NativeRender. Next, to load a Java class opengl.jni.Natives within C, you use the following:

```
jclass jNativesCls = (*env)->FindClass(env, "opengl/jni/Natives");
```

Here, env is a reference to the JNI environment obtained from the previous call. Note that the class name must be separated using /, not ..

Now, with a reference to the native class, you can call the static void method OnMessage:

```
jmethod mid = (*env)->GetStaticMethodID(env, jNativesCls, "GLSwapBuffers", "()V");
(*env)->CallStaticVoidMethod(env, jNativesCls, mid);
```

Note that to call this method, you need to obtain its JNI method ID using its name (GLSwapBuffers) and its signature "()V". The signature describes the method's arguments (void in this case) and the return type (void). With this information, you call the static void method sending the corresponding arguments.

Native Interface Function

The native interface function (see Listing 3–14) is the C implementation of the Java native method opengl.jni.Natives.NativeRender(). This function performs the following tasks:

- ▪ It saves a reference to the Java VM, required by the Java callbacks of the previous section.

- It initializes the scene.

- It renders one frame. This function is meant to be called multiple times within the rendering thread (implemented by GLThread.java).

Listing 3–14. *Native Interface Function from cuberenderer.c*

```
/*
 * Class:     opengl_jni_Natives
 * Method:    RenderTest
 * Signature: ()V
 */
JNIEXPORT jint JNICALL Java_opengl_jni_Natives_NativeRender
  (JNIEnv * env, jclass cls)
{

    (*env)->GetJavaVM(env, &g_VM);
    static int initialized = 0;

    if ( ! initialized ) {
        jni_printf("Native:RenderTest initscene");
        init_scene();

        initialized = 1;

    }
    drawFrame();
    return 1;
}
```

Native Cube

Native cube (cube.c) is the last file in the lot (see Listing 3–15). This file is a carbon copy of Cube.java. It defines the vertices, colors, and indices of the cube, and draws it in the same way as its Java counterpart.

> **TIP:** cube.c is located in the book source under ch03.OpenGL/jni.

Listing 3–15. *Native Implementation of Cube.java*

```
#include <stdio.h>
#include <unistd.h>
#include <stdlib.h>
#include <GLES/gl.h>

#define FIXED_ONE 0x10000
#define one 1.0f

typedef unsigned char byte;

extern void jni_printf(char *format, ...);

// Cube vertices
static GLfloat vertices[24] = {
```

```
            -one, -one, -one,
             one, -one, -one,
             one,  one, -one,
            -one,  one, -one,
            -one, -one,  one,
             one, -one,  one,
             one,  one,  one,
            -one,  one,  one,
};

// Colors
static GLfloat colors[] = {
             0,    0,    0,  one,
             one,   0,    0,  one,
             one,  one,    0,  one,
             0,  one,    0,  one,
             0,    0,  one,  one,
             one,   0,  one,  one,
             one,  one,  one,  one,
             0,  one,  one,  one,
};

static byte indices[] = {
            0, 4, 5,   0, 5, 1,
            1, 5, 6,   1, 6, 2,
            2, 6, 7,   2, 7, 3,
            3, 7, 4,   3, 4, 0,
            4, 7, 6,   4, 6, 5,
            3, 0, 1,   3, 1, 2
};


void Cube_draw()
{
    glFrontFace(GL_CW);

    glVertexPointer(3, GL_FLOAT, 0, vertices);
    glColorPointer(4, GL_FLOAT, 0 , colors);

    glDrawElements(GL_TRIANGLES, 36, GL_UNSIGNED_BYTE, indices);
}
```

Compiling and Running the Sample

Now let's run the sample in the emulator. But before that, we need to compile the native library using the NDK:

1. Start your cygwin console and change to the project work directory ch03.OpenGL (see Figure 3–6)

2. Type ndk-build to compile the library. An Android make file (Android.mk) is required to do so (see Listing 3–16).

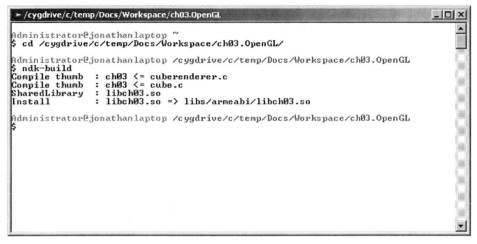

Figure 3–6. *Compiling the native library using the Cygwin console*

Listing 3–16. *Make File (Android.mk) for the Native Library*

```
LOCAL_PATH := $(call my-dir)

include $(CLEAR_VARS)

LOCAL_MODULE    := ch03

INCLUDES :=

LOCAL_CFLAGS := -O2 $(INCLUDES)


LOCAL_SRC_FILES := cuberenderer.c cube.c

LOCAL_LDLIBS := -llog -lGLESv1_CM


include $(BUILD_SHARED_LIBRARY)
```

Let's take a look at Android.mk to see what some of the lines mean. The most important are:

- LOCAL_MODULE: This is a required variable that defines the name of the library (ch03 in this case). After compilation the output file will be named libch03.so

- LOCAL_SRC_FILES: This is a required variable that defines the names of the source files.

- LOCAL_LDLIBS: This is an optional but critical variable. It defines the required C runtime libraries at link time. In our case we use the Android logging and OpenGL thus: -llog –lGLESv1_CM

Finally, to run the project, create a Run configuration.

1. From the main menu in Eclipse click **Run ➤ Run Configurations**.

2. Give it a name and select the ch03.OpenGL Project. Optionally select an activity you wish to run.

3. Click Run (see Figure 3–7).

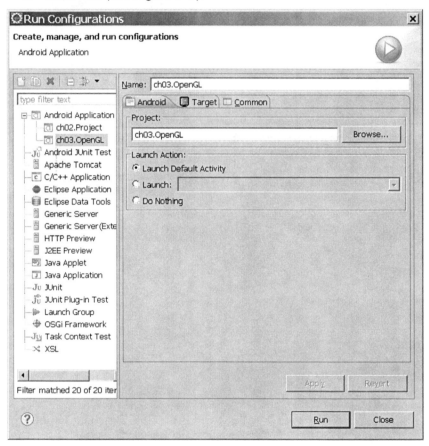

Figure 3–7. *Run configuration for the project.*

As shown in Figure 3–8, when the project is started in the device, two launchers will be placed in the device desktop: OpenGL Java and OpenGL Native.

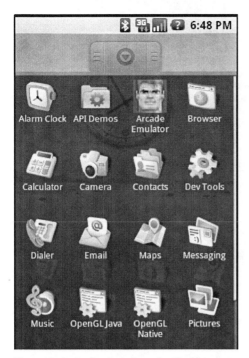

Figure 3–8. *Device launchers for the GL cubes sample*

Run both launchers and look at the device log (see Listing 3–17). On the native side, you should see the following messages:

Listing 3–17. *Device Logs for the Java and Native Implementations of GL Cubes*

```
// Java Device Log
07-28 19:46:04.568: INFO/ActivityManager(52): Start proc opengl.test for activity
opengl.test/.JavaGLActivity: pid=505 uid=10021 gids={}
07-28 19:46:04.857: INFO/jdwp(505): received file descriptor 10 from ADB
07-28 19:46:05.677: INFO/System.out(505): GLSurfaceView::setRenderer setting
07-28 19:46:06.347: INFO/System.out(505): Vendor:Google Inc.
07-28 19:46:06.376: INFO/System.out(505): Renderer:Android PixelFlinger 1.0
07-28 19:46:06.376: INFO/System.out(505): Version:OpenGL ES-CM 1.0
07-28 19:46:06.416: INFO/System.out(505): Vendor:Google Inc.
07-28 19:46:06.436: INFO/System.out(505): Renderer:Android PixelFlinger 1.0
07-28 19:46:06.476: INFO/System.out(505): Version:OpenGL ES-CM 1.0
07-28 19:46:06.546: INFO/ARMAssembler(505): generated 07-28 19:46:06.638:
INFO/ActivityManager(52): Displayed activity opengl.test/.JavaGLActivity: 2202 ms

// Native Log
07-28 19:56:57.167: INFO/ActivityManager(52): Start proc opengl.test for activity
opengl.test/.NativeGLActivity: pid=512 uid=10021 gids={}
07-28 19:56:57.357: INFO/jdwp(512): received file descriptor 10 from ADB
07-28 19:56:58.247: INFO/System.out(512): Loading JNI lib using abs
path:/data/libgltest_jni.so
07-28 19:56:58.267: DEBUG/dalvikvm(512): Trying to load lib /data/libgltest_jni.so
0x433a7258
07-28 19:56:58.376: DEBUG/dalvikvm(512): Added shared lib /data/libgltest_jni.so
0x433a7258
```

```
07-28 19:56:58.387: DEBUG/dalvikvm(512): No JNI_OnLoad found in /data/libgltest_jni.so
0x433a7258
07-28 19:56:58.548: INFO/System.out(512): GLSurfaceView::setRenderer setting natives
listener
07-28 19:56:59.777: INFO/System.out(512): Vendor:Google Inc.
07-28 19:56:59.816: INFO/System.out(512): Renderer:Android PixelFlinger 1.0
07-28 19:56:59.916: INFO/System.out(512): Version:OpenGL ES-CM 1.0
07-28 19:57:00.056: INFO/System.out(512): Vendor:Google Inc.
07-28 19:57:00.158: INFO/System.out(512): Renderer:Android PixelFlinger 1.0
07-28 19:57:00.187: INFO/System.out(512): Version:OpenGL ES-CM 1.0
07-28 19:57:00.187: INFO/System.out(512): GLThread::OnMessage Native:RenderTest
initscene
07-28 19:57:00.796: INFO/ActivityManager(52): Displayed activity
opengl.test/.NativeGLActivity: 3971 ms
```

Figure 3–9 shows the native renderer running in the emulator.

Figure 3–9. *GL cubes native renderer*

So far we have seen two ways of tackling OpenGL rendering: purely using Java versus a mix of a thin Java wrapper and a native renderer. Both are equally valid and can achieve the same results. However the later works better if you already have large portions of OpenGL code written in C and you wish to reuse them. The former will be the way to go if you plan to write your code entirely in Java. Choosing the right rendering technique is difficult but not the only challenge you will face when creating your game. Video scaling is another difficult subject that we'll tackle in the next section. Let's continue.

Scaling Video Buffers with Hybrid OpenGL ES

One of the trickiest parts of working with software-based games is scaling the video buffer to fit the display size. It is even more troublesome when you have a multitude of resolutions, such as in an open environment like Android. As a developer we must try to achieve the right balance of performance versus display quality. As we've seen in Chapter 2, video scaling can be of three kinds from slowest to the fastest:

- Software: Slowest of them all but the easiest to implement. Best for old devices with no GPUs. However most of today's phones are hardware accelerated.

- Hybrid: It uses a mix of software drawing (to create an image buffer), and hardware rendering (to draw into the display). It is fast and can render images at any resolution greater than 256x256.

- Hardware Only: The fastest of the bunch but the hardest to implement. Depending on the complexity of your game it may require a powerful GPU. If you have good hardware it can create games with amazing quality and effects. It is a tough choice in hardware fragmented platforms such as Android.

In this section we tackle the middle one. It is the best choice for a fragmented platform where you have a software renderer and wish to scale your game to any display resolution. It is perfect for games such as emulators, arcade, simple shooters, and others. It also works very well in low, middle, and high power devices.

We'll start with a general overview of hybrid scaling and why it is the preferable method to scale video. Next, we'll dig into the implementation, including how to initialize a surface, and drawing into the texture to perform the actual scaling.

Why Use Hybrid Scaling?

The principle behind this scaling technique is simple:

- Your game creates an image buffer (usually in pixel format RGB565 – the most common for mobile) at a given size. Let's say 320x240, the typical size of an emulator.

- The image 320x240 needs to be scaled to a tablet size (1024x768) or any device for that matter. Here we could use a software scaler but it would be painfully slow. Instead we create an OpenGL ES texture and render the image (320x240) into the texture using a GL Quad.

- By magic the texture will be scaled to the display size (1024x768) using hardware; thus gaining a significant performance boost to your game.

From the implementation point of view, the process can be described as follows:

- Initialize the OpenGL ES texture: at the stage of the game where the video gets initialized, a hardware surface must be created. This surface consists of a simple texture where the video image will be rendered (see Listing 3–18 and 3–19).

- Draw the image buffer into the texture: at the end of your game loop, render the video image into the texture which will be automatically scaled to fit any display size (see Listing 3–20).

Listing 3–18. *Create an Empty Texture as RGB656*

```
// Texture ID
static unsigned int mTextureID;

// These are used to compute an XY offset of the image drawn into the texture
static int xoffset;
static int yoffset;

/**
 * Create an empty texture as RGB565
 * params: (w,h) width, height of the texture
 * (x_offsety_offset): XY offset of the image drawn into the texture
 */
static void CreateEmptyTextureRGB565 (int w, int h, int x_offset, int y_offset)
{
  int size = w * h * 2;

  xoffset = x_offset;
  yoffset = y_offset;

  // buffer
  unsigned short * pixels = (unsigned short *)malloc(size);

  memset(pixels, 0, size);

  // Init GL sate
  glDisable(GL_DITHER);
  glHint(GL_PERSPECTIVE_CORRECTION_HINT, GL_FASTEST);

  glClearColor(.5f, .5f, .5f, 1);
  glShadeModel(GL_SMOOTH);
  glEnable(GL_DEPTH_TEST);
  glEnable(GL_TEXTURE_2D);

  // Create texture
  glGenTextures(1, &mTextureID);
  glBindTexture(GL_TEXTURE_2D, mTextureID);

  // texture params
  glTexParameterf(GL_TEXTURE_2D, GL_TEXTURE_MIN_FILTER,GL_NEAREST);
  glTexParameterf(GL_TEXTURE_2D, GL_TEXTURE_MAG_FILTER,GL_LINEAR);

  glTexParameterf(GL_TEXTURE_2D, GL_TEXTURE_WRAP_S, GL_CLAMP_TO_EDGE);
  glTexParameterf(GL_TEXTURE_2D, GL_TEXTURE_WRAP_T, GL_CLAMP_TO_EDGE);
```

```
// Texture is RGB565
 glTexImage2D(GL_TEXTURE_2D, 0, GL_RGB, w, h, 0, GL_RGB, GL_UNSIGNED_SHORT_5_6_5 ,
pixels);

 free (pixels);
}
```

Listing 3–18 shows CreateEmptyTextureRGB565 which creates an empty texture for drawing and has the following arguments:

- w,h: This is the size of the video image.

- x_offset, y_offset: This are XY offset coordinates at which the image will be rendered into the texture. Read on to see why we may need this.

To create a texture in OpenGL we simply call:

```
glGenTextures(1, &mTextureID);
glBindTexture(GL_TEXTURE_2D, mTextureID);
```

Where mTextureID is an integer that has stored the ID of our texture. Next it sets the following texture parameters:

- GL_TEXTURE_MIN_FILTER: This is the texture minifying function is used whenever the pixel being textured maps to an area greater than one texture element. The minifying function we use is: GL_NEAREST, which returns the value of the texture element that is nearest (in Manhattan distance) to the center of the pixel being textured.

- GL_TEXTURE_MAG_FILTER: This is the texture magnification function is used when the pixel being textured maps to an area less than or equal to one texture element. The magnification function we use is: GL_LINEAR which returns the weighted average of the four texture elements that are closest to the center of the pixel being textured.

- GL_TEXTURE_WRAP_S: It sets the wrap parameter for each texture coordinate S to GL_CLAMP which causes the coordinates to be clamped to the range [0,1] and is useful for preventing wrapping artifacts when mapping a single image onto an object.

- GL_TEXTURE_WRAP_T: It sets the wrap parameter for each texture coordinate T to GL_CLAMP.

Finally we specify a two-dimensional texture image with glTexImage2D with the following parameters:

- GL_TEXTURE_2D: It specifies the target texture.

- Level: Specifies the level-of-detail number. Level 0 is the base image level.

- Internal format: Specifies the color components in the texture. In this case RGB.

- Width and height: Size of the texture. It must be a power of two.

- Format: It specifies the format of the pixel data and must be the same as the internal format.

- Type: It specifies the data type of the pixel data. In this case RGB565 (16 bit).

- Pixels: It specifies a pointer to the image data in memory. It must be encoded as RGR656.

> **NOTE:** The size of the texture must be a power of two 256, 512, 1024, etc. However the size of the video image can be arbitrary. This means the size of the texture must be a power of two equal or greater to the size of the video. This is a caveat that will be explained later on.

Now, let's take a look at the actual implementation of the hybrid video scaler. The next two sections will show you how to initialize a surface for scaling and how to perform the actual drawing.

Initializing the Surface

It is critical for this scaler to work, that the size of the texture must be a power of two equal or greater than the size of the video. If we don't make sure this rule applies you will see a white or black screen whenever the image is rendered. In Listing 3–19 we have a function JNI_RGB565_SurfaceInit which makes sure this rule is obeyed. It takes the width and height of the image as arguments. It then calls getBestTexSize to obtain the closest texture size, and finally creates the empty texture by calling CreateEmptyTextureRGB565. Note that if the image is smaller than the texture, it will be centered on screen by calculating XY offset coordinates.

Listing 3–19. *Surface Initialization*

```
// Get the next POT texture size greater or equal to image size (wh)
static void getBestTexSize(int w, int h, int *tw, int *th)
{
  int width = 256, height = 256;

  #define MAX_WIDTH 1024
  #define MAX_HEIGHT 1024

  while ( width < w && width < MAX_WIDTH) { width *= 2; }
  while ( height < h && height < MAX_HEIGHT) { height *= 2; }

  *tw = width;
  *th = height;
}

/**
```

```
 * Ini an RGB565 surface
 * params: (w,h) width, height of the image
 */
void JNI_RGB565_SurfaceInit(int w, int h)
{
  // min texture w&h
  int texw = 256;
  int texh  = 256;

  // Get texture size (must be POT) >= WxH
  getBestTexSize(w, h, &texw, &texh);

 // Center image on screen?
  int offx = texw > w ? (texw - w)/2 : 0;
  int offy = texh > h ? (texh - h)/2 : 0;

  if ( w > texw || h > texh)
    printf ("Error: Invalid surface size %sx%d", w, h);

  // Create the OpenGL texture used to render
  CreateEmptyTextureRGB565 (texw, texh, offx, offy);
}
```

Drawing into the Texture

Finally, to render into the display (also known as surface flipping), we call
JNI_RGB565_Flip with an array of pixel data (encoded as RGB565) plus the size of the
image. JNI_RGB565_Flip draws into the texture by calling DrawIntoTextureRGB565 and
swaps the buffers. Note that the buffer swapping is done in Java not C, therefore we
need a way to tell Java it is time to swap. We can do this using JNI to call some Java
method to do the actual swapping (see Listing 3–20).

Listing 3–20. *Drawing an image Buffer into a Texture Using a Quad*

```
// Quad vertices X, Y, Z
static const float vertices[] = {
    -1.0f, -1.0f, 0,
    1.0f, -1.0f, 0,
    1.0f,  1.0f, 0,
    -1.0f, 1.0f, 0
};
// Quad coords (0-1)
static const float coords[] = {
    0.0f, 1.0f,
    1.0f, 1.0f,
    1.0f, 0.0f,
    0.0f, 0.0f,
 };

// Quad vertex indices
static const unsigned short indices[] = { 0, 1, 2, 3};

/**
 * Draw an array of pixels in the entire screen using a Quad
 *  pixels: unsigned short for RGB565
```

```
   */
static void DrawIntoTextureRGB565 (unsigned short * pixels, int w, int h)
{
  // clear screen
  glClear(GL_COLOR_BUFFER_BIT | GL_DEPTH_BUFFER_BIT);

  // enable vetices & and texture coordinates
  glEnableClientState(GL_VERTEX_ARRAY);
  glEnableClientState(GL_TEXTURE_COORD_ARRAY);

  glActiveTexture(GL_TEXTURE0);
  glBindTexture(GL_TEXTURE_2D, mTextureID);

  glTexSubImage2D(GL_TEXTURE_2D, 0, xoffset, yoffset, w, h, GL_RGB,
GL_UNSIGNED_SHORT_5_6_5 , pixels);

  // Draw quad
  glFrontFace(GL_CCW);
  glVertexPointer(3, GL_FLOAT, 0, vertices);
  glEnable(GL_TEXTURE_2D);
  glTexCoordPointer(2, GL_FLOAT, 0, coords);
  glDrawElements(GL_TRIANGLE_FAN, 4, GL_UNSIGNED_SHORT, indices);
}

// Flip surface (Draw into texture)
void JNI_RGB565_Flip(unsigned short *pixels , int width, int height)
{
  if ( ! pixels) {
    return;
  }
  DrawIntoTextureRGB565 (pixels, width, height);

  // Must swap GLES buffers here
  jni_swap_buffers ();
}
```

To render into the texture using OpenGL:

1. Clear the color and depth buffers using glClear(GL_COLOR_BUFFER_BIT |
    GL_DEPTH_BUFFER_BIT).

2. Enable the client state: vertex array and texture coordinates array for
    writing when glDrawElements is called.

3. Select active texture unit with glActiveTexture where the initial value is
    GL_TEXTURE0.

4. Bind a named texture to a texturing target. GL_TEXTURE_2D (a 2-D
    surface) is the default target to which the texture is bound. mTextureID is
    the ID of a texture.

5. Specify a two-dimensional texture subimage using glTexSubImage2D
    with the parameters:

    ▪   GL_TEXTURE_2D: It specifies the target texture.

- level: It specifies the level of detail number. Level 0 is the base image level.

- xoffset: It specifies a texel (texture pixel) offset in the x direction within the texture array.

- yoffset: It specifies a texel offset in the y direction within the texture array.

- width: It specifies the width of the texture subimage.

- height: It specifies the height of the texture subimage.

- format: It specifies the format of the pixel data.

- type: It specifies the data type of the pixel data.

- data: It specifies a pointer to the image data in memory.

6.   Draw the Quad vertices, coordinates and indices by calling:

- glFrontFace: It enables the front face of the Quad.

- glVertexPointer: It defines the array of the Quad's vertex data with a size of 3, of type GL_FLOAT, and a stride of 0.

- glTexCoordPointer: It defines the Quad's array of texture coordinates with a size of 2, of type GL_FLOAT, and a stride of 0

- glDrawElements: It renders primitives from the data array using triangles (GL_TRIANGLES), with 4 elements (hence a Quad) of type short (GL_UNSIGNED_SHORT) plus a pointer to the indices.

Note that from Listing 3–20 we see that the coordinates of the Quad range from [-1, 1] in both axes. This is because the OpenGL coordinate system ranges from (-1, 1) where the origin (0,0) is the center (see Figure 3–10).

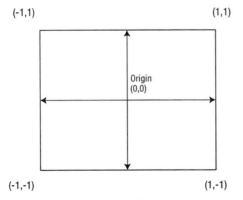

Figure 3–10. *OpenGL coordinate system*

In a perfect world we shouldn't have to worry much about the size of the video buffer (especially if using software only scalers/renderers). This is now true however when scaling video using OpenGL in Android. In this case the size of the buffer is crucial. In the next section you will learn how to deal with arbitrary video sizes that don't work very well with OpenGL.

What Happens when the Image is not a Power of Two

As mentioned before, hybrid scaling works flawlessly when the size if the image is a power of two. But, odds are that your image buffer won't be a power of two. For example, the chapter dealing with the Doom engine has a video size of 320x240. In that case, the image will still be scaled, but to a percentage of the size of the texture. To see this effect in action take a look at Figures 3–11 and 3–12.

Figure 3–11. *Scaling non power of two image*

In Figure 3–11 we have the following sizes:

```
Device display: 859x480
Texture: 512x256
Image: 320x240
```

As we can see the image is scaled but to a 62% (320/512*100) of the texture width, and 93% (240/256*100) of the height. Therefore, the image will be scaled to 62%x93% of any device resolution provided the resolution is greater than 256. Now let's take a look at Figure 3–12.

Figure 3–12. *Scaling a power of two image*

In Figure 3–12 we have the following sizes:

```
Device display: 859x480
Texture: 512x256
Image: 512x256
```

Zoom and Draw

In Figure 3–12 we see that the image will be scaled at 100% of any device resolution which is what we want. But what do we do when the image is not a power of two? To get passed this caveat, we could:

1. Zoom the 320x240 image to the closest power of two (512x256 in this case) using a software scaler.

2. Convert the scaled surface into a RGB656 image, compatible with DrawIntoTextureRGB565 from the previous section.

3. Draw into the texture thus performing hardware scaling to the display resolution.

This solution is a little slower than the previous section but still much faster than using a pure software scaler, especially if you run in high resolution devices such as tablets. Listing 3–21 shows how we can zoom an SDL surface using the popular SDL_gfx library

Listing 3–21. *Zooming an Image with SDL_gfx roto-zoom*

```
void JNI_Flip(SDL_Surface *surface )
{
  if ( zoom ) {
    // if surface is 8bit scaled will be 8bit else surface is 32 bit RGBA!
    SDL_Surface * sized = zoomSurface( surface, zoomx, zoomy, SMOOTHING_OFF);

    JNI_FlipByBPP (sized);

    // Must clean up!
```

```
      SDL_FreeSurface(sized);
   }
   else {
     JNI_FlipByBPP (surface);
   }
}
```

Zoom and Draw Implementation

To zoom/scale an SDL surface we simply call SDL_gfx zoomSurface with:

1. An SDL surface

2. Horizontal zoom factor:(0-1)

3. Vertical zoom factor, and

4. SMOOTHING_OFF: This disables anti-aliasing for faster drawing

Next we flip the SDL surface based on its resolution (bits per pixel). Listing 3–22 shows how this is done for an 8-bit RGB surface.

Listing 3–22. *Flipping an SDL Surface by Resolution*

```
/**
 * Flip SDL Surface by bits per pixel
 */
static void JNI_FlipByBPP (SDL_Surface *surface)
{
  int bpp = surface->format->BitsPerPixel;

  switch ( bpp ) {
    case 8:
      JNI_Flip8Bit (surface);
      break;
    case 16:
      // Flip 16bit RGB (surface);
      break;
    case 32:
      // flip 32 bit RGB (surface);
      break;
    default:
      printf("Invalid depth %d for surface of size %dx%d", bpp, surface->w, surface->h);
  }
}

/**
 * Flip 8bit SDL surface
 */
static void JNI_Flip8Bit(SDL_Surface *surface )
{
  int i;
  int size = surface->w * surface->h;
  int bpp = surface->format->BitsPerPixel;

  unsigned short pixels [size]; // RGB565
```

```
SDL_Color * colors = surface->format->palette->colors;

for ( i = 0 ; i < size ; i++ ) {
  unsigned char pixel =   ((unsigned char *)surface->pixels)[i];

  pixels[i] = ( (colors[pixel].r >> 3) << 11)
    | ( (colors[pixel].g >> 2) << 5)
    | (colors[pixel].b >> 3);   // RGB565

}

DrawIntoTextureRGB565 (pixels, surface->w,  surface->h);

jni_swap_buffers ();
}
```

Given an SDL surface, we simply check the format's bits per pixel: surface->format->BitsPerPixel and based on that value we create an RGB565 array of pixels that can be used by DrawIntoTextureRGB565:

```
for ( i = 0 ; i < size ; i++ ) {
    unsigned char pixel =   ((unsigned char *)surface->pixels)[i];

    // RGB565
    pixels[i] = ( (colors[pixel].r >> 3) << 11)
      | ( (colors[pixel].g >> 2) << 5)
      | (colors[pixel].b >> 3);
  }
```

Each pixel consists of a Red, Green, and Blue value extracted from the surface color palette with:

```
SDL_Color * colors = surface->format->palette->colors;
RED: colors[pixel].r
GREEN: colors[pixel].g
BLUE: colors[pixel].b
```

To build an RGB565 pixel, discard the least significant bits from each color component:

```
colors[pixel].r >> 3 (8 -3 = 5)
colors[pixel].g >> 2 (8 – 2 = 6)
colors[pixel].b >> 3 (8 – 3 = 5)
```

Then shift each component into the proper position of a 16-bit value (5+6+5 = 16 - hence RGB656).

```
pixels[i] = (RED << 11) | (GREEN << 5) | BLUE
```

Finally we send the new array to DrawIntoTextureRGB565 along with the image width and height. For the final piece of the puzzle, we need a way to tell if the surface requires zooming. This can be done at video initialization when the surface is created in the first place. Listing 3–23 shows how we can create a software surface using SDL.

Listing 3–23. *Zoom Surface Initialization*

```
// Should be zoom?
static char zoom = 0;

// Zoom scales [0,1]
static double zoomx = 1.0;
static double zoomy = 1.0;

/***********************************************************
 * Image Constructor
 * The image must be a power of 2 (256x256, 512x256,...)
 * to render full screen on the OpenGL texture. If the image
 * is not POT (320x240) it will be scaled
 ***********************************************************/
SDL_Surface * JNI_SurfaceNew(int width, int height, int bpp, int flags)
{
  Uint32 rmask = 0, gmask = 0, bmask =0 , amask = 0;

  // texture size & offset
  int realw = 256, realh = 256, offx = 0, offy = 0;

  // Image must be a power of 2 for OpenGL to scale it.
  if ( width > 512 ) {
    Sys_Error("ERROR: INVALID IMAGE WIDTH %d (max POT 512x512)", width);
  }

  // REAL W/H must be the closest POT value to wxh
  // Will scale to 512x256
  // could be 256 but 512 gives better res (slower)
  if ( width > 256 ) realw = 512;

  // size not POT , zoom to closest POT. Choices are:
  // 256x256 (fastest/low res) 512x256 (better res/slower)
  // 512x512 slowest.
  if ( ( width != 512 && width != 256) || ( height != 256 ) ) {
    zoom = 1;
    zoomx = realw / (float)width;
    zoomy = realh / (float)height;

    offx = offy = 0;

    printf("WARNING Texture of size %dx%d will be scaled to %dx%d zoomx=%.3f zoomy=%.3f"
      , width, height, realw, realh, zoomx, zoomy);
  }

  // Create the OpenGL texture used to render
  CreateEmptyTextureRGB565 (realw, realh, offx, offy);

  // This is the real surface used by the client to render the video
  return SDL_CreateRGBSurface (SDL_SWSURFACE, width, height, bpp, rmask, gmask, bmask,
amask);
}
```

If the size of the image is not a power of two, then the zoom flag will be set to 1 and the horizontal and vertical zoom factors will be computed. Then, the empty texture will be created by calling CreateEmptyTextureRGB565 with the width, height, and XY offset values of the texture. Finally, the SDL surface is created by calling SDL_CreateRGBSurface with:

- SDL_SWSURFACE: it tells SDL to create a software surface

- width, height: It defines the size of the surface

- bpp: It defines the bits per pixel (resolution) of the surface (8, 16, 24, or 32)

- rmask, gmask, bmask, amask: These are mask values for the red, green, blue, and alpha (transparency) components of the pixel format. Set them to 0 to let SDL take care of it.

Hybrid Scaler Rules of Thumb

To conclude things, always keep in mind the following rules of thumb when using a hybrid scaler like this in your games:

- Always set the video size, if you can, to a power of two: 256x256 or 512x56. Values above 512 are simply too big for this technique.

- If you cannot set the video size but still want a full screen display, use the SDL software scaler from the previous section to scale to the closest power of two resolution, then use the hardware scaler.

- This scaling technique may not be useful (performance wise) if your video size if greater than 512x512.

Summary

The veil has been lifted to reveal a new frontier of 3D development for Android. The techniques demonstrated in this chapter can help you to bring a large number of 3D PC games to the platform, at an enormous savings in development costs.

In this chapter, you have learned a trick to mix OpenGL code in Java and C to enable the reuse of large portions of C code along with Java code. We started by looking at the OpenGL tumbling cubes sample provided by Google, and how sections of the rendering process can be implemented in C. You saw that the sample's rendering process included EGL initialization, the main loop, drawing, buffer swap, and cleanup. Then you saw how to reimplement the cube rendering invoked within the main loop. You created the new components:

- The native activity used to launch the application from the device.

- The native interface class used to define the native methods and C callbacks.

- The cube renderer and cube class used to render the cubes.

Finally, we looked at the limitations of OpenGL ES when it comes to advanced 3D games.

I hope this chapter will help you get your own 3D games for Android with minimal effort and maximum code reuse. This is a prelude to the next chapters, where we will look at three of the greatest 3D shooters for the PC, Doom, Quake I, Quake II, and the minimal changes required to get them running on your phone.

## Chapter 4

Efficient Graphics with OpenGL ES 2.0

We have seen what OpenGL 1.0 can offer, but there is so much more to this API. In this chapter, we take a look at the cutting edge in graphics development: OpenGL ES 2.0, a subset of OpenGL. We'll start with a brief description of the most important features OpenGL ES 2.0 can offer, including shaders, GLSL, and how they affect the Android platform. Then, will take a deeper look into OpenGL ES Shading Language (GLSL) by creating a neat Android project to render a geometric shape—icosahedrons—using OpenGL ES 2.0. Let's get started.

OpenGL ES 2.0 and Android

OpenGL ES 2.0 is a set of enhancements to OpenGL ES 1.0. It emphasizes a programmable 3D graphics pipeline with the ability to create shader and program objects and the ability to write vertex and fragment shaders in the GLSL.

OpenGL ES 2.0 provides the following desirable qualities for current graphics programming:

- A wider range of precision options for use in embedded devices using shading language similar to the desktop OpenGL 2.0.

- Frame Buffer Objects to simplify surface management and offer a subset of functionality from the desktop FBO.

- One hundred percent backward compatible with OpenGL ES 1.x and built with the latest standards and most advanced ideas available for graphics development.

Android fully implements the OpenGL ES 2.0 specification. However, the following are some caveats you should consider before using this technology to build your games:

■   OpenGL ES 2.0 is not supported in all versions of Android. Thus if you are targeting the largest breath of devices out there, you should stick with OpenGL ES 1.x.

■   OpenGL ES 2.0 implements the slickest ideas and technology in graphics rendering; however, that doesn't necessarily mean that the code will be better or run faster.

It does provide a desirable characteristic, nevertheless. It is designed to reduce power consumption in embedded systems such as phones, thus it could reduce your game's overall power requirements and provide more efficient graphics rendering. All in all, having a solid knowledge of OpenGL ES 2.0 is a good thing for your résumé. Chances are that if you are a graphics developer looking for a job, the very first thing you'll be asked in a job interview is your knowledge about shaders and GLSL.

Shaders

A shader is a simple program that describes the traits of either a vertex or a pixel. At the low level, a shader defines a set of software instructions used to calculate rendering effects with a high degree of flexibility. Shaders were created to replace the traditional desktop OpenGL fixed-function pipeline that allowed only common geometry transformation and pixel-shading functions. They provide the following advantages over the traditional desktop OpenGL pipeline:

■   Customized effects can be applied for rendering

■   A higher degree of flexibility

■   Simplicity, and higher degree of reusability

There are three basic types of shaders implemented in OpenGL ES 2.0: vertex, fragment, and geometry.

Vertex Shaders

Vertex shaders are run once for each vertex given to the GPU and transform the 3D position in virtual space to the 2D coordinate for on-screen rendering. They can manipulate properties such as position, color, and texture coordinates, but cannot create new vertices.

Fragment Shaders

Fragment shaders (also known as pixel shaders) calculate the color of individual pixels. They are typically used for scene lighting and related effects, such as bump mapping and color toning, and are often called many times per pixel for every object that is in the corresponding space.

Geometry Shaders

Geometry shaders can add and remove vertices from a mesh. They are used to generate geometry or to add volumetric detail to existing meshes that would be too costly to process on the CPU.

GLSL

GLSL is the OpenGL ES 2.0 Shading Language for programming vertex and fragment shaders that has been adapted for embedded platforms. It is meant to work together with OpenGL ES 1.1 to minimize the cost and power consumption of embedded devices like smartphones.

> **TIP:** OpenGL ES 2.0 removes fixed-point functionality commonly used in desktop OpenGL and replaces it with shader for power savings critical on smartphones and other embedded systems.

At the implementation level, GLSL is actually two closely-related languages: vertex shader and fragment shader.

Vertex Shader Language (VSL)

At its simplest, VSL is a C style program to manipulate the attributes of a vertex. The following fragment defines a very simple vertex shader to set the rendering position to the position of the current vertex.

```
void main(void)
{
  // This is a C++ style comment
 /* This is a C style comment */
  gl_Position = gl_Vertex;
}
```

As we can see, the shader has a C-style syntax with main function where you simply declare GLSL instructions. In this case, we use two built-in variables:

- gl_Position: Sets the position of the vertex to be rendered

- gl_Vertex: Contains the position of the current vertex being processed

Fragment Shader Language (FSL)

The FSL is used to change the color attributes (RGBA) of the current pixel. For example, the following fragment sets the color of the current pixel to red RGBA (1, 0, 0, 0).

```
void main(void)
{
   gl_FragColor = vec4(1.0, 0.0, 0.0, 0.0);
}
```

gl_FragColor is the built-in variable used to set the color of the current pixel. As with any programming language, GLSL provides all the things you would expect from a computer language, including:

- *Variables and functions*: All variables and functions must be declared before being used

- *Basic types*: This includes void, bool, int, float, vec2 (two-component float point vector), boolean or integer 2, 3 or 4 component vectors, 2×2, 3×3, or 4×4 float matrices

- *Declaration scope*: Determines where the declaration is visible; this includes global and local variables, name spaces, plus re-declarations within the same scope

- *Storage qualifiers*: Qualifiers specified in front of the type—pure traditional C-style—including: local variables and constants

  New to GLSL, we also have:

  - attribute: defines the linkage between a vertex shader and OpenGL ES for per-vertex data

  - uniform: tells that the value does not change across the primitive being processed; forms the linkage between a shader, OpenGL ES, and the application

  - varying: defines that linkage between a vertex shader and a fragment shader for interpolated data

- *Parameter qualifiers*: These are the qualifiers passed to the arguments of a function, including:

  - in: a parameter is passed into a function

  - out: a parameter passed back out of a function, but not initialized

  - inout: a parameter is passed both into and out of a function

- *Precision qualifiers*: For floating point precision including: highp, mediump, and lowp for high, medium, and low precision, respectively

- *Variance and the invariant qualifier*: These are used to handle the possibility of getting different values from the same expression in different shaders. It is possible, in independent compilation, that two identical shaders are not exactly the same when they run, in which case there are two qualifiers—invariant and varying—to prevent or allow this.

- *Operators and expressions*: All the common operators and expression you would expect from your typical programming language (see the following sidebar for more details)

■ *Many other powerful features*: These include built-in angle, trigonometry, exponential, matrix, and vector functions; built-in variables, and more

---

NEED GLSL HELP?

There is so much to the GLSL language. The best source on GLSL is probably the OpenGL Software Development Kit available at www.opengl.org/sdk/docs/manglsl/. Another great source on the GLSL syntax is available from the Khronos Group at www.khronos.org/files/opengles_shading_language.pdf.

These sites can help you learn more about GLSL features and syntax, so make sure to check them out.

Now let's take a look at how we can implement a shader and use it in an Android program.

Anatomy of a Shader

The anatomy of a shader is defined by the following steps:

1. Create a program. The very first step is to create a shader program to be run within your main program—a program within a program, if you will.

2. Load the shader. Once you create the shader, you must load it from a string variable or file.

3. Attach. Next, you must attach the shader to the main program.

4. Link. This step compiles the shader code and checks for syntax errors.

5. Optional validation. It is always a good idea to validate the link status and handle errors appropriately.

6. Enable and use. Finally, you can enable it and use it against a set of vertices.

Creating the Shader Program

To create a shader object or program, we use the glCreateShader API call. It takes as a parameter a shader type: either GL_VERTEX_SHADER or GL_FRAGMENT_SHADER for vertex or fragment respectively. glCreateShader returns a non-zero value by which it can be referenced. The following fragment creates two shaders to load a vertex, and fragment shaders to draw an icosahedron (described later in this chapter).

```
   int      Shader[2]
// Create 2 shader programs
  Shader[0] = glCreateShader(GL_VERTEX_SHADER);
  Shader[1] = glCreateShader(GL_FRAGMENT_SHADER);
```

```
    // Load VertexShader: It has the GLSL code
    LoadShader((char *)VertexShader, Shader[0]);

    // Load fragment shader: FragmentShaderBlue has the GLSL code
    LoadShader((char *)FragmentShaderBlue, Shader[1]);

    // Create the program and attach the shaders & attributes
    int Program   = glCreateProgram();
```

We also make an API call to glCreateProgram, which creates an empty program object
and returns a non-zero value by which it can be referenced. Shaders must be attached
to a program. This provides a mechanism to specify the shader objects that will be
linked to create a program. It also provides a means for checking the compatibility of the
shaders that will be used to create a program. Next, we load it.

Loading the Shader

A shader object is used to maintain the source code strings that define a shader. For
this purpose, we can create a load function that invokes: glShaderSource and
glCompileShader. glShaderSource takes as arguments the ID of the shader, the number
of elements, a string containing the source code to be loaded, and an array of string
lengths (NULL in this case). glCompileShader compiles the shader described by its
reference ID. The following fragment describes the load function that will be used to
draw the Icosahedron for an upcoming project.

```
// Simple function to create a shader
void LoadShader(char *Code, int ID)
{
    // Compile the shader code
    glShaderSource  (ID, 1, (const char **)&Code, NULL);
    glCompileShader (ID);

    // Verify that it worked
    int ShaderStatus;
    glGetShaderiv(ID, GL_COMPILE_STATUS, &ShaderStatus);

    // Check the compile status
    if (ShaderStatus != GL_TRUE) {
        printf("Error: Failed to compile GLSL program\n");
        int Len = 1024;
        char Error[1024];
        glGetShaderInfoLog(ID, 1024, &Len, Error);
        printf("%s\n", Error);
        exit (-1);
    }
}
```

As a bonus, you can also check the compilation status using the API call glGetShaderiv.
It takes as arguments: a shader ID, a query constant (GL_COMPILE_STATUS, in this case,
to check the compilation status), and the status of the query. If the status is not GL_TRUE,
then the compilation errors can be extracted by calling glGetShaderInfoLog with the ID

of the shader and a string buffer that described the nature of the error. The next step is attaching the shader to a program.

Attaching to the Shader

To attach our shader to the main program, use the API call glAttachShader. It takes as arguments the ID of the program object, to which a shader object will be attached, and the shader object that is to be attached, as shown in the following fragment.

```
glAttachShader(Program, Shader[0]);
glAttachShader(Program, Shader[1]);
glBindAttribLocation(Program, 0, "Position");
glBindAttribLocation(Program, 1, "Normal");
```

We also use glBindAttribLocation to associate a user-defined attribute variable in the program object with a generic vertex attribute index. The name of the user-defined attribute variable is passed as a null-terminated string in the last argument. This allows the developer to declare variables in the master program and bind them to variables in the shader code.

Linking the Shader Program

To use the shaders, we must link the program that contains them by calling glLinkProgram with the reference ID of the program. Behind the scenes, OpenGL will create an executable that will run on the programmable fragment processor.

```
// Link
glLinkProgram(Program);
```

Getting the Link Status

The status of the link operation will be stored as part of the program object's state. It is always a good idea to check for errors by getting the status of the link using glGetProgramiv, very similar to the way we checked the compilation status but using the GL_LINK_STATUS constant in this particular case. The following fragment demonstrates how to do so.

```
// Validate our work thus far
int ShaderStatus;
glGetProgramiv(Program, GL_LINK_STATUS, &ShaderStatus);
if (ShaderStatus != GL_TRUE) {
    printf("Error: Failed to link GLSL program\n");
    int Len = 1024;
    char Error[1024];
    glGetProgramInfoLog(Program, 1024, &Len, Error);
    printf("%s\n", Error);
    exit(-1);
}
```

Optional: Program Validation and Status

You should always validate program objects. It helps to see if you have syntax errors in your shader code. To validate a program, use the API call glValidateProgram with the reference ID of the program. Next, call glGetProgramiv with the program validation constant GL_VALIDATE_STATUS. The result of the validation will be returned in the last argument (ShaderStatus in this case). Then, simply check the status and handle the error accordingly, as shown in the following fragment.

```
glValidateProgram(Program);
glGetProgramiv(Program, GL_VALIDATE_STATUS, &ShaderStatus);

if (ShaderStatus != GL_TRUE) {
    printf("Error: Failed to validate GLSL program\n");
    exit(-1);
}
```

Finally, enable and use the program.

Enabling and Using the Program

To starts things off, use glUseProgram with the program ID to install a program object as part of a current rendering state. A program object will contain an executable that will run on the vertex processor if it contains one or more shader objects of type GL_VERTEX_SHADER that have been successfully compiled and linked.

```
// Enable the program
glUseProgram              (Program);
glEnableVertexAttribArray (0);
glEnableVertexAttribArray (1);
```

Remember the two local attributes (Position and Normal) we declared in the attach step? They must be enabled before they can take effect. By default, all client-side capabilities are disabled, including all generic vertex attribute arrays. If enabled, the values in the generic vertex attribute array will be accessed and used for rendering when calls are made to vertex array commands such as glDrawArrays, glDrawElements, glDrawRangeElements, glArrayElement, glMultiDrawElements, or glMultiDrawArrays.

Now let's put what we have learned so far into practice by building a neat Android project to draw an icosahedron using shaders.

Invoking OpenGL ES 2.0 in Android

Before we jump into the Android project, there are three steps that we should keep in mind when using OpenGL ES 2.0 in Android as opposed to OpenGL ES 1.x.

1. The surface view Java class must use a custom context factory to enable 2.0 rendering.

2. The surface view class must use a custom `EGLConfigChooser` to be able to select an `EGLConfig` that supports 2.0. This is done by providing a config specification to `eglChooseConfig()` that has the attribute `EGL10.ELG_RENDERABLE_TYPE` containing the `EGL_OPENGL_ES2_BIT` flag set.

3. The surface view class must select the surface's format, then choose an `EGLConfig` that matches it exactly (with regards to red/green/blue/alpha channels bit depths). Failure to do so will result in an `EGL_BAD_MATCH` error.

Project Icosahedron

This is where we put our skills to the test with a cool Android project to draw an icosahedron using vertex and fragment shaders. The goals of the exercise are to:

- Demonstrate the use of vertex and fragment shaders using OpenGL ES 2.0.

- Demonstrate the use of hybrid activities (both Java and C++) to perform the geometry rendering. The project launcher, surface, and rendering thread will be created in Java. All OpenGL ES 2.0 rendering will be performed in C++, using JNI to glue both parts together.

- Demonstrate Android multi-touch functionality to manipulate the rotation speed (using swipes) and the zooming (using pinching) of the shape.

But before we start, let's take a look at what an icosahedron is.

Reviewing the Shape

An icosahedron is a regular polyhedron with 20 identical equilateral triangular faces, 30 edges, and 12 vertices (see Figure 4–1).

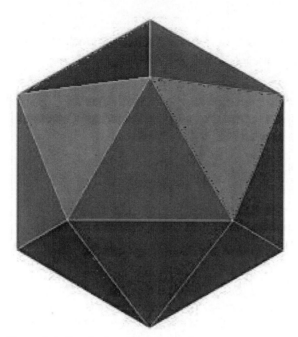

Figure 4–1. *Regular icosahedron*

The following Cartesian coordinates define the vertices of an icosahedron with edge-length 2, centered at the origin:

(0, ±1, ±)

(±1, ± , 0)

(± , 0, ±1)

where φ = (1+√5)/2 is the golden ratio (also written as τ). Note that these vertices form five sets of three concentric, mutually orthogonal golden rectangles. In the OpenGL coordinate system, which ranges from [-1, 1] in all axes. The 12 vertices of the icosahedron are defined as the following:

```
// Vertex information
float PtData[][3] = {
        {0.5f, 0.0380823f, 0.028521f},
        {0.182754f, 0.285237f, 0.370816f},
        {0.222318f, -0.2413f, 0.38028f},
        {0.263663f, -0.410832f, -0.118163f},
        {0.249651f, 0.0109279f, -0.435681f},
        {0.199647f, 0.441122f, -0.133476f},
        {-0.249651f, -0.0109279f, 0.435681f},
        {-0.263663f, 0.410832f, 0.118163f},
        {-0.199647f, -0.441122f, 0.133476f},
        {-0.182754f, -0.285237f, -0.370816f},
        {-0.222318f, 0.2413f, -0.38028f},
        {-0.5f, -0.0380823f, -0.028521f},
};
```

The 20 triangular faces (that map to the vertices) are defined as follows:

```
// Face information
unsigned short FaceData[][3] = {
        {0,1,2,},
        {0,2,3,},
        {0,3,4,},
        {0,4,5,},
        {0,5,1,},
        {1,5,7,},
        {1,7,6,},
        {1,6,2,},
        {2,6,8,},
        {2,8,3,},
        {3,8,9,},
        {3,9,4,},
        {4,9,10,},
        {4,10,5,},
        {5,10,7,},
        {6,7,11,},
        {6,11,8,},
        {7,10,11,},
        {8,11,9,},
        {9,11,10,},
};
```

This information will be used by the shaders in our C++ program to render the scene on screen, as you'll see later on. But first, let's take a look at the project in more detail.

Tackling the Project

We'll start by creating a new Android project to host the code. Start the Eclipse Android project wizard and create a new project, as shown in Figure 4–2.

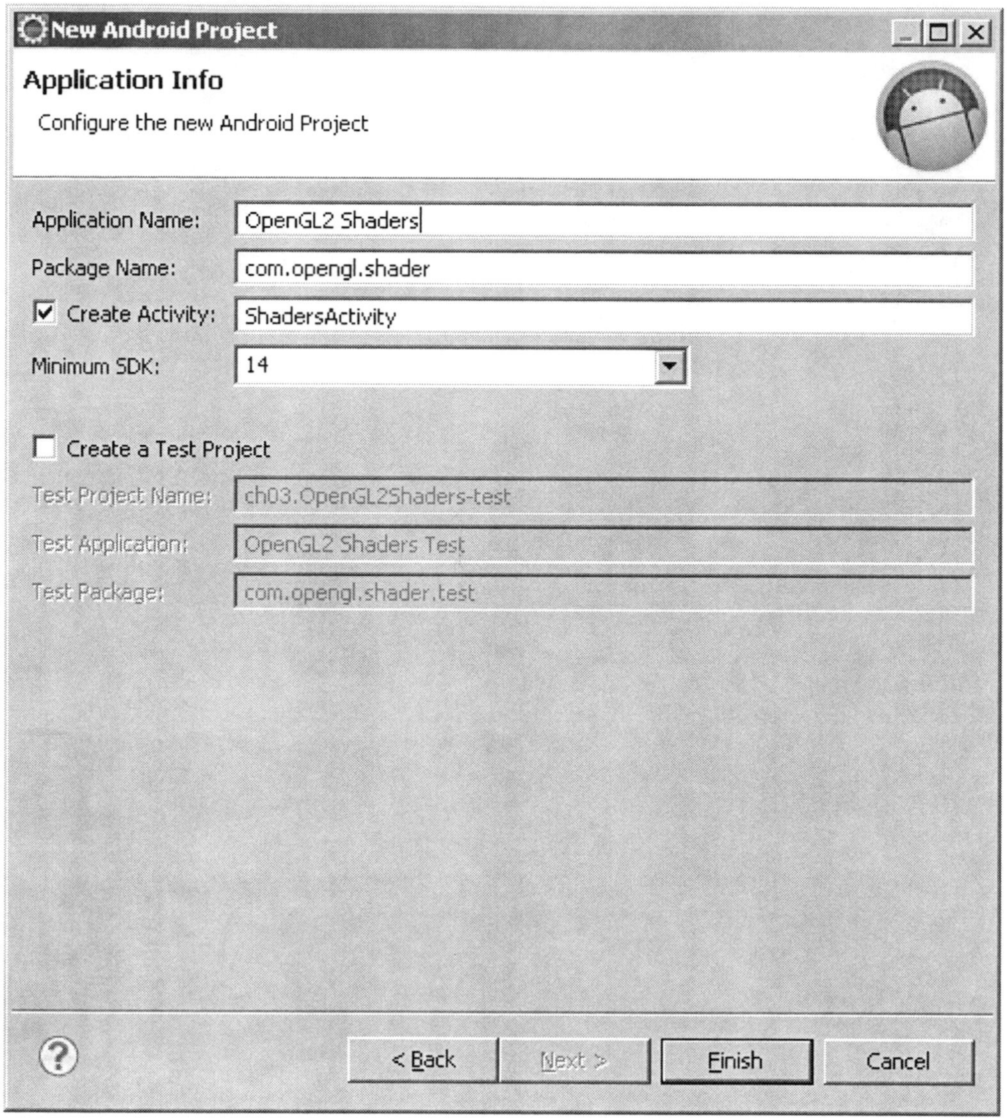

Figure 4–2. *Project properties for the icosahedron*

Next, perform the following `steps`:

1. Give the application a name (anything you choose).

2. Enter a package name; com.opengl.shader in this case.

3. Select a main Activity name (ShadersActivity).

4. Select a minimum SDK API number (14 for Android 4) and click Finish.

Your project should look as shown in Figure 4–3.

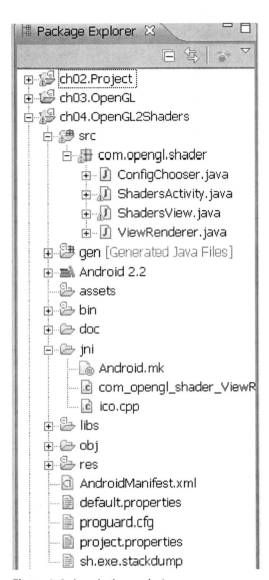

Figure 4–3. *Icosahedron project*

Table 4–1 lists the files that compose the project.

Table 4–1. *Files for the Icosahedron project*

Language	File Name	Description
XML	AndroidManifest.xml	This is the file descriptor for the application. It describes the package information, SDK requirements and the main activity or starting point of the application.
Java	ShadersActivity.java	This is the entry point of the application. It will be invoked by android when the application is launched from the device.
Java	ShadersView.java	This is the GL surface view that contains the OpenGL scene to be rendered.
Java	ViewRenderer.java	The renderer is in charge of initializing the scene and drawing the frames.
Java	ConfigChooser.java	The configuration chooser is used to tell Android that we wish to use OpenGL ES 2.0.
C++	ico.cpp	This is the C++ code that contains all shader and OpenGL rendering code. Plus the icosahedron vertex and face information.
Make	Android.mk	This is the compilation file for ico.cpp.

TIP: If you get stuck, get the source for this project is under ch04.OpenGLES2Shaders, available from the publisher.

Now let's look at the files in more detail.

Manifest

Listing 4–1 is the XML file created by the wizard. The most important thing to remember is to use the OpenGL ES 2.0 feature and set the required attribute to true.

Listing 4–1. *Android Manifest for the Project*

```
<?xml version="1.0" encoding="utf-8"?>
<manifest xmlns:android="http://schemas.android.com/apk/res/android"
    package="com.opengl.shader"
    android:versionCode="1"
    android:versionName="1.0" >

<uses-sdk
        android:minSdkVersion="14"
        android:targetSdkVersion="14" />
```

```
<uses-feature
        android:glEsVersion="2"
        android:required="true" />

<application
        android:icon="@drawable/ic_launcher"
        android:label="@string/app_name" >
<activity
            android:label="@string/app_name"
            android:name=".ShadersActivity" >
<intent-filter >
<action android:name="android.intent.action.MAIN" />
<category android:name="android.intent.category.LAUNCHER" />
</intent-filter>
</activity>
</application>
</manifest>
```

The next step is the main activity.

Activity

Listing 4–2 shows the main program of an Android application. It is very simple: when the application starts, the onCreate method will be invoked. Within this method, a ShadersView object is created and set as the content view. A set of arguments may be passed to the C++ layer by invoking the setrenderer method with an array of strings.

Listing 4–2. *Main Application Activity*

```
public class ShadersActivity extends Activity {
  ShadersView view;
  int width;
  int height;

  @Override
  public void onCreate(Bundle savedInstanceState) {
    super.onCreate(savedInstanceState);
      width = getWindowManager().getDefaultDisplay().getWidth();
    height = getWindowManager().getDefaultDisplay().getHeight();

    String[] args = {};

    view = new ShadersView(this);
    view.setRenderer(args, false, 0, 0);

    setContentView(view);
  }
}
```

Now, on to the surface view.

Surface View

The surface view is in charge of creating an OpenGL-capable, hardware-accelerated surface where objects can be drawn. The process is triggered by the setRenderer method. Because Android supports a plethora of graphics configuration, resolutions, and hardware specs, we don't know if the running device is set up to perform OpenGL ES 2.0 calls. Thus we must create a context factory class ContextFactory, which implements GLSurfaceView.EGLContextFactory. This class can then be used to tell Android that we wish to use an OpenGL ES 2.0-enabled context by giving the version as an attribute (see Listing 4–3).

```
int[] attrib_list = {EGL_CONTEXT_CLIENT_VERSION, 2, EGL10.EGL_NONE };
EGLContext context = egl.eglCreateContext(display, eglConfig, EGL10.EGL_NO_CONTEXT,
attrib_list);
```

Listing 4–3. *Surface View Class*

```
public class ShadersView extends GLSurfaceView {
  private static final String TAG = "View";

  private String[] mArgs;
  private ViewRenderer mRenderer;

  public ShadersView(Context context) {
    super(context);
  }

  public void setRenderer(String[] args, boolean translucent, int depth,
      int stencil) {
    Log.d(TAG, "Setting startup args & renderer");

    mArgs = args;

    /*
     * Setup the context factory for 2.0 rendering. See ContextFactory class
     * definition below
     */
    setEGLContextFactory(new ContextFactory());

    /*
     * We need to choose an EGLConfig that matches the format of our surface
     * exactly. This is going to be done in our custom config chooser. See
     * ConfigChooser class definition below.
     */
    setEGLConfigChooser(translucent ? new ConfigChooser(8, 8, 8, 8, depth,
        stencil) : new ConfigChooser(5, 6, 5, 0, depth, stencil));

    mRenderer = new ViewRenderer();
    setRenderer(mRenderer);
  }

  private static class ContextFactory implements
      GLSurfaceView.EGLContextFactory {
    private static int EGL_CONTEXT_CLIENT_VERSION = 0x3098;
```

```
    public EGLContext createContext(EGL10 egl, EGLDisplay display,
        EGLConfig eglConfig) {
      Log.w(TAG, "creating OpenGL ES 2.0 context");

      checkEglError("Before eglCreateContext", egl);

      int[] attrib_list = { EGL_CONTEXT_CLIENT_VERSION, 2, EGL10.EGL_NONE };
      EGLContext context = egl.eglCreateContext(display, eglConfig,
          EGL10.EGL_NO_CONTEXT, attrib_list);

      checkEglError("After eglCreateContext", egl);
      return context;
    }

    public void destroyContext(EGL10 egl, EGLDisplay display,
        EGLContext context) {
      egl.eglDestroyContext(display, context);
    }
  }

  private static void checkEglError(String prompt, EGL10 egl) {
    int error;
    while ((error = egl.eglGetError()) != EGL10.EGL_SUCCESS) {
      Log.e(TAG, String.format("%s: EGL error: 0x%x", prompt, error));
    }
  }

  public void setRotationSpeed(int speed) {
    ViewRenderer.setRotationSpeed(speed);
  }

  public void setVideoSize(final int width, final int height) {
    queueEvent(new Runnable() {
      public void run() {
        ViewRenderer.initialize(width, height);
      }
    });
  }
}
```

ShadersView is also in charge of the following:

   ▪ Choosing an EGLConfig that matches the format of the surface
     exactly. This is going to be done in the configuration chooser class
     later on. For example, the following fragment tells the surface to use
     an RGB565 configuration with a depth and stencil size.

```
setEGLConfigChooser( new ConfigChooser(5, 6, 5, 0, depth, stencil) );
```

   ▪ Creating a setting for the surface renderer.

```
mRenderer = new ViewRenderer();
setRenderer(mRenderer);
```

Surface Renderer

The surface renderer (ViewRenderer) contains the following methods, which trigger on different stages of the surface lifecycle, as shown in Listing 4–4:

- onSurfaceCreated: fires only once when the surface is first created

- onSurfaceChanged: may fire multiple times whenever a surface change occurs; for example, when the device is rotated

- onDrawFrame: fires many times by the rendering thread when a frame is drawn

Listing 4–4. *Surface Renderer*

```java
public class ViewRenderer implements GLSurfaceView.Renderer {

  private static final String TAG = "ViewRenderer";

  // native initializer
  native static void initialize(int width, int height);
  // native draw frame
  native static void drawFrame(int ticks);
  // native set rotation speed
  native static void setRotationSpeed(int speed);

  static {
    System.loadLibrary("icosahedron");
  }

  @Override
  public void onDrawFrame(GL10 arg0) {
    // Log.d(TAG, "onDrawFrame");
    int ticks = (int) System.currentTimeMillis();

    drawFrame(ticks);
  }

  @Override
  public void onSurfaceChanged(GL10 arg0, int w, int h) {
    Log.d(TAG, "onSurfaceChanged w=" + w + " h=" + h);
    initialize(w, h);
  }

  @Override
  public void onSurfaceCreated(GL10 arg0, EGLConfig conf) {
    Log.d(TAG, "onSurfaceCreated " + conf);
  }
}
```

Viewrenderer also declares the native C++ methods that will be invoked to initialize the scene, draw a frame, and set the rotation speed of the object. It also loads the native C++ library libicosahedron.so which contains the C++ implementations of these methods:

```java
native static void initialize(int width, int height);
native static void drawFrame(int ticks);
native static void setRotationSpeed(int speed);
static {
```

```
        System.loadLibrary("icosahedron");
}
```

Next comes the critical GLES 2.0 configuration chooser.

OpenGL ES 2.0 Configuration Chooser

The configuration chooser is critical to select an EGLConfig that supports OpenGL ES 2.0.
ConfigChooser implements the Android interface GLSurfaceView.EGLConfigChooser and
must receive a configuration spec with the attribute EGL10.ELG_RENDERABLE_TYPE
containing the EGL_OPENGL_ES2_BIT flag. With this information, it queries the display for
all available configurations (see Listing 4–5).

```
// Get the number of minimally matching EGL configurations
int[] num_config = new int[1];
egl.eglChooseConfig(display, s_configAttribs2, null, 0, num_config);

int numConfigs = num_config[0];
// Allocate then read the array of minimally matching EGL configs
EGLConfig[] configs = new EGLConfig[numConfigs];
egl.eglChooseConfig(display, s_configAttribs2, configs, numConfigs, num_config);
```

With this information, it chooses the best configuration that matches the original
configuration spec.

Listing 4–5. *Configuration Chooser*

```
class ConfigChooser implements GLSurfaceView.EGLConfigChooser {
    private static final String TAG = "ConfigChooser";
    private boolean DEBUG = false;

    public ConfigChooser(int r, int g, int b, int a, int depth, int stencil) {
        mRedSize = r;
        mGreenSize = g;
        mBlueSize = b;
        mAlphaSize = a;
        mDepthSize = depth;
        mStencilSize = stencil;
    }

    /*
     * This EGL config specification is used to specify 2.0 rendering. We use a
     * minimum size of 4 bits for red/green/blue, but will perform actual matching
     * in chooseConfig() below.
     */
    private static int EGL_OPENGL_ES2_BIT = 4;
    private static int[] s_configAttribs2 = { EGL10.EGL_RED_SIZE, 4,
        EGL10.EGL_GREEN_SIZE, 4, EGL10.EGL_BLUE_SIZE, 4,
        EGL10.EGL_RENDERABLE_TYPE, EGL_OPENGL_ES2_BIT, EGL10.EGL_NONE };

    public EGLConfig chooseConfig(EGL10 egl, EGLDisplay display) {

        /*
         * Get the number of minimally matching EGL configurations
         */
        int[] num_config = new int[1];
```

```java
        egl.eglChooseConfig(display, s_configAttribs2, null, 0, num_config);

        int numConfigs = num_config[0];

        if (numConfigs <= 0) {
          throw new IllegalArgumentException("No configs match configSpec");
        }

        /*
         * Allocate then read the array of minimally matching EGL configs
         */
        EGLConfig[] configs = new EGLConfig[numConfigs];
        egl.eglChooseConfig(display, s_configAttribs2, configs, numConfigs,
            num_config);

        if (DEBUG) {
          printConfigs(egl, display, configs);
        }
        /*
         * Now return the "best" one
         */
        return chooseConfig(egl, display, configs);
      }

      public EGLConfig chooseConfig(EGL10 egl, EGLDisplay display,
          EGLConfig[] configs) {
        for (EGLConfig config : configs) {
          int d = findConfigAttrib(egl, display, config, EGL10.EGL_DEPTH_SIZE,
              0);
          int s = findConfigAttrib(egl, display, config,
              EGL10.EGL_STENCIL_SIZE, 0);

          // We need at least mDepthSize and mStencilSize bits
          if (d < mDepthSize || s < mStencilSize)
            continue;

          // We want an *exact* match for red/green/blue/alpha
          int r = findConfigAttrib(egl, display, config, EGL10.EGL_RED_SIZE, 0);
          int g = findConfigAttrib(egl, display, config, EGL10.EGL_GREEN_SIZE,
              0);
          int b = findConfigAttrib(egl, display, config, EGL10.EGL_BLUE_SIZE,
              0);
          int a = findConfigAttrib(egl, display, config, EGL10.EGL_ALPHA_SIZE,
              0);

          if (r == mRedSize && g == mGreenSize && b == mBlueSize
      && a == mAlphaSize)
            return config;
        }
        return null;
      }

      private int findConfigAttrib(EGL10 egl, EGLDisplay display,
          EGLConfig config, int attribute, int defaultValue) {

        if (egl.eglGetConfigAttrib(display, config, attribute, mValue)) {
          return mValue[0];
```

```
    }
    return defaultValue;
  }

  private void printConfigs(EGL10 egl, EGLDisplay display,
      EGLConfig[] configs) {
    int numConfigs = configs.length;
    Log.w(TAG, String.format("%d configurations", numConfigs));
    for (int i = 0; i < numConfigs; i++) {
      Log.w(TAG, String.format("Configuration %d:\n", i));
      printConfig(egl, display, configs[i]);
    }
  }

  private void printConfig(EGL10 egl, EGLDisplay display, EGLConfig config) {
      // code removed for simplicity
    }
  }

  // Subclasses can adjust these values:
  protected int mRedSize;
  protected int mGreenSize;
  protected int mBlueSize;
  protected int mAlphaSize;
  protected int mDepthSize;
  protected int mStencilSize;
  private int[] mValue = new int[1];
}
```

That will take care of the Java side of things; now let's shift gears to the C++ rendering. Table 4–1 described the native side of the project (contained in the ico.cpp file), which is the last piece of the puzzle. This file is in charge of the JNI function implementation; it also contains the source of the shaders, plus scene initialization and rendering. Let's take a look.

Native Icosahedron

The Java native functions declared in ViewRenderer.java are implemented in C++ using the syntax shown in Listing 4–6.

Listing 4–6. *C++ Native Functions for the Project*

```
// Java
static {
System.loadLibrary("icosahedron");
}
native static void initialize(int width, int height);
native static void drawFrame(int ticks);
native static void setRotationSpeed(int speed);

// C++
extern "C" {
 JNIEXPORT void JNICALL Java_com_opengl_shader_ViewRenderer_initialize
  (JNIEnv * env, jclass cls, jint w, jint h)
 {
      Init(w,h);
```

```
    }

JNIEXPORT void JNICALL Java_com_opengl_shader_ViewRenderer_drawFrame
  (JNIEnv * env, jclass cls, jint ticks)
{
      Display(ticks);
}

JNIEXPORT void JNICALL Java_com_opengl_shader_ViewRenderer_setRotationSpeed
  (JNIEnv * env, jclass cls, jint val)
{
      doSetRotationSpeed((double)val);
}
}
```

We have the following three C++ functions:

- Init: to initialize the scene

- Display: to draw a frame of the scene

- doSetRotationSpeed: to set the rotation speed

Before we look at the implementations, we must create the two shader programs, vertex and fragment, which will be used to draw the icosahedron.

Project Shaders

Listing 4–7 declares the two shader programs that will be used to compute the position and color of the vertices and the faces of the icosahedron.

Listing 4–7. *Shaders Used in the Icosahedron Project*

```
// vertex Shader
attribute vec3 Position;
attribute vec3 Normal;

uniform mat4 Proj;
uniform mat4 Model;

varying vec3 NormVec;
varying vec3 LighVec;

void main(void)
{
vec4 Pos = Model * vec4(Position, 1.0);
gl_Position = Proj * Pos;
NormVec     = (Model * vec4(Normal,0.0)).xyz;
LighVec     = -Pos.xyz;
}

// Fragment Shader
varying highp vec3 NormVec;
varying highp vec3 LighVec;


void main(void)
```

```
{
  lowp vec3 Color = vec3(1.0, 0.0, 0.0);
  mediump vec3 Norm  = normalize(NormVec);
  mediump vec3 Light = normalize(LighVec);
  mediump float Diffuse = dot(Norm, Light);
  gl_FragColor = vec4(Color * (max(Diffuse, 0.0) * 0.6 + 0.4), 1.0);
}
```

Scene Initialization

The scene initialization in Listing 4–8 performs the following steps:

1. It creates two shader programs, vertex, and fragment.

```
Shader[0] = glCreateShader(GL_VERTEX_SHADER);
Shader[1] = glCreateShader(GL_FRAGMENT_SHADER);
```

2. It loads the vertex shader.

```
LoadShader((char *)VertexShader, Shader[0]);
```

3. It loads the fragment shader. Note that VertexShader and FragmentShaderRed are two strings describing the shaders in Listing 3-28 from Chapter 3.

```
LoadShader((char *)FragmentShaderRed, Shader[1]);
```

4. It creates the program and attaches the shaders and attributes.

```
Program   = glCreateProgram();
glAttachShader(Program, Shader[0]);
glAttachShader(Program, Shader[1]);
```

5. It attaches the attributes or variables (Position and Normal) used by the master and shader programs to manipulate the vertex and face information of the icosahedron.

```
glBindAttribLocation(Program, 0, "Position");
glBindAttribLocation(Program, 1, "Normal");
```

6. It links the program using its program ID: glLinkProgram(Program).

7. It validates the program status by querying the status using the GL_VALIDATE_STATUS constant.

```
glValidateProgram(Program);
glGetProgramiv(Program, GL_VALIDATE_STATUS, &ShaderStatus);
if (ShaderStatus != GL_TRUE) {
  // handle error
}
```

8. It enables the program and attributes: Position (0) and Normal (1).

```
glUseProgram           (Program);
glEnableVertexAttribArray  (0);
glEnableVertexAttribArray  (1);
```

Listing 4–8. *Scene Initialization*

```
int Init(int w, int h) {
  width = w;
  height = h;

  LOGD("Init: w=%d h=%d", width, height);

// Vertex shader from listing 3-28
  const char VertexShader[] = " ... ";

  // Fragment Shader (see listing 3-28)
  const char  FragmentShaderRed[] = "...";

  // Create 2 shader programs
  Shader[0] = glCreateShader(GL_VERTEX_SHADER);
  Shader[1] = glCreateShader(GL_FRAGMENT_SHADER);

  LoadShader((char *) VertexShader, Shader[0]);

  if (id == 2) {
    LoadShader((char *) FragmentShaderBlue, Shader[1]);
  } else {
    LoadShader((char *) FragmentShaderRed, Shader[1]);
  }

  // Create the program and attach the shaders & attributes
  Program = glCreateProgram();

  glAttachShader(Program, Shader[0]);
  glAttachShader(Program, Shader[1]);

  glBindAttribLocation(Program, 0, "Position");
  glBindAttribLocation(Program, 1, "Normal");

  // Link
  glLinkProgram(Program);

  // Validate our work thus far
  int ShaderStatus;
  glGetProgramiv(Program, GL_LINK_STATUS, &ShaderStatus);

  if (ShaderStatus != GL_TRUE) {
    LOGE("Error: Failed to link GLSL program\n");
    int Len = 1024;
    char Error[1024];
    glGetProgramInfoLog(Program, 1024, &Len, Error);
    LOGE(Error);
    exit(-1);
  }

  glValidateProgram(Program);

  glGetProgramiv(Program, GL_VALIDATE_STATUS, &ShaderStatus);

  if (ShaderStatus != GL_TRUE) {
    LOGE("Error: Failed to validate GLSL program\n");
    exit(-1);
```

```
}

   // Enable the program
   glUseProgram(Program);
   glEnableVertexAttribArray(0);
   glEnableVertexAttribArray(1);

   // Setup the Projection matrix
   Persp(Proj, 70.0f, 0.1f, 200.0f);

   // Retrieve our uniforms
   iProj = glGetUniformLocation(Program, "Proj");
   iModel = glGetUniformLocation(Program, "Model");

   // Basic GL setup
   glClearColor(0.0, 0.0, 0.0, 1.0);
   glEnable ( GL_CULL_FACE);
   glCullFace ( GL_BACK);

   return GL_TRUE;
}
```

Initialization is the first step and it is performed only once. Next, we tackle rendering.

Scene Rendering

Scene rendering is performed multiple times when a frame is to be drawn. Listing 4–9 defines the Display C++ function.

Listing 4–9. *Scene Rendering*

```
void Display(int time) {
   // Clear the screen
   glClear ( GL_COLOR_BUFFER_BIT);

   float Model[4][4];

   memset(Model, 0, sizeof(Model));

   // Setup the Proj so that the object rotates around the Y axis
   // We'll also translate it appropriately to Display
   Model[0][0] = cosf(Angle);
   Model[1][1] = 1.0f;
   Model[2][0] = sinf(Angle);
   Model[0][2] = -sinf(Angle);
   Model[2][2] = cos(Angle);
   Model[3][2] = -1.0f;
   Model[3][3] = 1.0f;

   // Constantly rotate the object as a function of time
   int ticks = time;
   int thisTicks = ticks - lastTicks; // note delta time
   if (thisTicks > 200)
     thisTicks = 200; // throttling
   Angle += ((float) thisTicks) * RotationSpeed; // apply animation
   lastTicks = ticks; // note for next loop
```

```
// Vertex information
float PtData[][3] = {
// see source (removed for simplicity)
};

// Face information
unsigned short FaceData[][3] = {
// see source (removed for simplicity)
};

// Draw the icosahedron
glUseProgram(Program);
glUniformMatrix4fv(iProj, 1, false, (const float *) &Proj[0][0]);
glUniformMatrix4fv(iModel, 1, false, (const float *) &Model[0][0]);

glVertexAttribPointer(0, 3, GL_FLOAT, 0, 0, &PtData[0][0]);
glVertexAttribPointer(1, 3, GL_FLOAT, GL_TRUE, 0, &PtData[0][0]);

glDrawElements(GL_TRIANGLES, sizeof(FaceData) / sizeof(unsigned short),
GL_UNSIGNED_SHORT, &FaceData[0][0]);
}
```

The Display C++ function performs the following steps:

1. It clears the screen with glClear (GL_COLOR_BUFFER_BIT);.

2. It creates a model matrix float Model[4][4] to set up a projection so that the object rotates around the Y axis. It also translates it appropriately to display.

3. It then constantly rotates the object as a function of time.

4. It enables the program with glUseProgram (Program);.

5. It binds the shader attributes Position (iProj) and Normal (iModel) to the projection (Proj) and Model matrices.

```
glUniformMatrix4fv    (iProj, 1, false, (const float *)&Proj[0][0]);
glUniformMatrix4fv    (iModel, 1, false, (const float *)&Model[0][0]);
```

6. It sets the icosahedron vertex information with

```
glVertexAttribPointer    (0, 3, GL_FLOAT, 0, 0, &PtData[0][0]);
glVertexAttribPointer    (1, 3, GL_FLOAT, GL_TRUE, 0, &PtData[0][0]);
```

7. Finally, it draws the icosahedron using the GL_TRIANGLES and the face information array described at the beginning of the project.

```
glDrawElements (GL_TRIANGLES, sizeof(FaceData) / sizeof(unsigned short),
GL_UNSIGNED_SHORT, &FaceData[0][0]);
```

Setting the Rotation Speed

The rotation speed function in Listing 4–10 is a bonus C++ call that will be used in the next section to change the rotation speed whenever a finger is swiped in the display. To do so, it updates a global variable RotationSpeed, which is, in turn, used by the Display function to update the angle of the Model matrix used by the shaders. Because RotationSpeed is read by multiple threads, it is declared as volatile that tells the compiler to always re-read from memory when used.

Listing 4–10. *Setting the Rotation Speed*

```
volatile float RotationSpeed = 0.001f; // Rotation speed of our object
void doSetRotationSpeed(double val)
{
    // we'll make the slowest it goes 0.001, and
    // the fastest 0.01
    double slowest = -0.005;
    double fastest = 0.005;
    double range = fastest - slowest;
    RotationSpeed = (float)(slowest + ((range*val)/100.0f));
}
```

This takes care of the C++ side of things. As a bonus, let's add swipe and pinch zooming functionality with Android's multi-touch APIs.

Adding Swipe and Multi-Touch Pinch for Zooming

As a bonus, this section describes how to use the Android multi-touch APIs to increase the rotation speed of the icosahedron by:

- Increasing the speed whenever finger-swiped to the right, or decrease it when swiping to the left. The rotation will switch from left to right whenever a threshold value is reached.

- Zooming the shape in or out whenever pinching inward or outward with two fingers.

Listing 4–11 describes the additions to the ShadersActivity class to perform such tasks.

Listing 4–11. *Swipe and Pinch Zooming with Multi-Touch*

```
// default rotation speed
int speed = 10;

// pointer 1,2 XY coords
float p1X, p1Y, p2X, p2Y;

// deltas
float DX1, DX2;

// # of fingers
int fingers = 0;

@Override
public boolean onTouchEvent(MotionEvent e) {
  int count = e.getPointerCount();
  int action = e.getAction();
  float X1 = 0f, Y1 = 0f, X2 = 0f, Y2 = 0f;

// finger 1 down
```

```java
            if (action == MotionEvent.ACTION_DOWN) {
              p1X = e.getX(0);
              p1Y = e.getY(0);
              fingers = 1;
            }

// finger 2 down
        if (action == MotionEvent.ACTION_POINTER_2_DOWN) {
          p2X = e.getX(1);
          p2Y = e.getY(1);
          fingers = 2;
        }

        // pointer 1 up
        if (action == MotionEvent.ACTION_UP) {
          X1 = e.getX(0);
          Y1 = e.getY(0);
          DX1 = X1 - p1X;

          X2 = e.getX(1);
          Y2 = e.getY(1);
          DX2 = X2 - p2X;
        }

      // 1 or 2 up
      if (action == MotionEvent.ACTION_UP
          || action == MotionEvent.ACTION_POINTER_2_UP) {

        if (fingers == 1) {
          // Swipe
          setRotationSpeed(DX1);
        } else if (fingers == 2) {
          // Pinching
          setPinch(DX1, DX2);
        }
        p1X = p1Y = p2X = p2Y = DX1 = DX2 = 0f;
        fingers = 0;
      }
      return super.onTouchEvent(e);
    }

  // Pinch: Set Zoom
  private void setPinch(float DX1, float DX2) {
    // Pinch inwards: zoom in
    if (DX1 > 0 && DX2 < 0) {
      width *= 0.6;
      height *= 0.8;
      view.setVideoSize(width, height);
    } else {
// Pinch outwards: zoom out
      width *= 1.4;
      height *= 1.2;
      view.setVideoSize(width, height);
    }
  }

  // Swipe Left/right: Set rotation speed
```

```
// 0-50 left, 50-100 right
private void setRotationSpeed(float DX) {
  if (DX < 0) {
    speed -= 20;
  } else {
    speed += 20;
  }
  // clamp 0-100
  if (speed < 0)
    speed = 0;
  if (speed > 100)
    speed = 100;

  view.setRotationSpeed(speed);
}
```

To listen for touch events, an activity can overload the Android method:

```
public boolean onTouchEvent(MotionEvent e)
```

The MotionEvent type contains all the information we need to access single or multitouch attributes of the event. Among the most important are the following:

- getPointerCount: returns the number of pointers (or fingers) on screen

- getAction: returns the action constant being performed; for example,

    - ACTION_DOWN when the first pointer goes down

    - ACTION_UP when the first pointer goes up

    - ACTION_MOVE when the first pointer is dragged

Android supports up to four simultaneous pointers, thus when a second pointer goes down when the action returned will be ACTION_POINTER_2_DOWN, and so forth. When the user swipes on finger the pointer count will be 1. In that case, we simply save the XY coordinates of the finger and set the number of fingers to 1.

```
// finger 1 down
if (action == MotionEvent.ACTION_DOWN) {
  p1X = e.getX(0);
  p1Y = e.getY(0);
  fingers = 1;
}
```

If pinching, the pointer count will be 2 and the action will be ACTION_POINTER_2_DOWN when the second finger goes down. In such case, we save the down coordinates of the second pointer by calling MotionEvent.getX and MotionEvent.getY with the index of the desired pointer. Also, set the number of fingers to 2.

```
// finger 2 down
if (action == MotionEvent.ACTION_POINTER_2_DOWN) {
  p2X = e.getX(1);
  p2Y = e.getY(1);
  fingers = 2;
}
```

Finally, when the swipe or pinch gesture completes, the `MotionEvent.ACTION_UP` or `MotionEvent.ACTION_POINTER_2_UP` actions will fire. Here, we calculate the delta coordinates for both fingers in the X and Y coordinates.

```
X1 = e.getX(0);
Y1 = e.getY(0);
DX1 = X1 - p1X;
X2 = e.getX(1);
Y2 = e.getY(1);
DX2 = X2 - p2X;
```

Next, we simply check the number of active fingers. A value of 1 indicates a swipe, 2 indicates a pinch. If swiping, we call the `setRotationSpeed(DX1)` function with the delta coordinates for the first finger in the X axis. If pinching, we call `setPinch(DX1, DX2)` with the deltas for both fingers in the X coordinate.

When swiping to the left, the delta X value will be negative; it will be positive when swiping to the right. In either case, we decrease or increase the rotation speed and call the view's `setRotationSpeed` function, which will invoke doSetRotation in C++.

```
if (DX < 0) {
  speed -= 20;
} else {
  speed += 20;
}
// clamp 0-100
if (speed < 0)
  speed = 0;
if (speed > 100)
  speed = 100;
view.setRotationSpeed(speed);
```

For a pinch gesture, we must check if we are pinching inward or outward. When the deltas are `DX1 > 0 && DX2 < 0`, we have an inward pinch or zoom in; otherwise, it's a zoom out. In either case, we modify the width and height of the display by an arbitrary factor and invoke the view's `setVideoSize(width, height)` method. This method will invoke the C++ `Init(w,h)` subroutine.

```
// Pinch inwards: zoom in
if (DX1 > 0 && DX2 < 0) {
  width *= 0.6;
  height *= 0.8;
  view.setVideoSize(width, height);
} else {
  // Pinch outwards: zoom out
  width *= 1.4;
  height *= 1.2;
  view.setVideoSize(width, height);
}
```

Now let's compile and run the project in the device.

Compiling and Running

To compile the native library, start the Cygwin console in Windows, change to the project folder ch03.OpenGLES2Shaders, and use the Android compilation script:

```
$ ndk-build
```

The compilation script Android.mk is very simple, as shown in the following fragment. It defines a module called libicosahedron that is bound to the libraries: log (for text logging) and GLESv2 for OpenGL ES 2.0. When compilation completes, the shared library libicosahedron.so will be created in the libs/armeabi folder of your project.

```
LOCAL_PATH:= $(call my-dir)
include $(CLEAR_VARS)
LOCAL_MODULE    := libicosahedron
LOCAL_CFLAGS    := -Werror
LOCAL_SRC_FILES := ico.cpp
LOCAL_LDLIBS    := -llog -lGLESv2
include $(BUILD_SHARED_LIBRARY)
```

The library can now be loaded within Java with the system call:
System.loadLibrary("icosahedron"). We're done! Connect the device to your computer, create a run configuration for the project, and launch it in your device. The result is shown in Figure 4–4. Try swiping a finger to the left or right to change the rotation speed or pinching to zoom in/out—and have some fun with OpenGL 2.0.

Figure 4–4. *Icosahedron in action*

Summary

We have seen the most important features of OpenGL ES 2.0 and how they can be used to create a complex shape using vertex and fragment shaders. Remember the following when looking at using OpenGL ES 2.0 in Android:

- ▓ OpenGL ES 2.0 is not supported in all versions of Android, thus if you want to reach the largest amount of users and devices, you should use OpenGL ES 1.x instead.

- ▓ OpenGL ES 2.0 provides more efficient power consumption than 1.x. Always keep that in mind when working on embedded devices.

- ▓ If you are interested in the latest and greatest techniques in graphics rendering, then OpenGL 2.0 is definitely the way to go.

In the following chapters, you will learn how easy it is to bring powerful PC hardware-accelerated game engines to the platform in record time and with minimal development costs. Carry on.

3D Shooters for Doom

This chapter looks at another great PC game: Doom. It came along shortly after Wolfenstein 3D and put id Software at the lead of the pack in 3D graphics gaming for the PC. In this chapter, you'll learn how to bring the open source Doom engine (PrBoom) to the Android platform.

The chapter starts with fun facts about Doom itself, which will help you understand the breadth of this project. Bringing a PC game to a mobile device with little change to the original code is a difficult task. As you can probably tell from reading the previous chapters, I embrace the Java/C power combo for maximum performance.

Next, we dig into the game itself, which is divided into two big layers: Java and native. This makes sense, as the game is a mix of original C wrapped in Java code. In the Java layer are classes for the main activity, audio, and JNI interface (what I call the native interface class). The native layer has the native method implementations (using JNI), plus changes to the original C code. The latter is required to glue both layers together and requires less than 50 lines of new code (I consider this to be the most difficult to follow, as there are close to 80,000 lines of original C code, but I will explain the new C code as clearly as possible.)

Finally, we get to compilation, deployment, and playing Doom in the emulator! You will learn awesome tips for native library compilation—a subject that is obscure to the average Java developer.

This is a long and complex chapter, and I have tried my best to make it as simple and clean as possible. For the sake of simplicity, I have omitted some of the lengthier code. Even so, there are some big listings throughout this chapter and a lot of things to cover. To make the most of this chapter, you should grab the chapter source distributed with this book. The project has been built with Eclipse Galileo and can be imported into your workspace. The source will help you to understand the layout of the resources as you read through the chapter.

The Sky Is the Limit with the Java/C Power Combo

The goal here is not to try to explain how the game itself works (that would take a complete book), but to show the kinds of things that can be accomplished by combining the elegant object-oriented features of Java with the raw power of C. Most Java developers dismiss procedural languages like C, failing to see what can be accomplished when this duo coexists harmoniously. The trick is to find the right balance that combines the best of both worlds to solve a complex task with minimal time and effort. Here, you will learn how a task that would take a team of Java developers possibly months to complete can be done in a matter of days by someone who understands that object-oriented and procedural languages are not enemies, but simply pieces of the same puzzle.

Consider Tables 5–1 and 5–2. They show the total number of lines of new Java code, plus the number of lines inserted in the existing C code in Doom for Android.

Table 5–1. *Estimated Number of Lines for Java Files of Doom for Android*

File	Description	Lines of Code
DoomClient.java	Main game activity	700
DialogTool.java	Methods to create help dialogs	300
DoomTools.java	Miscellaneous helper subs	450
GameFileDownloader.java	A class to install game files to the SD card	180
WebDownload.java	Web download tool	200
AudioManager.java	Singleton for audio management	200
AudioClip.java	Wrapper for Android MediaPlayer to play sounds	110

Table 5–2. *Estimated Number of Lines Changed from the Original Doom C Code*

File	Description	Lines of Code
jni_doom.c (new)	Implementation of the JNI native methods plus C to Java callbacks	450
i_sound.c	C to Java callbacks to send sound events to Java	3
s_sound.c	C to Java callbacks to send sound events to Java	6
i_video.c	C to Java callbacks to send video events to Java	10

The following is the rundown of the estimated totals:

- Total number of lines of new Java code = 2,140

- Total number of lines of original C code = 80,000

- Total number of lines of new C code = 469

The bottom line? One developer has managed to reuse about 80,000 lines of C code, thus bringing a PC game to Android with a few thousand lines of new code in a couple of days. Imagine the potential savings in development costs and time. Now compare this to a team of three developers trying to port the 80,000 lines of raw C to pure Java. It would probably take them months of head-pounding work with no financial gain (as the code is open sourced). This simply makes no sense. I hope that at this point you understand why this chapter is my personal favorite and a must-read for the aspiring Android game developer. So get the source code for the chapter—and let's get started.

Bringing Doom to a Mobile Device

I was excited about the challenge of bringing the great game of Doom to the mobile platform. But I had my doubts that this could even be achieved once I looked at the complexity and the amount of original C code. Listing 5–1 shows a portion of the total number of lines of C code of the popular Doom engine, PrBoom (available from `http://prboom.sourceforge.net/`).

I knew I had two choices for this project:

- Port the C code line by line to Java. I even started porting a few files to Java. Believe me when I say that this is not a good idea. The amount of time that it would take to do this makes the project unfeasible, especially considering that the hard work must be done *pro bono*.

- Find a way to pack the game as a dynamic shared object (DSO) and call it from Java using JNI. This option seems to be simpler and quicker, but requires expert knowledge of C and JNI, as well as changes to the original game to glue both languages together.

Given these two options, the latter is the best approach to the problem, so I decided to build a DSO and glue it to Java with JNI.

Listing 5–1. *Portion of Code for the PrBoom Doom Engine (Approximately 80,000 Lines in Total)*

```
$ wc -l *.c
   1585 am_map.c
    554 d_client.c
   3093 d_deh.c
    140 d_items.c
   1744 d_main.c
    759 d_server.c
     48 doomdef.c
    108 doomstat.c
     85 dstrings.c
```

```
    668 f_finale.c
    202 f_wipe.c
   2979 g_game.c
   2717 gl_main.c
    957 gl_texture.c
    767 hu_lib.c
   1593 hu_stuff.c
    866 mmus2mid.c
    467 p_ceilng.c
// …
    450 r_fps.c
    649 r_main.c
    788 r_patch.c
    468 r_plane.c
    854 r_segs.c
     56 r_sky.c
   1077 r_things.c
    714 s_sound.c
    245 sounds.c
    374 st_lib.c
   1160 st_stuff.c
    128 tables.c
   1037 v_video.c
     38 version.c
    166 w_memcache.c
    335 w_mmap.c
    476 w_wad.c
   1968 wi_stuff.c
    123 z_bmalloc.c
    705 z_zone.c
  73176 total

$ wc -l *.h
    111 am_map.h
    209 config.h
   1118 d_deh.h
    707 d_englsh.h
    125 d_event.h
     59 d_items.h
     82 d_main.h
    214 d_net.h
    234 d_player.h
     94 d_think.h
     59 d_ticcmd.h
    204 doomdata.h
// …
     64 r_bsp.h
    109 r_data.h
    428 r_defs.h
     45 r_demo.h
    163 r_draw.h
    174 r_filter.h
    100 s_sound.h
    305 sounds.h
    209 st_lib.h
    102 st_stuff.h
     93 tables.h
```

```
  207 v_video.h
   40 version.h
  146 w_wad.h
   64 wi_stuff.h
   52 z_bmalloc.h
  131 z_zone.h
13460 total
```

As I've noted, I chose to use the PrBoom Doom engine. Even though the game was created by id Software and released under the GNU license in 1993 (see http://en.wikipedia.org/wiki/ Doom_(video_game)), there are many Doom engines out there. I did try a few engines before settling on PrBoom.

The first engine I tried was the original code from id Software—after all, it is the original creator. But I had a lot of trouble with id Software's Linux implementation of the game, due to two main issues:

- *Color palette*: The Linux flavor supports an 8-bit color palette, which looks pretty bad on 32-bit machines. This code was written for old machines (it has not been updated for a long time). There should be a more modern implementation out there.

- *Sine and cosine tables*: These are used for ray casting. I had many compiler idiosyncrasies (using the CodeSourcery GCC 4.3.*x* compiler) where these tables, which have hard-coded values, were not filled in correctly, making sprites go through walls or move in the wrong way and creating many other display problems.

PrBoom is a modern Doom engine. It is highly portable, although it is much bigger than the original game. I found it to be the best choice due to the plethora of platforms it has been ported to and the powerful support available for it from the developer community.

Game Architecture for Doom

When the user starts the game, the main activity, org.doom.DoomClient, will start (see Figure 5–1). This activity is bound to the other pieces in the following manner:

- The main activity is bound to the device UI through an XML layout (doom.xml). This layout defines an image buffer used to display the graphics and a set of controller buttons for navigation (see the "Game Layout" section for details).

- The Doom engine is written in C and compiled as a DSO (libdoom_jni.so). All communication with the DSO goes through the JNI layer (or native interface class Natives.java). Events are cascaded back to the main activity, which dispatches them to their respective handler. Game files are read from the SD card by the DSO, which handles all game aspects except sound.

- Sound requests are delegated by the native library to the native interface class to the main activity, and finally to the sound classes, which play them using the Android `MediaPlayer`.

- Video buffers (pixels) are cascaded by the native library to the native interface class to the main activity, which renders them into the `ImageView` of the layout XML.

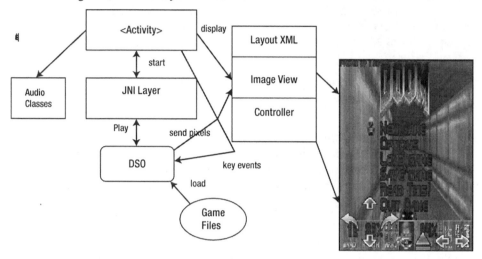

Figure 5–1. *Doom for Android architecture*

This process continues in an endless loop, where key and touch events are dispatched back to the DSO, which updates the game accordingly.

The game is composed of the following Java packages:

- `org.doom`: This is the main game package and contains the main activity `DoomClient.java`. This class controls the application life cycle and the key and touch events, dispatches sound and music requests to the audio classes, and dispatches user events to the DSO through the native interface class.

- `doom.audio`: This package contains the audio classes `AudioManager` and `AudioClip`.

  - `AudioManager`: This class is in charge of playing sounds and background music using `AudioClip`. It also caches sounds for better performance.

  - `AudioClip.java`: This class is capable of playing, stopping, and looping a sound using the Android `MediaPlayer`. Sound files use the WAVE format.

- `doom.jni`: This JNI package contains the native interface class `Natives.java`. This class is a two-way pipe for all access with the DSO. This includes native Java methods and C to Java callbacks.

- `doom.util`: This package contains the following utility classes:

  - `DialogTool.java`: This class contains miscellaneous dialogs to start the game and install shareware game files, message boxes, and other items.

  - `DoomTools.java`: This class contains basic game constants and commonly used subroutines.

  - `GameFileDownloader.java`: This class is capable of downloading shareware game files from the Internet into the SD card.

  - `LibraryLoader.java`: This class loads the DSO, which is required before the native methods can be invoked.

  - `WebDownload.java`: This is a web download tool used by the `GameFileDownloader` class.

Again, before we look at these components in more detail, make sure you have the chapter code at hand; most of the listings have been stripped down for simplicity.

Java Main Activity

The main activity class is invoked when the user starts the game and controls the life cycle of the application. In Doom, this life cycle is handled by the following:

- *Creation handler*: This handler is implemented by `onCreate` and it is called when the activity is first created. It sets the UI layout XML (doom.xml) and initializes the game.

- *Menu handlers*: Here, we have `onCreateOptionsMenu` and `onOptionsItemSelected`. The first method creates the game menu, and the latter processes the menu when the user selects an option.

- *Key and touch handlers*: These methods receive key and touch events and dispatch them to the right JNI component.

- *Native callback handlers*: These methods receive video and sound updates from the native interface and dispatch them.

- *Controller toolbar*: The controller toolbar is a set of image buttons displayed at the bottom of the screen for navigation. It is helpful for devices that do not have a keyboard.

Creation Handler

The creation handler is defined by onCreate (see Listing 5–2). For Doom, this method performs the following steps:

- Sets the display to full screen and hides the title

- Sets the content view layout to R.layout.doom, which maps to doom.xml

- Gets a reference to the video buffer (R.id.doom_iv), which will be used to display the pixels sent by the DSO

- Sets the navigation controls

Listing 5–2. *Main Activity Life Cycle*

```
public void onCreate(Bundle savedInstanceState) {
    super.onCreate(savedInstanceState);

    // Full screen
    getWindow().setFlags(WindowManager.LayoutParams.FLAG_FULLSCREEN,
            WindowManager.LayoutParams.FLAG_FULLSCREEN);

    // No title
    requestWindowFeature(Window.FEATURE_NO_TITLE);

    setContentView(R.layout.doom);

    mView = (ImageView)findViewById(R.id.doom_iv);

    if (mGameStarted) {
        setGameUI();
        setupPanControls();
        return;
    }

    // Pan controls
    setupPanControls();

}
```

onCreate() is the very first function called when the game starts, and it is called only once while the application is in memory. Next, let's look at the game layout loaded by this function.

Game Layout

GUIs in Android are defined by XML layouts, where visual components are placed in a variety of layout schemes. Doom's layout (doom.xml) is a relative layout, which has widgets placed relative to each other (meaning they can overlap depending on the widget size). The master layout contains an image view and two table layouts.

In Android, an image view encapsulates an array of pixels representing an image. The great thing about image views is that they have efficient automatic resize capabilities. This will allow the game to be resized on the fly!

The two table layouts are for the navigation controls (see Figure 5–2). The first table layout defines a three-row table that contains image buttons for up, down, left, and right navigation. The second table layout is a one-row table that contains buttons for the level map, object pick up, and strafing left and right.

Figure 5–2. *Doom displaying the game layout*

Listing 5–3 shows Doom's relative layout XML. The most important attributes are explained in Table 5–3.

Table 5–3. *Main Attributes of doom.xml*

Attribute	Meaning
`android:id="@+id/doom_iv"`	Defines the ID of the widget, which can be used for programmatic access. The format must be @+id/NAME.
`android:layout_width="fill_parent"`	Defines the width of the widget. The values can be `fill_parent` or `wrap_content`.
`android:focusableInTouchMode="true"`	Specifies that the widget should be focusable and receive touch events from the main activity.
`android:focusable="true"`	Specifies that the widget should be focusable and receive key events from the main activity.

Table 5–3. *Main Attributes of doom.xml (continued)*

Attribute	Meaning
`android:src="@drawable/up"`	Defines the bitmap source of the widget (applies to image view only). The format is `@drawable/NAME`, where NAME is the bitmap filename saved under the `res/drawable` folder of the project.
`android:layout_alignParentBottom="true"`	Tells the relative layout to align the widget to the bottom of the parent, possibly overlapping other widgets.
`android:layout_alignParentLeft="true"`	Tells the relative layout to align the widget to the left of the parent, possibly overlapping other widgets.
`android:visibility="gone"`	Sets the visibility of the widget. Possible values are `visible` or `gone` (indicates the widget occupies no space).

Listing 5–3. *Doom Game UI Layout doom.xml*

```xml
<?xml version="1.0" encoding="utf-8"?>
<RelativeLayout
    xmlns:android="http://schemas.android.com/apk/res/android"
    android:layout_width="fill_parent"
    android:layout_height="fill_parent"
    >

    <!-- GAME IMAGE -->
    <ImageView android:id="@+id/doom_iv"
        android:layout_width="fill_parent"
        android:layout_height="fill_parent"
        android:adjustViewBounds="true"
        android:visibility="visible"
        android:background="@drawable/doom"
        android:focusableInTouchMode="true"
```

```
            android:focusable="true"/>

    <!-- Nav Controls -->
    <TableLayout android:id="@+id/pan_ctls"
            android:layout_width="wrap_content"
            android:layout_height="wrap_content"
            android:layout_alignParentBottom="true"
            android:layout_alignParentLeft="true"
            android:visibility="gone"
            android:focusable="false"
            android:focusableInTouchMode="false">

        <TableRow>
        <ImageButton android:id="@+id/btn_upleft"
            android:layout_width="wrap_content"
            android:layout_height="wrap_content"
            android:background="#00000000"
            android:layout_margin="0px"
            android:src="@drawable/blank"
            />
        <ImageButton android:id="@+id/btn_up"
            android:layout_width="wrap_content"
            android:layout_height="wrap_content"
            android:src="@drawable/up"
            android:background="#00000000"
            android:layout_margin="0px"
            />
        <ImageButton android:id="@+id/btn_upright"
            android:layout_width="wrap_content"
            android:layout_height="wrap_content"
            android:src="@drawable/blank"
            android:background="#00000000"
            android:layout_margin="0px"
            />
        </TableRow>
    </TableLayout>

    <!-- Other controls: Map, Open, strafe -->
    <!--  This XML has been removed for simplicity →
    <!-- See the file doom.xml for details -->
</RelativeLayout>
```

Once the GUI is all set, the next step is to provide a menu and handlers for the application.

Menu and Selection Handlers

The application menu can be easily defined by overriding the following methods:

- onCreateOptionsMenu(Menu menu): Override this method to add items to the menu. To do this, use menu.add(groupId, itemId, order, Menu Label), where groupId is the ID of the group for this item. This can be used to define groups of items for batch state changes. itemId is the unique item ID. order is the order for the item.

- ◾ onOptionsItemSelected(MenuItem item): Override this method to process menu selections. The item selected can be obtained with item.getItemId().

The following menus are defined for Doom (see Listing 5–4):

- ◾ *Start*: to run the native game loop

- ◾ *Install Game*: to download and install game files

- ◾ *Navigation*: to switch the navigation controls between the keyboard and touch screen

- ◾ *Exit*: to quit the application

Listing 5–4. *Game Menu and Selection*

```
public boolean onCreateOptionsMenu(Menu menu) {
    super.onCreateOptionsMenu(menu);
    menu.add(0, 0, 0, "Start").setIcon(R.drawable.icon);
    menu.add(0, 2, 2, "Install Game").setIcon(R.drawable.install);
    menu.add(0, 3, 3, "Navigation").setIcon(R.drawable.nav);
    menu.add(0, 6, 6, "Exit").setIcon(R.drawable.exit);
    return true;
}

/**
 * Menu selection
 */
public boolean onOptionsItemSelected(MenuItem item) {
    super.onOptionsItemSelected(item);
    switch (item.getItemId()) {
    case 0:
        if ( mGameStarted) {
            MessageBox("Game already in progress.");
            return true;
        }
        mMultiPlayer = false;
        showLauncherDialog(this, mMultiPlayer);

        return true;
    case 2:
        if ( mGameStarted) {
            MessageBox("Can't install while game in progress.");
            return true;
        }

        // SD card required
        if ( ! DoomTools.checkSDCard(this) ) return true;

        // Download Game file
        DialogTool.showDownloadDialog(this);
        return true;

    case 3:
        DialogTool.showNavMethodDialog(this);
        return true;
```

```
    case 6:
        // Exit
        DoomTools.hardExit(0);
        return true;

    }
    return false;
}
```

Key and Touch Event Handlers

Key and touch handlers can be overridden to process key and touch events. Doom handles key and touch events as follows (see Listing 5–5):

- ■ The Android keyCode is first translated to an ASCII key symbol by calling int sym = DoomTools.keyCodeToKeySym(keyCode).

- ■ The ASCII symbol is the sent to the DSO through the native interface class Natives.keyEvent(EVENT_TYPE, SYMBOL), where the event type must be either Natives.EV_KEYUP or Natives.EV_KEYDOWN. Note that any errors in the native side (such as a missing symbol or invalid signature) will throw an UnsatisfiedLinkError.

Listing 5–5. *Key and Touch Handlers*

```
public boolean onKeyUp(int keyCode, KeyEvent event) {
    //
    if (keyCode == KeyEvent.KEYCODE_MENU) {
        return false;
    }

    int sym = DoomTools.keyCodeToKeySym(keyCode);

    try {
        Natives.keyEvent(Natives.EV_KEYUP, sym);

    } catch (UnsatisfiedLinkError e) {
        // Should not happen
        Log.e(TAG, e.toString());
    }
    return false;
}

public boolean onKeyDown(int keyCode, KeyEvent event) {
    // Ignore menu key
    if (keyCode == KeyEvent.KEYCODE_MENU) {
        return false;
    }

    int sym = DoomTools.keyCodeToKeySym(keyCode);

    try {
        Natives.keyEvent(Natives.EV_KEYDOWN, sym);
    }
```

```
        catch (UnsatisfiedLinkError e) {
            // Should not happen
            Log.e(TAG, e.toString());
        }
        return false;
    }
    public boolean onTouchEvent(MotionEvent event)
    {

        try {
            if ( event.getAction() == MotionEvent.ACTION_DOWN) {
                // Fire on tap R-CTL
                Natives.keyEvent(Natives.EV_KEYDOWN, DoomTools.KEY_RCTL);
            }
            else if ( event.getAction() == MotionEvent.ACTION_UP) {
                Natives.keyEvent(Natives.EV_KEYUP, DoomTools.KEY_RCTL);
            }
            else if ( event.getAction() == MotionEvent.ACTION_MOVE) {
                // Motion event
            }
            return true;
        }
        catch (UnsatisfiedLinkError e) {
            // Should not happen!
            Log.e(TAG, e.toString());
            return false;
        }
    }
}
```

For touch events, Android provides three actions: ACTION_DOWN, ACTION_UP, and
ACTION_MOVE, when the user is pressing, releasing, and dragging fingers in the device
screen, respectively. When a finger press or release occurs, Doom will send a right
control (KEY_RCTL) to the native layer, which will result in the weapon being fired.

Native Callback Handlers

The native callback handlers are implemented by the main activity (DoomClient.java) via
the Natives.EventListener interface. This allows the activity to listen for native
callbacks. The handlers are divided in the following categories:

- *Graphics initialization*: This handler receives information when the
  native graphics have been initialized. It receives the width and height
  of the video buffer.

- *Image update*: This handler receives video buffer updates and fires
  multiple times per second.

- *Message update*: This handler receives string messages from the
  native rendering engine.

- *Fatal errors*: This handler will fire whenever an unrecoverable error
  occurs.

- *Sound and music requests*: A series of handlers handle audio.

Graphics Initialization Handler

The graphics initialization handler is critical and must be the first to fire before the game can start. It receives the width and height of the video buffer, which are used to create the Android bitmap that renders the video on the device (see Listing 5–6). To create a 32-bit ARGB bitmap in Android, you use the following call:

```
Bitmap.createBitmap(width, height, Config.ARGB_8888)
```

Config.ARGB_8888 tells the system you wish to use a 4-byte (32-bit) ARGB bitmap. You will use this bitmap to set pixels for the video in later sections. Note that this callback fires only once during the lifetime of the game. To set the width and height of the video buffer ImageView, use a call to ImageView.getLayoutParams().

Listing 5–6. *Graphics Initialization*

```
public void OnInitGraphics(int w, int h) {
    Log.d(TAG, "OnInitGraphics creating Bitmap of " + w + " by " + h);
    mBitmap = Bitmap.createBitmap(w, h, Config.ARGB_8888);
    LayoutParams lp = mView.getLayoutParams();
    mWidth = w;
    mHeight = h;
    lp.width = w;
    lp.height = h;
}
```

Image Update Handler

The image update handler receives an array of ARGB packed pixels representing a color (see Listing 5–7). It fires multiple times per second, and its job is to replace pixels in the bitmap with the colors in the array by calling the following method:

```
mBitmap.setPixels(pixels, offset, stride, x, y, width, height)
```

The arguments are as follows:

- pixels is the colors to write to the bitmap.

- offset is the index of the first color to read from pixels[].

- stride is the number of colors in pixels[] to skip between rows (normally, this value will be the same as the width of the bitmap.

- x is the x coordinate of the first pixel to write to in the bitmap.

- y is the y coordinate of the first pixel to write to in the bitmap.

- width is the number of colors to copy from pixels[] per row.

- height is the number of rows to write to the bitmap.

Listing 5–7. *Image Update Handler*

```
public void OnImageUpdate(int[] pixels) {
    mBitmap.setPixels(pixels, 0, mWidth, 0, 0, mWidth, mHeight);
    mHandler.post(new Runnable() {
        public void run() {
            mView.setImageBitmap( mBitmap);
        }
    });
}
```

Note that because this handler fires from a non-UI thread, you cannot set the pixels directly into the ImageView, but must use an android.os.Handler to post a Runnable to the message queue:

```
Handler.post(new Runnable() {
    public void run() {
        // Code that updates the UI goes here
    }
});
```

> **NOTE:** A handler allows you to send and process message and runnable objects associated with a thread's message queue. Each handler instance is associated with a single thread and that thread's message queue. When you create a new handler, it is bound to the thread and message queue of the thread that is creating it. Always use a handler when updating UI widgets from a non-UI thread!

Message Updates

The message updates handler receives native messages, which are very helpful for debugging. Listing 5–8 shows this handler, which logs the text to the Android console.

Listing 5–8. *Message Update Handler*

```
/**
 * Fires on DSO message
 */
public void OnMessage(String text, int level) {
    Log.d(TAG, "**Doom Message: " + text);
}
```

Fatal Error Handler

The fatal error handler deals with unrecoverable errors. This means displaying a message to the user and exiting gracefully. There are many things that can cause unrecoverable errors, such as code bugs, corrupted game files, I/O errors, and network failures.

Listing 5–9 shows the way Doom deals with this situation. It uses a message handler to display a message box to the user (remember that this method fires from a non-UI thread, where all UI widget access must go through an OS handler). It then waits for a while so the user can read the message, and finally exits gracefully.

Listing 5–9. *Fatal Error Handler*

```
public void OnFatalError(final String text) {
    mHandler.post(new Runnable() {
        public void run() {
            MessageBox("Fatal Error",
                    text + " - Please report this error.");
        }
    });

    // Wait for the user to read the box
    try {
        Thread.sleep(8000);
    } catch (InterruptedException e) {

    }
    // Must quit here or the LIB will crash
    DoomTools.hardExit(-1);
}
```

Audio Request Handlers

The native Doom engine cannot access the sound device directly. This is due to the nonstandard audio library used by Android (Enhanced Audio System, EAS, by SoniVOX, and in Ice Cream Sandwich, Vorbis). To overcome this very serious limitation, audio requests are cascaded back to these handlers, which start sound events at a given volume, start and stop background music events, and set the background music.

Listing 5–10 shows the audio handlers for Doom. Note that all requests are delegated to the doom.audio.AudioManager class, which deals with the Android audio system.

Listing 5–10. *Sound and Music Handlers*

```
public void OnStartSound(String name, int vol)
{
    if ( mSound && mAudioMgr == null)
        Log.e(TAG, "Bug: Audio Mgr is NULL but sound is enabled!");

    try {
        if ( mSound && mAudioMgr != null)
            mAudioMgr.startSound( name, vol);

    } catch (Exception e) {
        Log.e(TAG, "OnStartSound: " + e.toString());
    }
}

/**
 * Fires on background music
 */
public void OnStartMusic(String name, int loop) {
    if ( mSound && mAudioMgr != null)
        mAudioMgr.startMusic(DoomClient.this, name, loop);
}
```

```
/**
 * Stop bg music
 */
public void OnStopMusic(String name) {
    if ( mSound &&  mAudioMgr != null)
        mAudioMgr.stopMusic( name);
}

public void OnSetMusicVolume(int volume) {
    if ( mSound &&  mAudioMgr != null)
        mAudioMgr.setMusicVolume(volume);
}
```

> **NOTE:** Even though cascading audio in this way will make the game slower, it will provide high-quality sound to the game. It also provides a format-independent way of handling audio. Whatever the format of your sound file, Android will detect it behind the scenes and call the appropriate audio driver—as long as your sound file uses any format supported by the platform.

Navigation Controls

Older Android devices feature a trackball, which is cumbersome for mobile games. In fact, most gaming devices, such as PlayStation Portable (PSP) and Game Boy, feature multiple keypad arrows, which are great for navigation. On the plus side, the QWERTY keyboard is helpful for PC games. But the latest Android devices have neither a keyboard nor a trackball. This is where the navigation controls can help. Figure 5–3 shows the navigation controls in action during a game.

Figure 5–3. *Navigation controls for Doom*

The controls themselves are implemented as image buttons within the game layout (see the "Game Layout" section). The RelativeLayout of the game allows the controls to overlap the video ImageView, as shown in Figure 5–3. To set up events for the buttons, simply load the button widget using its ID and set a touch listener:

```
findViewById(R.id.BUTTON_ID).setOnTouchListener(new View.OnTouchListener(){
  public boolean onTouch(View v, MotionEvent evt) {
      // ACTION_DOWN or ACTION_UP
      int action = evt.getAction();
```

```
    // ...
  }
});
```

Depending on the touch event action, `ACTION_DOWN` or `ACTION_UP`, you simply send a key event to the native layer with the following code:

```
public static void sendNativeKeyEvent (int type, int sym) {
    try {
        Natives.keyEvent(type, sym);
    } catch (UnsatisfiedLinkError e) {
        Log.e(TAG, e.toString());
    }
}
```

Listing 5–11 shows the `setupPanControls()` function for the up, down, left, and right buttons of the Doom controller.

Listing 5–11. *Controller Event Setup*

```
private void setupPanControls() {
    // Up
    findViewById(R.id.btn_up).setOnTouchListener(
            new View.OnTouchListener(){
        public boolean onTouch(View v, MotionEvent evt) {
            int action = evt.getAction();
            if ( action == MotionEvent.ACTION_DOWN) {
                Natives.sendNativeKeyEvent(Natives.EV_KEYDOWN
                        , DoomTools.KEY_UPARROW);
             }
            else if ( action == MotionEvent.ACTION_UP) {
                Natives.sendNativeKeyEvent(Natives.EV_KEYUP
                        , DoomTools.KEY_UPARROW);
            }
            return true;
        }
    });

    // Down
    findViewById(R.id.btn_down).setOnTouchListener(
            new View.OnTouchListener(){
        public boolean onTouch(View v, MotionEvent evt) {
            int action = evt.getAction();
            if ( action == MotionEvent.ACTION_DOWN) {
                Natives.sendNativeKeyEvent(Natives.EV_KEYDOWN
                        , DoomTools.KEY_DOWNARROW);
            }
            else if ( action == MotionEvent.ACTION_UP) {
                Natives.sendNativeKeyEvent(Natives.EV_KEYUP
                        , DoomTools.KEY_DOWNARROW);
            }
            return true;
        }
    });

    // Right
    findViewById(R.id.btn_right).setOnTouchListener(
            new View.OnTouchListener(){
```

```
    public boolean onTouch(View v, MotionEvent evt) {
        int action = evt.getAction();
        if ( action == MotionEvent.ACTION_DOWN) {
            Natives.sendNativeKeyEvent(Natives.EV_KEYDOWN
                    , DoomTools.KEY_RIGHTARROW);
        }
        else if ( action == MotionEvent.ACTION_UP) {
            Natives.sendNativeKeyEvent(Natives.EV_KEYUP
                    , DoomTools.KEY_RIGHTARROW);
        }
        return true;
    }
});

// More ...
}
```

Handling Audio Independently of the Format

The audio classes are implemented in the package doom.audio and consist of two files: AudioManager and AudioClip.

AudioManager is a singleton class very similar to the AudioManager class presented in the previous chapter. Some of the method signatures are different to accommodate the Doom engine:

- preloadSounds(): This method preloads the most common Doom sounds to improve performance. Sounds are encoded in WAVE format.

- startSound(String name, int vol): This method starts the sound given by a name key at volume vol. The key does not include the file extension, and the volume ranges from 0 to 100.

- startMusic (Context ctx, String key, int loop): This method starts a background music file given by key and loops if loop is set to anything other than 0. An Android context is required by the background AudioClip.

- stopMusic (String key): This method stops the background music given by key.

- setMusicVolume (int vol): This method sets the background music volume. vol ranges from 0 to 100.

A great thing about AudioClip is that it provides a format independent way of playing sound (behind the scenes Android will take care of the dirty work of dealing with the format drivers), plus it will work in all versions of Android thus giving you the widest range of device support.

Because the audio files (including background music) can occupy more than 5 MB, files have been packed in a zip archive and installed at runtime into the SD card. This will save precious disk space in the main file system. The zip archive lives in the assets folder of the Doom project.

> **TIP:** Android features an automated media scanner service that searches for audio files within the file system. This can be really annoying, as your media player will suddenly display a few hundred unwanted Doom sounds and music. You can fix the problem by adding an empty file called .nomedia to the sound folder. This will tell the media scanner to bypass this directory.

Native Interface Class

The native interface class is the two-way pipe that sends messages from Java to the Doom engine through native methods, and from the engine to Java using C to Java callbacks (see Listing 5–12). This class consists of three parts: callback listener, native methods, and C to Java callbacks.

Callback Listener

The callback listener is implemented by the interface EventListener. It must be implemented by clients that wish to receive C to Java callbacks (in this case, by the main activity DoomClient.java). The C to Java callbacks are as follows:

- OnMessage(String text, int level): This is mostly a debug callback that sends messages to let Java know what is happening on the native side.

- OnInitGraphics(int w, int h): This is the very first callback and fires only once after graphics initialization. It tells Java the width and height of the video buffer.

- OnImageUpdate(int[] pixels): This fires many times per second and sends an Android packed video buffer to Java, which will use it to render the game bitmap.

- OnFatalError(String text): This callback fires when there is an unrecoverable error in the engine. The receiver should display the message and terminate.

- OnQuit(int code): This callback fires when the user exits the game. It sends a return code back to the receiver.

- OnStartSound(String name, int vol): This fires when the native engine starts a sound. It delegates to the receiver.

- OnStartMusic(String name, int loop): This fires on background music. It delegates to the receiver.

- OnStopMusic(String name): This fires on stop music background. It delegates to the receiver.

- OnSetMusicVolume(int volume): This fires when the user sets the music volume. It delegates to the receiver.

Native Methods

The native methods invoke the native Doom engine. There are three basic native methods:

- static native int DoomMain(String[] argv): This method invokes the main game loop of the Doom engine.

- static native int keyEvent(int type, int key): This method sends a key event to the engine. The event type is either EV_KEYDOWN or EV_KEYUP. The argument key must be an ASCII symbol, not an Android key code. This means the key code must be translated before being sent to the engine.

- static native int motionEvent(int b, int x, int y): This method sends a motion event to the engine (such as when the user drags a finger on the display). The first argument is a mouse button (always zero in this case), plus the x and y coordinates of the event itself.

static native int DoomMain(String[] argv) requires a list or arguments and blocks execution, so it must be run within a thread. The following are the most important arguments:

- width defines the width of the video buffer.

- height defines the height of the video buffer.

- iwad defines the game to be played. The following game files are supported by the engine:

    - doom1.wad: This is the shareware episode of Doom.

    - doom.wad: This is the retail episode.

    - doom2.wad: This is the second episode in the Doom series.

    - plutonia.wad: This is the Plutonia Experiment episode, part of the Ultimate Doom series.

    - tnt.wad: This is an episode dubbed Evilution, also part of the ultimate Doom series.

- file defines extra game files to be used by the engine.

For example, to play Doom shareware in landscape mode, the list arguments that must be sent to DoomMain (as a String array) would be doom -width 480 -height 320 -iwad doom1.wad.

C to Java Callbacks

C to Java callbacks are used to delegate engine messages to the listener activity. To do so, the native interface class uses a private listener and a static setter method:

```
private static EventListener listener;
public static void setListener(EventListener l) {
      listener = l;
}
```

Note that there can be only one listener. When the Doom engine sends a message (such as "have some text"), the native interface class simply delegates to the listener, which deals with the event:

```
private static void OnMessage(String text, int level) {
      if (listener != null)
          listener.OnMessage(text, level);
}
```

In the preceding example, the engine is saying "have some text," along with an integer log level. The rest of callbacks are shown in Listing 5–12.

Listing 5–12. *Native Interface Class (Natives.java)*

```
package doom.jni;

import android.util.Log;

public class Natives {
    public static final String TAG = "Natives";

    private static EventListener listener;

    public static final int EV_KEYDOWN = 0;
    public static final int EV_KEYUP = 1;
    public static final int EV_MOUSE = 2;

    public static interface EventListener {
        void OnMessage(String text, int level);
        void OnInitGraphics(int w, int h);
        void OnImageUpdate(int[] pixels);
        void OnFatalError(String text);
        void OnQuit(int code);
        void OnStartSound(String name, int vol);
        void OnStartMusic(String name, int loop);
        void OnStopMusic(String name);
        void OnSetMusicVolume(int volume);
    }

    public static void setListener(EventListener l) {
        listener = l;
    }
    /**
     * Send a key event to the native layer
     *
     * @param type : key up down or mouse
     * @param sym: ASCII symbol
```

```java
    */
    public static void sendNativeKeyEvent(int type, int sym) {
        try {
            Natives.keyEvent(type, sym);
        } catch (UnsatisfiedLinkError e) {
            Log.e(TAG, e.toString());
        }
    }

    // Native Main Doom Loop: @param argv: program arguments
    public static native int DoomMain(String[] argv);

    /**
     * Send a Key Event
     * @param type: event type: UP/DOWN
     * @param key: ASCII symbol
     */
    public static native int keyEvent(int type, int key);


    /***********************************************************
     * C to Java - Callbacks
     ***********************************************************/

    /**
     * This fires on messages from the C layer
     */
    private static void OnMessage(String text, int level) {
        if (listener != null)
            listener.OnMessage(text, level);
    }

    private static void OnInitGraphics(int w, int h) {
        if (listener != null)
            listener.OnInitGraphics(w, h);
    }

    private static void OnImageUpdate(int[] pixels) {
        if (listener != null)
            listener.OnImageUpdate(pixels);

    }

    private static void OnFatalError(String message) {
        if (listener != null)
            listener.OnFatalError(message);
    }
    private static void OnQuit(int code) {
        if (listener != null)
            listener.OnQuit(code);
    }
    /**
     * Fires when a sound is played in the C layer.
     */
    private static void OnStartSound(byte[] name, int vol) {
        if (listener != null)
            listener.OnStartSound(new String(name), vol);
    }
```

```java
/**
 * Start background music callback
 */
private static void OnStartMusic(String name, int loop) {
    if (listener != null)
        listener.OnStartMusic(name, loop);
}

/**
 * Stop background music
 * @param name
 */
private static void OnStopMusic(String name) {
    if (listener != null)
        listener.OnStopMusic(name);
}

/**
 * Set background music volume
 * @param volume Range: (0-255)
 */
private static void OnSetMusicVolume(int volume) {
    if (listener != null)
        listener.OnSetMusicVolume((int) (volume * 100.0 / 15.0));
}
}
```

Native Layer

The native layer glues the Java and C code together by defining three types of tasks to be performed:

- *Native method implementations*: These are the C implementations of the native Java methods defined by the native interface class. This code lives in the file jni_doom.c.

- *Original game changes*: The original Doom engine needs to be modified slightly to accommodate the JNI glue. This consists of inserting calls to the C to Java callbacks in the correct files.

- *Removal of invalid dependencies*: Invalid dependencies in the original code must be removed. For example, the original Simple DirectMedia Layer (SDL) dependency used by the PC code must be deleted.

Let's look a these tasks in more detail.

Native Method Implementations

Table 5–4 shows the Java native signatures and their C counterparts in jni_doom.c.

Table 5–4. *Java Native Methods and Their Native Counterparts*

Java Method	C Method
static native int DoomMain(String[] argv)	JNIEXPORT jint JNICALL Java_doom_jni_Natives_DoomMain(JNIEnv * env, jclass class, jobjectArray jargv)
static native int keyEvent(int type, int key)	JNIEXPORT jint JNICALL Java_doom_jni_Natives_keyEvent(JNIEnv * env, jclass cls, jint type, jint key)
static native int motionEvent(int btn, int x, int y)	JNIEXPORT jint JNICALL Java_doom_jni_Natives_motionEvent(JNIEnv * env, jclass cls, jint btn, jint x, jint y)

Before you can proceed with the implementation, the javah command must be used to generate the required header files and signatures:

```
javah -jni -classpath PATH_TO_PROJECT_FOLDER/bin -d include doom.jni.Natives
```

Note that a class path to the bin folder is required for javah to find the doom.jni.Natives class. The output file doom_jni_Natives.h will be dumped in the include folder by using -d. The header file is then used by jni_doom.c, as shown in this fragment:

```
#include <stdio.h>
#include "include/doom_jni_Natives.h"
#include "include/jni_doom.h"
#include "doomdef.h"
#include "d_event.h"
```

The code will use Doom code, thus the inclusion of doomdef.h and d_event.h. The header jni_doom.h defines prototypes for the C to Java callbacks and miscellaneous constants.

You also need a static reference to the JVM used by the C to Java callbacks, as in the following fragment:

```
// Global  Java VM  reference
static JavaVM *g_VM;
```

For improved performance, static references to the Java native interface class (doom.jni.Natives) are kept in jNativesCls. References to the Java methods to send the video image (jSendImageMethod) and sound file (jStartSoundMethod) are also kept. This is because these methods will be invoked multiple times, and looking up these names every time can slow things.

```
static jclass jNativesCls;
static jmethodID jSendImageMethod;
static jmethodID jStartSoundMethod;
```

Also, since you may send a pixel buffer (image) multiple times per second, you should keep a reference to the Java array and its size, as in the following fragment:

```
static jintArray jImage;
static int iSize;
extern int doom_main(int argc, char **argv);
```

The line extern int doom_main defines the main engine function and tells the compiler it is defined somewhere else in the library. The header jni_doom.h included up front defines the constants and method signatures required to invoke the C to Java callbacks. For example, the following fragment of the header defines constants for the Java native interface class (doom/jni/Natives), and the method names and signatures for the callbacks OnImageUpdate and OnStartSound (see the "C to Java Callbacks" section for more details).

```
#define CB_CLASS "doom/jni/Natives"
#define CB_CLASS_IU_CB  "OnImageUpdate"
#define CB_CLASS_IU_SIG  "([I)V"

#define CB_CLASS_SS_CB  "OnStartSound"
#define CB_CLASS_SS_SIG  "([BI)V"
```

Let's take a look at the actual implementations. They are divided into the following three groups:

- *Native game loop*: This invokes the engine loop doom_main.

- *Key and motion events*: These post key and motion events to the engine.

- *C to Java callbacks*: These callbacks are critical for the Java code to receive information from the Doom engine.

Native Game Loop

The native game loop's job is to extract the arguments sent as a jobjectArray into a C char ** array and invoke the main Doom engine function (doom_main). This function performs the following additional steps:

- Obtain a reference to the JVM using (*env)->GetJavaVM(env, &g_VM). This reference will be used by the C to Java callbacks.

- Load the doom.jni.Natives class, also used by the C to Java callbacks: jNativesCls = (*env)->FindClass(env, "doom/jni/Natives").

- Load the doom.jni.Natives.OnImageUpdate and doom.jni.natives.OnStartSound Java methods. This is done for performance reasons, as these methods are called many times.

Listing 5–13 shows the native game loop.

Listing 5–13. *JNI Call to the Main Game Loop*

```
/*
 * Class:     doom_jni_Natives
 * Method:    DoomMain
 * Signature: ([Ljava/lang/String;)V
 */
JNIEXPORT jint JNICALL Java_doom_jni_Natives_DoomMain
  (JNIEnv * env, jclass class, jobjectArray jargv)
{
    // Obtain a global ref to the Java VM
    (*env)->GetJavaVM(env, &g_VM);

    // Extract char ** args from Java array
    jsize clen =  getArrayLen(env, jargv);

    char * args[(int)clen];

    int i;
    jstring jrow;
    for (i = 0; i < clen; i++)
    {
        jrow = (jstring)(*env)->GetObjectArrayElement(env, jargv, i);
        const char *row  = (*env)->GetStringUTFChars(env, jrow, 0);

        args[i] = malloc( strlen(row) + 1);
        strcpy (args[i], row);

        jni_printf("Main argv[%d]=%s", i, args[i]);

        // Free Java string jrow
        (*env)->ReleaseStringUTFChars(env, jrow, row);
    }

    /*
     * Load the Image update class (called many times)
     */
    jNativesCls = (*env)->FindClass(env, CB_CLASS);

    if ( jNativesCls == 0 ) {
        jni_printf("Unable to find class: %s", CB_CLASS);
        return -1;
    }

// Load doom.util.Natives.OnImageUpdate(char[])
    jSendImageMethod = (*env)->GetStaticMethodID(env, jNativesCls
            , CB_CLASS_IU_CB
            , CB_CLASS_IU_SIG);

    if ( jSendImageMethod == 0 ) {
        jni_printf("Unable to find method OnImageUpdate(): %s"
                , CB_CLASS);
        return -1;
    }

    // Load OnStartSound(String name, int vol)
    jStartSoundMethod = (*env)->GetStaticMethodID(env, jNativesCls
            , CB_CLASS_SS_CB
```

```
          , CB_CLASS_SS_SIG);

    if ( jStartSoundMethod == 0 ) {
        jni_printf("Unable to find method OnStartSound signature: %s "
                , CB_CLASS_SS_SIG);
        return -1;
    }

    // Invoke Doom's main sub. This will loop forever
    doom_main (clen, args);

    return 0;
}
```

Key and Motion Events

Key and motion events are posted via the extern symbol D_PostEvent, as shown in
Listing 5–14. The event type (event_t) is defined by the engine and consists of the
following:

- A type (0 for key down, 1 for key up, and 2 for mouse events)

- An ASCII key stored in event.data1 for key events

- A mouse button and x and y coordinates for mouse events, stored as
  event.
  data1 = MOUSE BUTTON, event.data2 = x, and event.data3 = y. Mouse
  buttons can be 1 for left, 2 for middle, or 3 for right.

Listing 5–14. *Posting Key and Motion Events with JNI*

```
/*
 * Class:     doom_util_Natives
 * Method:    keyEvent
 * Signature: (II)V
 */
extern void D_PostEvent (event_t* ev);

JNIEXPORT jint JNICALL Java_doom_jni_Natives_keyEvent
  (JNIEnv * env, jclass cls, jint type, jint key)
{
    event_t event;
    event.type = (int)type;
    event.data1 = (int)key;
    D_PostEvent(&event);

    return type + key;
}

/*
 * Class:     doom_util_Natives
 * Method:    motionEvent
 * Signature: (II)I
 */
JNIEXPORT jint JNICALL Java_doom_jni_Natives_motionEvent
  (JNIEnv * env, jclass cls, jint x, jint y, jint z)
```

```
{
    event_t event;
    event.type = ev_mouse;
    event.data1 = x;
    event.data2 = y;
    event.data3 = z;
    D_PostEvent(&event);
    return 0;
}
```

C to Java Callbacks

Table 5–5 shows the callbacks on the left side and the Java methods they invoke on the right. The callbacks can be divided into the following types:

- Graphics initialization (jni_init_graphics)

- Video buffer (jni_send_pixels)

- Sound and music (jni_start_sound, jni_start_music, jni_stop_music and jni_set_music_volume)

- Fatal errors (jni_fatal_error)

Table 5–5. *C to Java Callbacks in jni_doom.c*

C Method	Invoked Java Method
void jni_init_graphics(int width, int height)	static void OnInitGraphics(int w, int h)
void jni_send_pixels(int * data)	static void OnImageUpdate(int[] pixels)
void jni_start_sound (const char * name, int vol)	static void OnStartSound(byte[] name, int vol)
void jni_start_music (const char * name, int loop)	static void OnStartMusic(String name, int loop)
void jni_stop_music (const char * name)	static void OnStopMusic(String name)
void jni_set_music_volume (int vol)	static void OnSetMusicVolume(int volume)
void jni_fatal_error(const char * text)	static void OnFatalError(String message)

The callbacks must be inserted in the C code, as explained in the following sections.

Graphics Initialization

Constants for the graphics initialization callback are defined in jni_doom.h, as shown in Listing 5–15. CB_CLASS_IG_CB indicates the Java method name OnInitGraphics.

CB_CLASS_IG_SIG "(II)V" defines the signature: two integer parameters and a void return type, as shown in the following fragment:

```
#define CB_CLASS_IG_CB  "OnInitGraphics"
#define CB_CLASS_IG_SIG  "(II)V"
```

This callback also performs some critical steps:

- It attaches to the current thread with (*g_VM)->AttachCurrentThread (g_VM, &env, NULL). This is where the global JVM reference comes into play. Furthermore, the JNI environment (env) will be used to invoke the callback.

- It allocates space for the Java pixel array (video buffer) used by jni_send_pixels using the width and height of the display: jImage = (*env)-> NewIntArray(env, width * height).

- It invokes the static void method doom.util.Natives.OnInitGraphics(width, height) using its method ID: (*env)->CallStaticVoidMethod(env, jNativesCls, METHOD_ID, ARGUMENTS), where ARGUMENTS are the width and height of the display. Note that the arguments must match the arguments in the Java method!

Listing 5–15. *Graphics Initialization*

```
/**
 * Fires when Doom graphics are initialized.
 * params: img width, height
 */
void jni_init_graphics(int width, int height)
{
    JNIEnv *env;

    if ( !g_VM) {
        printf("No JNI VM available.\n");
        return;
    }

    (*g_VM)->AttachCurrentThread (g_VM, (void **) &env, NULL);


    iSize = width * height;

    // Create a new int[] used by jni_send_pixels
    jImage = (*env)-> NewIntArray(env, iSize);

    // Call doom.util.Natives.OnInitGraphics(w, h);
    jmethodID mid = (*env)->GetStaticMethodID(env, jNativesCls
            , CB_CLASS_IG_CB
            , CB_CLASS_IG_SIG);

    if (mid) {
        (*env)->CallStaticVoidMethod(env, jNativesCls
                , mid
                , width, height);
    }
}
```

Video Buffer Callback

The video buffer callback is critical, and it must be lean and mean. It gets called continuously and must not create any objects (see Listing 5–16). Like the previous callback, it attaches to the current thread. It also calls the static void method doom.jni.Natives.OnImageUpdate(int[] pixels). But before calling this method, it must set the pixels into the Java array (jImage):

```
(*env)->SetIntArrayRegion(env, jImage, 0, iSize, (jint *) data)
```

data is an array of integers already formatted as 32-bit ARGB pixels, as required by Android, and iSize is the size of the display calculated in the previous callback.

Listing 5–16. *Sending Video Pixels*

```
/**
 * Image update Java callback. Gets called many times per sec.
 * It must not look up JNI classes/methods or create any objects; otherwise
 * the local JNI ref table will overflow & the app will crash
 */
void jni_send_pixels(int * data)
{
    JNIEnv *env;
    if ( !g_VM) {
        return;
    }

    (*g_VM)->AttachCurrentThread (g_VM, (void **) &env, NULL);

    // Send img back to Java.
    if (jSendImageMethod) {
        (*env)->SetIntArrayRegion(env, jImage, 0, iSize, (jint *) data);

        // Call Java method
        (*env)->CallStaticVoidMethod(env, jNativesCls
                , jSendImageMethod
                , jImage);
    }

}
```

Sound and Music Callbacks

The sound and music callbacks fire from the engine when a sound or background music must be played. In a perfect world, sound would be handled in the native layer; however, due to the lack of documentation and support for open audio standards in Android, requests are cascaded back to Java for processing.

There are four sound and music callbacks in Doom, with their names and signatures defined in the header jni_doom.h:

```
// doom.jni.Natives.OnStartSound(byte[] name, int volume)
#define CB_CLASS_SS_CB  "OnStartSound"
#define CB_CLASS_SS_SIG  "([BI)V"
```

```
// doom.jni.Natives.OnStartMusic (String name , int loop)
#define CB_CLASS_SM_CB  "OnStartMusic"
#define CB_CLASS_SM_SIG  "(Ljava/lang/String;I)V"

// doom.jni.Natives.OnStopMusic (String name )
#define CB_CLASS_STOPM_CB  "OnStopMusic"
#define CB_CLASS_STOPM_SIG  "(Ljava/lang/String;)V"

//   doom.jni.Natives.OnSetMusicVolume (int volume)
#define CB_CLASS_SETMV_CB  "OnSetMusicVolume"
#define CB_CLASS_SETMV_SIG  "(I)V"
```

Note the method signature for OnStartSound with ([BI)V, where [B represents an array of bytes (the name of the sound), I represents an integer (volume), and V is the return type of the method (void). Another interesting signature is OnStartMusic with (Ljava/lang/String;I)V, where Ljava/lang/String; means the class java.lang.String (enclosed in L;).

Listing 5–17 shows the implementation of these callbacks. They are pretty similar in nature, in that they all must attach to the current thread using the global JVM (g_VM). The following are some of the key aspects of the code:

- To create a Java byte array, you can use jbyteArray ARRAY = (*env)-> NewByteArray(env, SIZE), where the words byte/Byte can be replaced with boolean/Boolean, int/Int, object/Object, and other primitive types, depending on your needs.

- To insert data into the array, use (*env)->SetByteArrayRegion(env, ARRAY, START, SIZE, (jbyte *) C_ARRAY), where Byte can be replaced with any Java primitive type.

- To call a static void method, use (*env)->CallStaticVoidMethod(env, CLASS, METHOD_ID, ARG1, ARG2,…).

- To release resources for an array, use (*env)->DeleteLocalRef(env, ARRAY).

Listing 5–17. *Cascading Sound and Music Requests Back to Java*

```
/**
 * Fires multiple times when a sound is played
 * @param name Sound name
 * @param volume
 */
void jni_start_sound (const char * name, int vol)
{
    /*
     * Attach to the curr thread; otherwise we get JNI WARNING:
     * threadid=3 using env from threadid=15 which aborts the VM
     */
    JNIEnv *env;

    if ( !g_VM) {
        return;
    }
```

```
    (*g_VM)->AttachCurrentThread (g_VM, (void **) &env, NULL);

    if ( jStartSoundMethod == 0 ) {
        jni_printf("BUG: Invalid Doom JNI method OnStartSound %s"
        , CB_CLASS_SS_SIG);
        return ;
    }

    // Create a new char[] used by jni_send_pixels
    // Used to prevent JNI ref table overflows
    int iSize = strlen(name);
    jbyteArray jSound = (*env)-> NewByteArray(env, iSize);

    (*env)->SetByteArrayRegion(env, jSound, 0, iSize, (jbyte *) name);

    // Call Java method
    (*env)->CallStaticVoidMethod(env, jNativesCls
            , jStartSoundMethod
            , jSound //(*env)->NewStringUTF(env, name)
            , (jint) vol);

    (*env)->DeleteLocalRef(env,jSound);
}

/**
 * Fires when a background song is requested
 */
void jni_start_music (const char * name, int loop)
{
    /*
     * Attach to the curr thread; otherwise we get JNI WARNING:
     * threadid=3 using env from threadid=15 which aborts the VM
     */
    JNIEnv *env;

    if ( !g_VM) {
        return;
    }

    (*g_VM)->AttachCurrentThread (g_VM, (void **) &env, NULL);

    jmethodID mid = (*env)->GetStaticMethodID(env, jNativesCls
        , CB_CLASS_SM_CB
        , CB_CLASS_SM_SIG);

    if (mid) {
        (*env)->CallStaticVoidMethod(env, jNativesCls
                , mid
                , (*env)->NewStringUTF(env, name)
                , (jint) loop );

    }
}

/**
 * Fires when a background song is stopped
 */
```

```
void jni_stop_music (const char * name)
{
    /*
     * Attach to the curr thread; otherwise we get JNI WARNING:
     * threadid=3 using env from threadid=15 which aborts the VM
     */
    JNIEnv *env;

    if ( !g_VM) {
        return;
    }

    (*g_VM)->AttachCurrentThread (g_VM, (void **) &env, NULL);
    jmethodID mid = (*env)->GetStaticMethodID(env, jNativesCls
        , CB_CLASS_STOPM_CB
        , CB_CLASS_STOPM_SIG);

    if (mid) {
        (*env)->CallStaticVoidMethod(env, jNativesCls
                , mid
                , (*env)->NewStringUTF(env, name)
                );
    }
}

/**
 * Set bg msic vol callback
 */
void jni_set_music_volume (int vol) {
    JNIEnv *env;

    if ( !g_VM) {
        return;
    }

    (*g_VM)->AttachCurrentThread (g_VM, (void **) &env, NULL);

    jmethodID mid = (*env)->GetStaticMethodID(env, jNativesCls
        , CB_CLASS_SETMV_CB
        , CB_CLASS_SETMV_SIG);

    if (mid) {
        (*env)->CallStaticVoidMethod(env, jNativesCls
                , mid
                , (jint) vol
                );
    }
}
```

Fatal Errors

Fatal or unrecoverable errors occur in any type of software. In Doom, these errors are cascaded back to Java, where a message is presented to the user, and then the application aborts. The following fragment from jni_doom.h shows the callback name and signature for this task:

```
#define CB_CLASS_FATAL_CB  "OnFatalError"
#define CB_CLASS_FATAL_SIG  "(Ljava/lang/String;)V"
```

This callback is simple (see Listing 5–18). It works as follows:

- It attaches to the current thread, aborting if no JNI environment is available.

- It looks up the doom.jni.Natives Java class, aborting if not found.

- It looks up the doom.jni.Natives.OnFatalError(String) using the method name and signature.

- It calls the static void method.

Listing 5–18. *Cascading Fatal Errors*

```
/**
 * Called when a fatal error has occurred.
 * The receiver should terminate
 */
void jni_fatal_error(const char * text) {
    JNIEnv *env;

    if ( !g_VM) {
        printf("JNI FATAL: No JNI Environment available. %s\n", text);
        exit(-1);
    }

    (*g_VM)->AttachCurrentThread (g_VM, (void **) &env, NULL);

    if ( !env) {
        printf("JNI FATAL: Unable to attach to thread: %s.\n", text);
        exit(-1);
    }

    if ( !jNativesCls ) {
        jNativesCls = (*env)->FindClass(env, CB_CLASS);

        if ( jNativesCls == 0 ) {
                printf("JNI FATAL: Unable to find class: %s", CB_CLASS);
                exit(-1);
        }
    }
    jmethodID mid = (*env)->GetStaticMethodID(env, jNativesCls
        , CB_CLASS_FATAL_CB
        , CB_CLASS_FATAL_SIG);

    if (mid) {
        (*env)->CallStaticVoidMethod(env, jNativesCls
```

```
                , mid
                , (*env)->NewStringUTF(env, text) );
    }
    else {
        printf("JNI FATAL: Unable to find method: %s, signature: %s\n"
                , CB_CLASS_MSG_CB, CB_CLASS_MSG_SIG );
        exit (-1);
    }
}
```

Original Game Changes

In order for the JNI glue to work, changes are required to the original game engine. Some are simple, such as inserting calls to the C to Java callbacks; some are not so simple, such as removing invalid dependencies. Table 5–6 shows the original files and the changes required. Considering that the engine has a total of 90,000 lines of code, these changes are not that bad.

Table 5–6. *Changes Required to the Original Engine to Insert the JNI Glue*

File	Changes
i_main.c	Rename the main subroutine to doom_main.
i_system.c	In I_Error, insert jni_fatal_error.
i_sound.c	Comment SDL dependencies. In I_StartSound, insert start sound callback jni_start_sound.
s_sound.c	In S_SetMusicVolume, insert volume callback jni_set_music_volume.
i_video.c	Comment SDL dependencies. Insert code to build an Android ARBG pixel array from the video buffer. In I_SetRes, add JNI callback to initialize graphics. In I_FinishUpdate, send pixels to Java with jni_send_pixels.

These changes are explained in more detail in the following sections.

Renaming main

Let's start with the simplest change: renaming the main() subroutine in i_main.c so it can be invoked from the Java native Java_doom_jni_Natives_DoomMain, which will start the game from Java, as shown in the following fragment:

```
// In i_main.c
int main(int argc, char **argv)
int doom_main(int argc, char **argv)

// In jni_doom.c
extern int doom_main(int argc, char **argv);
```

```
JNIEXPORT jint JNICALL Java_doom_jni_Natives_DoomMain

  (JNIEnv * env, jclass class, jobjectArray jargv)

{
  ...
  doom_main (clen, args);
  ...
}
```

Once main is renamed to doom_main, simply add the extern symbol extern int doom_main(int argc, char **argv) to jni_doom.c and invoke it from the game starter function.

Inserting the Fatal Error Callback

Another simple change is to insert the C to Java callback jni_fatal_error whenever an unrecoverable error occurs. The changes occur in the I_Error function in the i_system.c file, as shown in Listing 5–19.

Listing 5–19. *Changes Required to i_system.c*

```
void I_Error (char *error, ...)
{
    va_list     argptr;
    static char string[1024];

    // Message first.
    va_start (argptr,error);
    vsprintf (string, error ,argptr);
    va_end (argptr);

    // Shutdown. Here might be other errors.
    if (demorecording)
      G_CheckDemoStatus();

    D_QuitNetGame ();
    I_ShutdownGraphics();

    // Send the error back to JNI layer
    jni_fatal_error(string);

    // Something wrong has happened
    // OLD CODE -> exit(-1);
}
```

Commenting SDL Occurrences

The Doom engine is built on top of SDL, which is an open framework to access system resources such as sound and video hardware. Doom uses SDL to display video and play music. This is a relatively hard problem, as Android has no support for SDL. Thus, any SDL occurrence must be commented or removed and replaced by a JNI equivalent. This happens in two files: i_sound.c and i_video.c.

Changes to i_sound.c are simple and consist of commenting the sdl.h header file and inserting jni_doom.h instead, as shown in the following fragment:

```
#include <sdl.h>
#include "include/jni_doom.h"
```

Furthermore, any function that starts with SDL_ must be commented. Luckily, these functions do not affect the game flow itself, and thus they can be safely commented.

Sound System Changes

Other changes are required to i_sound.c to insert a call to jni_start_sound, as shown in Listing 5–20. The global variable S_sfx[id].name provides the sound name, which will be sent back to Java and loaded from the file system, along with its volume.

Listing 5–20. *Changes Required to i_sound.c to Insert the jni_start_sound Callback*

```c
int I_StartSound(int id, int channel, int vol, int sep, int pitch, int priority)
{
  const unsigned char* data;
  int lump;
  size_t len;

  // ...

 // The entries DSBSPWLK, DSBSPACT, DSSWTCHN
 // and DSSWTCHX are all zero-length sounds
  if (len<=8) return -1;

  /* Find padded length */
  len -= 8;
  // Do the lump caching outside the SDL_LockAudio/SDL_UnlockAudio pair
  // Use locking which makes sure the sound data is in a malloced area and
  // not in a memory mapped one
  data = W_LockLumpNum(lump);

  // JNI changes: Send a sound request to Java
  // id is the sound index, S_sfx[id].name (soundname)
  // vol = volume
  jni_start_sound(S_sfx[id].name , vol);

  // ...

  return channel;
}
```

Changes are also required to s_sound.c to insert a call to jni_set_music_volume (volume) to send the background music volume back to Java (see Listing 5–21). Note that this function is called within the game when the user changes the music volume from the options menu.

Listing 5–21. *Changes Required to s_sound.c to Insert the Music JNI Callback*

```c
void S_SetMusicVolume(int volume)
{
  // Return if music is not enabled
```

```
    if (!mus_card || nomusicparm)
      return;

    if (volume < 0 || volume > 15)
      I_Error("S_SetMusicVolume: Attempt to set music volume at %d", volume);

    // JNI Changes: Send a volume request to Java
    // volume = [0..100]
    jni_set_music_volume (volume);

    I_SetMusicVolume(volume);
    snd_MusicVolume = volume;
}
```

Video Buffer Changes

This is where the toughest changes must be done. The file i_video.c is the one that renders the video buffer and uses SDL heavily. All SDL references must be removed and replaced with structures compatible with Android.

Down to the pipe, a video buffer is simply an array of packed colors, represented as either bytes indicating the index of a color in a color palette or integers specifying an RGB color. SDL uses a structure called SDL_Surface to encapsulate the video buffer as an array of bytes plus a palette used to map colors to the buffer. Consider the following fragment, which replaces the SDL screen with a similar structure called XImage (actually taken from the X11 structure of the same name).

```
static SDL_Surface *screen;    // OLD CODE
static XImage * image;         // NEW CODE
```

In Doom, SDL_Surface will be replaced with the equivalent XImage that holds the array of bytes for the video buffer. Note that the video buffer cannot be rendered directly to a display. Instead, it must be cascaded back to Java using the C to Java callbacks, where Android will take care of the actual rendering.

Because XImage doesn't exist, it must be written. This isn't difficult, as XImage is simply a C struct holding the width, height, and array of bytes for the video buffer, as shown in Listing 5–22.

Listing 5–22. *Video Buffer Image Object from i_video.c*

```
/*********************************************************
 * Class XImage
 *********************************************************/
typedef struct Image XImage;

struct Image
{
  int width;
  int height;
  byte * data;
};

/**
 * Class Color
```

```
 */
typedef struct Color XColor;

struct Color
{
  int red;
  int green;
  int blue;
};

// The Image
XImage *              image;

/**
 * XImage Constructor
 */
XImage * XCreateImage(int width, int height)
{
    XImage * this = (XImage*) malloc(sizeof(XImage));

    // set width, height
    this->width = width;
    this->height = height;

    // allocate image buffer
    this->data = (byte *)malloc (width * height);

    return this;
}
/**********************************************************
 * Class XImage
 **********************************************************/
```

In addition to XImage, you need a color palette used to map the bytes on XImage to
ARGB colors used by Android. For this purpose, you use the struct XColor, which
holds the red, green, and blue values of a color. You also need a function to allocate
memory for the XImage given its width and height (XCreateImage). This function will
allocate space for the image byte buffer. You must modify the palette upload function
(I_UploadNewPalette) in i_video.c to use the new XColor structure, as shown in
Listing 5–23.

Listing 5–23. *Setting the Color Palette in i_video.c*

```
// Color palette
static XColor * colours;

static void I_UploadNewPalette(int pal)
{
  // This is used to replace the current 256 colour cmap with a new one
  // Used by 256 colour PseudoColor modes

  static int cachedgamma;
  static size_t num_pals;

  if (V_GetMode() == VID_MODEGL)
    return;
  if ((colours == NULL) || (cachedgamma != usegamma)) {
```

```
    int pplump = W_GetNumForName("PLAYPAL");
    int gtlump = (W_CheckNumForName)("GAMMATBL",ns_prboom);

    register const byte * palette = W_CacheLumpNum(pplump);
    register const byte * const gtable = (const byte *)W_CacheLumpNum(gtlump)
     + 256*(cachedgamma = usegamma);

    register int i;

    num_pals = W_LumpLength(pplump) / (3*256);
    num_pals *= 256;

    if (!colours) {
      // First call - allocate and prepare colour array
      colours = malloc(sizeof(*colours)*num_pals);
    }

    // set the colormap entries
    for (i=0 ; (size_t)i<num_pals ; i++) {
      colours[i].red    = gtable[palette[0]];
      colours[i].green = gtable[palette[1]];
      colours[i].blue   = gtable[palette[2]];
      palette += 3;
    }

    W_UnlockLumpNum(pplump);
    W_UnlockLumpNum(gtlump);
    num_pals/=256;
  }
}
```

In Listing 5–23, the original SDL palette has been replaced by XColor * colours. Note that the Doom engine uses a 768-color palette (256 colors each for red, green, and blue). The palette is read from the game file, along with a gamma table (used to apply a brightness factor to each color). With this information, the palette is filled and kept in memory for later use.

The final change to i_video.c is the function that does the actual rendering, I_FinishUpdate (see Listing 5–24). This function uses the width and height of the screen to create an array of pixels (each one representing an Android-packed ARGB color). It then loops through the array and uses the byte value from the screen buffer to look up the color from the palette:

```
byte b = screens[0].data[i];  // Video buffer byte
XColor color = colours[b];  // Palette color for that byte
```

It then constructs a 32-bit pixel using the RGB values of color:

```
pixels[i] = (0xFF << 24) | (color.red << 16) | (color.green << 8) | color.blue
```

NOTE: 0xFF << 24 represents the alpha (opacity) value of the pixel—fully visible in this case.

Finally, the array is sent back using the callback jni_send_pixels(pixels), where Android will do the rendering.

Listing 5–24. *Video Buffer Renderer Function from i_video.c*

```
void I_FinishUpdate (void)
{
  if (I_SkipFrame()) return;

  // Screen size
  int size = SCREENWIDTH * SCREENHEIGHT;

  // ARGB pixels
  int pixels[size], i;

  for ( i = 0 ; i < size ; i ++) {
      byte b = screens[0].data[i];

      XColor color = colours[b];

      pixels[i] = (0xFF << 24)
          | (color.red << 16)
          | (color.green << 8)
          | color.blue;
  }

  // Send pixels to Java
  jni_send_pixels(pixels);

}
```

At this point, the Doom engine is all set and ready for compilation.

Compiling Doom with the NDK

With the release of the NDK 1.6 and later, Google has made a lot of nice improvements to support native development. The following are the highlights of this new version:

- The sources folder from the NDK folder structure is gone (see the section on Wolf 3D and NDK 1.5). Now, all code (Java and native) lives in the apps folder. Within the apps folder, the project folder contains the Android Java project, and within project, the jni folder contains the native code and the Makefile Android.mk.

- NDK 1.6 adds support for OpenGL ES 2.0. This welcome addition will help many 3D games out there.

I would recommend the NDK over the CodeSourcery G++ compiler (or any other ARM compiler) if you have a slow system such as a laptop or VMware combination or if your library crashes mysteriously, perhaps because of GNU compiler version issues, which can happen in programs that are not highly portable. Discrepancies in the GNU compiler version (for example, CodeSourcery uses GCC 4.3.x instead of Android's 4.2.x) can cause optimization errors and other types of runtime errors that ultimately crash the game.

All in all, the NDK is a good improvement but still has far to go to catch up with other powerful tools, such as Apple's iPhone Xcode platform. For example, the NDK will recompile the entire library if you change the Makefile, `Android.mk` (too add a new source file for example). This is really annoying when you have a big library with lots of source files. Other tools such as `GNU` make will detect the changes and recompile only the right files in the library. Anyway, for Doom, the folder structure for NDK should look as follows:

- ▩ `NDK_ROOT/apps/Doom/Application.mk`: This file defines the module name to be built.

- ▩ `NDK_ROOT /apps/Doom/project`: This folder contains the actual Android project for the game.

- ▩ `NDK_ROOT /apps/Doom/project/jni`: This folder contains the native code and the Makefile, `Android.mk`.

The following steps show you how to get Doom to compile with NDK 1.6:

1. Create `android-ndk-1.6_r1/apps/Doom/Application.mk`. This file contains the module (doom) that we are building:

```
APP_PROJECT_PATH := $(call my-dir)/project
APP_MODULES      := doom
```

2. Create the folder `NDK_ROOT/apps/Doom/project`. Copy the Android project from `Android.Doom` to this folder. You don't need to copy the `native` folder (this is the native code).

3. Create the folder `android-ndk-1.6_r1/apps/Doom/project/jni`, and copy the native code from `ch07.Android.Doom/native/prboom`.

4. Create a Makefile called `Android.mk` in `NDK_ROOT/apps/Doom/ project/jni`. This make file should look as follows:

```
LOCAL_PATH := $(call my-dir)

# clear vars
include $(CLEAR_VARS)

# module name
LOCAL_MODULE := doom
LP := $(LOCAL_PATH)

# doom folder
DOOM := apps/Doom/project/jni

# includes
INC := -I$(DOOM) -I$(DOOM)/include

DOOM_FLAGS := -DNORMALUNIX -DLINUX -DHAVE_CONFIG_H

OPTS := -O3 -ffast-math  -fexpensive-optimizations
```

```
LOCAL_CFLAGS := $(DOOM_FLAGS)  $(OPTS) $(INC)

# sources
LOCAL_SRC_FILES        := \
 am_map.c    m_cheat.c    p_lights.c p_user.c    sounds.c \
 hu_lib.c       md5.c       p_map.c    r_bsp.c    s_sound.c \
 d_deh.c     hu_stuff.c    m_menu.c    p_maputl.c r_data.c    st_lib.c \
 d_items.c       m_misc.c     p_mobj.c    r_demo.c    st_stuff.c \
 d_main.c    info.c         p_plats.c   r_draw.c    tables.c \
 doomdef.c       m_random.c   p_pspr.c    r_filter.c  version.c \
 doomstat.c       p_ceilng.c   p_saveg.c   r_fps.c     v_video.c \
 p_checksum.c p_setup.c   r_main.c    wi_stuff.c \
 dstrings.c  p_doors.c   p_sight.c   r_patch.c   w_memcache.c \
 f_finale.c      p_enemy.c     p_spec.c    r_plane.c   w_mmap.c \
 f_wipe.c    lprintf.c    p_floor.c   p_switch.c r_segs.c    w_wad.c \
 g_game.c    m_argv.c     p_genlin.c  p_telept.c r_sky.c     z_bmalloc.c \
 m_bbox.c      p_inter.c    p_tick.c    r_things.c z_zone.c \
 d_client.c   d_server.c \
 droid/i_video.c droid/i_network.c droid/i_joy.c \
 droid/i_system.c droid/i_main.c droid/i_sound.c \
 droid/jni_doom.c

# Build libdoom.so
include $(BUILD_SHARED_LIBRARY)
```

5. Finally, run make APP=Doom from the NDK root folder. The output library libdoom.so will be stored in Doom/project//libs/armeabi and ready to use. Import Doom/project into your Eclipse workspace, and start the game.

Testing Doom in the Emulator

To test the game in the emulator, create a launch configuration within your Eclipse IDE, as follows:

1. From the main menu, select **Run ➤ Run Configurations**.

2. Enter a name for the configuration (Doom) and select the project ch05.Android.Doom.

3. Set the Launch Action as Launch Default Activity. Figure 5–4 shows the completed Run Configurations dialog box for this example.

4. Click Run.

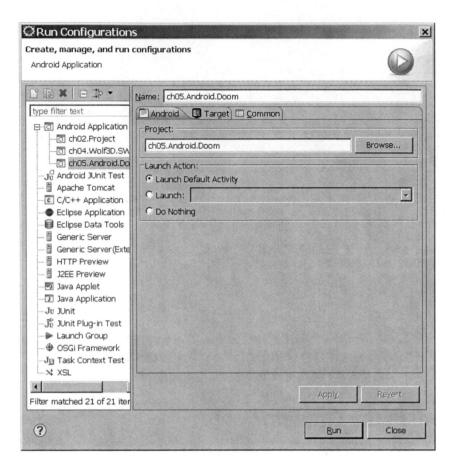

Figure 5–4. *Android run configuration for Doom*

Now let's play some Doom. From the emulator, click **Menu ➤ Start** and monitor the log view to make sure everything works. Consider the log fragment in Listing 5–25.

Listing 5–25. *Log Fragment from a Doom Run*

```
DEBUG/DoomClient(23981): Loading JNI librray from doom_jni
DEBUG/LibLoader(23981): Trying to load library doom_jni from LD_PATH: /system/lib
DEBUG/dalvikvm(23981): Trying to load lib /data/data/org.doom/lib/libdoom_jni.so
0x43733de8
DEBUG/dalvikvm(23981): Added shared lib /data/data/org.doom/lib/libdoom_jni.so
0x43733de8
DEBUG/dalvikvm(23981): No JNI_OnLoad found in /data/data/org.doom/lib/libdoom_jni.so↵
 0x43733de8
DEBUG/DoomTools(23981): Sound folder: /sdcard/doom/sound
DEBUG/DoomClient(23981): Starting doom thread with wad doom1.wad sound enabled? true↵
 Orientation:1
DEBUG/DoomClient(23981): **Doom Message: Main argv[0]=doom
DEBUG/DoomClient(23981): **Doom Message: Main argv[1]=-width
DEBUG/DoomClient(23981): **Doom Message: Main argv[2]=480
DEBUG/DoomClient(23981): **Doom Message: Main argv[3]=-height
```

```
DEBUG/DoomClient(23981): **Doom Message: Main argv[4]=320
DEBUG/DoomClient(23981): **Doom Message: Main argv[5]=-iwad
DEBUG/DoomClient(23981): **Doom Message: Main argv[6]=doom1.wad
DEBUG/DoomClient(23981): **Doom Message: I_UpdateVideoMode: 480x320 (fullscreen)↵
 default VM=8
DEBUG/DoomClient(23981): **Doom Message: I_SetRes: Creating 480x320 image.
```

The following two lines show the native library is loaded successfully by the JVM:

```
Trying to load lib /data/data/org.doom/lib/libdoom_jni.so
Added shared lib /data/data/org.doom/lib/libdoom_jni.so
```

So far, so good. Next, the game arguments are displayed:

```
**Doom Message: Main argv[0]=doom
**Doom Message: Main argv[1]=-width
**Doom Message: Main argv[2]=480
**Doom Message: Main argv[3]=-height
**Doom Message: Main argv[4]=320
**Doom Message: Main argv[5]=-iwad
**Doom Message: Main argv[6]=doom1.wad
```

This tells us the size of the display, 480 × 20 (landscape mode), plus the name of the game file, doom1.wad. At this point, the game has successfully loaded and is ready for action (see Figure 5–5).

Figure 5–5. *Doom running in the Android emulator*

Summary

Congratulations! You have seen how easy it is to bring one of the first PC shooters to Android using a mix of Java and the original C engine. We have looked at the complexity of the game and the best way to implement it. We covered the following topics:

- The game architecture, where Java activities and UI XML layouts are glued with C subroutines using JNI native methods and C to Java callbacks

- The main activity, which is the Java class that controls the life cycle of the application, along with a UI layout

- User interface handlers, such as menus and key and touch event handlers, and native callback handlers for graphics initialization, video buffer updates, fatal errors, and audio requests

We have also looked at custom touch screen controls for phones that do not have a keyboard. You saw that the native interface class has callback listeners for clients that wish to receive C to Java callbacks, native methods invoked through JNI to start the game loop and send key and motion event information to the Native library, and C to Java callbacks used to delegate engine messages to the listener activity.

We have looked at the native layer that glues the Java and C code together and provides the native method implementations. Changes to the original code are also required to remove invalid dependencies and insert the C to Java callbacks. Finally, you saw the Makefile required to compile the Native library and the IDE launch configuration to test the game in the emulator.

Using the Java/C power combo, we have brought one of the great PC games, Doom, to the platform. Even though Google is pushing for Java-only development and provides little or no support for native development, Java alone is not the best choice when it comes to advanced mobile gaming. Java-only code works fine for the regular mobile app, but it is not enough for high-performance graphics.

I hope that the material in this book has opened a new frontier for you to explore, and you're excited about the possibility of bringing thousands of PC games to Android—with minimal time and effort.

## Chapter 6

3D Shooters for Quake

This is where things start to get really exiting. I've always been a huge fan of First Person Shooters (FPS), and when Android came along, I had to jump at the chance of getting involved in bringing this gem (Quake) to the platform in all its beauty. Almost everybody knows of or has played this astounding game for the PC. It was created in 1996 by the great game developer John Carmack for id Software and later released under the GNU General Public License.

In this chapter, you will learn how minimum investment in development time can translate into maximum ROI for your organization. That is my goal. I am sure you have a lot of invested PC code or engines gathering dust somewhere on your servers. Well, why not reuse that code for your mobile projects? The GPL Quake I Engine brought to Android kept 98 percent of the original code intact. This chapter will demonstrate the power of code reuse.

A Little About the Quake Jargon

I do not wish to present a study or to try to explain the inner workings of the Quake engine (an entire book will not be enough for that), but to demonstrate how we can get this engine up and running in no time in Android. But before I do, I thought it would be nice at least to have an idea of the basic lingo used in this 3D engine. It would help you understand some of the code if you decide to dig into the engine source. Some of the Quake jargon includes the following:

- *Quake*: A true 3D game that uses a map design system to display a pre-rendered 3D environment to reduce the processing in slow CPUs.

- *Maps*: A 3D environment where the game takes place. Maps are created with a map editor program that uses a number of simple convex 3D geometric objects known as brushes.

- *Brushes*: Brushes are placed and oriented to create an enclosed, empty, volumetric space; they then run through the rendering preprocessor.

- *Pruning*: Maps are preprocessed to reduce polygon count from the original unprocessed. This step is called pruning.

- *Quake sky*: The famous cloudy sky in Quake is, in fact, closed space covered over and enclosed with brushes and textured with a special skybox texture that always looks the same from any viewing position, giving the illusion of a distant sky.

- *Lightmaps and 3D light sources*: An id Software's innovation that has since become common in many 3D games.

- *Map sectioning*: A technique to increase rendering speed by sectioning off large regions of the map that are currently not visible to the player, and to render those unseen spaces. With this engine optimization, if the player could not see into a nearby region, the 3D engine could be alerted to not include any of the objects in that space in the rendering calculations, greatly reducing the rendering load on the CPU.

- *Binary space partitioning* (BSP): A technique used to section a map by building a tree from the map. Each leaf represents an area of 3D space. The leaves of this binary tree have polygons of the original map associated with them, which are then used for computing each area's visibility. This process uses large amounts of memory and takes a time complexity of O(n2) (where n is the number of polygons).

- *Run-length encoding* (RLE): A simple form of data compression where sequences of the same data value occur in many consecutive data elements and are stored as a single data value and count, rather than as the original run. This encoding is used to compress sections of the BSP tree and is what allowed Quake's sophisticated graphics to run so quickly on low-end hardware.

- *Overdraw*: The process of rendering a new pixel that hides a previously rendered point, meaning the previous work was wasted. To minimize overdraw, the environment was displayed first, from front to back.

- *ZBuffering*: A technique used to decide which elements of a rendered scene are visible and which are hidden by using a two-dimensional array (x-y) with one element for each screen pixel of an object that is rendered. If another object of the scene must be rendered in the same pixel, the graphics card compares the two depths and chooses the one closer to the observer. The chosen depth is then saved to the z-buffer, replacing the old one.

- *Surface cache*: A cache that contains new pre-lighted textures combined with the base and lightmap textures. It is used to speed up the rendering of walls and their lightmap textures.

The Power of Code Reuse: Quake in Less Than 500 Lines of New Code

If I was a full-time PC game developer and was told that we could have Quake (with the full OpenGL renderer) running in Android with less than 500 lines of new code, while keeping most of the original game intact, I'd probably say, "Are you crazy?" Once you start digging into the source of the OpenGL renderer of the engine, then you realize how hard it is to bring this engine to a mobile device. Let's examine why.

OpenGL Is Not the Same as OpenGL ES

As mentioned, Quake is an engine written for the PC in 1996; nevertheless even a PC of the '90s could be arguably more powerful than some of today's phones. The problem is that the renderer in Quake uses OpenGL, which is a superset of OpenGL ES (used in phones/tablets). We'll take a look at some of the differences between OpenGL and OpenGL ES.

Immediate Mode Drawing

Immediate mode drawing is perhaps the biggest caveat for our Android version of Quake. Immediate mode is a technique used to for specifying geometry; for example, consider the following snippet to render an arbitrary polygon and corresponding texture:

```
// Bind some texture
glBegin (GL_POLYGON);
glTexCoord2f (...);
glVertex3fv (...);
...
glEnd ();
```

This code is typical of a desktop application; however, it is not valid in Android (which implements OpenGL ES). This is because OpenGL ES does not support immediate mode (glBegin/glEnd) for simple geometry. Porting this code will require line-by-line changes, which can consume significant resources (especially for a game like Quake, which has approximately 100,000 lines of C source).

In OpenGL ES, geometry must be specified using vertex arrays, so the preceding code becomes something like the following:

```
const GLbyte Vertices []= { ...};
const GLbyte TexCoords []= { ...};
...
glEnableClientState (GL_VERTEX_ARRAY);
glEnableClientState (GL_TEXTCOORD_ARRAY);

glVertexPointer (..., GL_BYTE , 0, Vertices);
glTexCoordPointer (..., GL_BYTE , 0, TexCoords);
glDrawArrays (GL_TRIANGLES, 0, ...);
```

This code achieves a similar result as the previous one by using arrays of vertices and coordinates to describe the polygon, and then drawing using triangles (GL_POLYGON does not exist in OpenGL ES). Now, the renderer of Quake is full (and I mean full) of immediate mode calls. Believe me when I say that translating immediate mode into array pointers is not an option. As a matter of fact, there is a project called GLES Quake (http://grammerjack.blogspot.com/2009/10/gles-quake-port-of-quake-to-android.html) that did just that. The guy even took the time to convert all the C files into C++. Oh my, I feel sorry for the poor soul that did this work. It must have been painful.

Floating Point Issues

You must also consider floating-point issues. OpenGL ES defines functions that use fixed-point values, as many devices do not have a floating-point unit (FPU). Fixed-point math is a technique to encode floating-point numbers using only integers. OpenGL ES uses 16 bits to represent the integer part, and another 16 bits to represent the fractional part. The following is an example of using a fixed-point translation function:

```
glTranslatex (10 << 16, 0, 0, 2 << 16); // glTranslatef (10.0f, 0.0f, 0.0f, 2.0f);
```

Other Issues

The following are other differences between OpenGL and OpenGL ES:

- OpenGL ES does not render polygons as wireframe or points (only solid).

- There is no GLU (OpenGL Utility Library) in OpenGL ES. It is possible, however, to find implementations of GLU functions on the internet.

- The GL_QUADS, GL_QUAD_STRIP, and GL_POLYGON primitives are not supported.

- The attribute stack used to save OpenGL state is not supported. This essentially means that calls such as: glPushAttrib, glPopAttrib are not supported, including their associated constants GL_COLOR_BUFFER_BIT , GL_CURRENT_BIT, GL_ENABLE_BIT, GL_HINT_BIT, etc.

- Quake uses OpenGL standard extensions not supported by ES; for example GL_ARB_multitexture, which is an Architecture Review Board (hence ARB) standard introduced in OpenGL version 1.2.1 is not available on OpenGL ES.

These are some of the things to watch for when you decide to port your OpenGL game to an embedded device. When thinking about a powerful game engine like Quake (or any other engine for that matter), there are two basic trains of thought when it comes to graphics rendering: software or hardware (OpenGL). Each has its advantages and disadvantages. Let's take a look at each one and the reason I chose to use hardware acceleration.

Is the Software Renderer a Possible Solution?

It certainly is. We could drop the Quake OpenGL (hardware) renderer and use the software renderer also provided with the source; however, this will make the game painfully slow, playable to around 15–20 frames per second (FPS) in a mid-size device. On the positive side, it will also be simpler to compile—but it is not a good solution because we can achieve over 50 FPS if we use a hardware renderer.

NanoGL: The Live Saver

We will definitely drop the software renderer, but how can we fix the big problem: immediate mode? Enter NanoGL (www.ohloh.net/p/nanogl). This is a wonderful tiny piece of software written by Oli Hinka for the Nokia N97 hardware. It is available under the GNU General Public License. Now, if we could only get past the fact that is was written for Nokia. No matter. We can get this library up and running for Android in no time. Because it is very well-written, we can actually keep around 98 percent of the original C++ code. The only thing we need to do is some initialization and dynamic loading logic, as shown in Listing 6–1.

> **TIP:** The entire NanoGL project is available from this book's source, in the NanoGL folder.

Listing 6–1. *NanoGL initializer for Android: nanogl.cpp.*

```
// nanogl.cpp: Some code has been removed for simplicity
// GLES structure with GL function pointers
#include "glesinterface.h"

#define GL_ENTRY(_r, _api, ...) #_api,

// function pointer names. Must match glesinterface.h
static char const * const gl_names[] = {
    #include "gl_entries.in"
    NULL
};

// OpenGL ES lib pointer
static void* glesLib = NULL;

GlESInterface* glEsImpl = NULL;

extern void InitGLStructs();

static void gl_unimplemented() {
  LOGE ("Called unimplemented OpenGL ES API\n");
}

// Create GLES interface
// name : Library name
// lib, lib1: 2 shared libraries to try to load GL symbols from
// defaut_func: Function to call if load symbol fails
```

```
static int CreateGlEsInterface( const char * name, void * lib, void * lib1, void *
default_func )
{
  // alloc space
  if ( !glEsImpl )
    glEsImpl = (GlESInterface *) malloc(sizeof(GlESInterface));

  if (!glEsImpl) {
      return 0;
    }

  // load GL API calls
  char const * const * api;
  api = gl_names;

  // nanoGL interface pointer
  void ** ptr = (void **)(glEsImpl);

  while (*api)
  {
    void * f;

    f = dlsym(lib, *api); // ltry ibGLESxx_CM.so

    if (f == NULL) {
      LOGW( "<%s> not found in %s. Trying libEGL.so.", *api, name); //driver);

      // try lib1
      if ( lib1 ) {
        f = dlsym(lib1, *api); // libEGL.so

        if ( f == NULL ) {
          LOGE ( "<%s> not found in libEGL.so", *api);
          f = default_func; //(void*)gl_unimplemented;
        }
        else {
          LOGD ("<%s> @ 0x%p\n", *api, f);
        }
      }
      else
        f = default_func;
    }
    else {
      LOGD ("<%s> @ 0x%p\n", *api, f);
    }

      *ptr++ = f;
        api++;
    }

  return 1;
}

// Load using the dynamic loader
static int loadDriver(const char * name) {
  glesLib = dlopen(name, RTLD_NOW | RTLD_LOCAL);
  int rc = (glesLib) ? 1 : 0;
```

```
    return rc;
}

/**
 * Initialize interface
 */
int nanoGL_Init()
{
  const char * lib1 = "libGLESv1_CM.so";   // Opengl ES lib
  const char * lib2 = "libGLESv2.so";
  const char * lib3 = "libEGL.so";
  const char * driver;

  // load lib1: libGLESv1_CM.so
  LOGI("nanoGL: Init loading driver %s\n", lib1);

  if ( ! loadDriver(lib1) )
  {
    LOGE("Failed to load driver %s. Trying %s\n", lib1, lib2);

    if ( ! loadDriver(lib2) ) {
      LOGE ("Failed to load  %s.\n", lib2);
      return 0;
    }
    else
      driver = lib2;
  }
  else
    driver = lib1;

  void * eglLib;

   LOGD ("**** Will Load EGL subs from %s ****", lib3);

   eglLib = dlopen(lib3, RTLD_NOW | RTLD_LOCAL);

   if ( ! eglLib ) {
      LOGE ( "Failed to load %s", lib3);
   }

  // Load API gl* for 1.5+  else egl* gl*
  if ( !CreateGlEsInterface(driver, glesLib, eglLib, (void *) gl_unimplemented) == -1)
    {
    // release lib
    LOGE ( "CreateGlEsInterface failed.");

    dlclose(glesLib);
      return 0;
    }

  // Init nanoGL
  InitGLStructs();
  return 1;
}

void nanoGL_Destroy()
{
```

```
    LOGD ("nanoGL_Destroy");

    if (glEsImpl) {
          free( glEsImpl);
          glEsImpl = NULL;
      }

    // release lib
    dlclose(glesLib);
}
```

Listing 6–1 has the following two public functions and one private function, which drive
the entire process:

- nanoGL_Init(): This function is meant to be called from your code to
  initialize the NanoGL interface, and it must be called before any
  OpenGL operations. Its job is to load the OpenGL ES library and
  create an interface between itself and OpenGL ES by calling
  CreateGlEsInterface. After this process completes, any OpenGL calls
  (such as immediate mode drawing) will be filtered through this
  interface and sent transparently to the OpenGL ES backend.

- nanoGL_Destroy(): This function can be called when you are done with
  OpenGL and wish to release resources. It is usually called when your
  program terminates.

- CreateGlEsInterface(): This is where all the magic happens. This is a
  private function that loads the OpenGL interface in a very clever way,
  as explained in the "Quake for Android Architecture" section.

nanoGL_Init starts by searching for an OpenGL ES library to load:

```
const char * lib1 = "libGLESv1_CM.so";
const char * lib2 = "libGLESv2.so";
const char * driver;

if ( ! loadDriver(lib1) )  {
  // failed to load libGLESv1_CM.so

  if ( ! loadDriver(lib2) ) {
    // failed to load libGLESv2.so. Abort.
    return 0;
  }
  else
    driver = lib2; // use libGLESv2.so
}
else
  driver = lib1;   // use libGLESv1_CM.so
```

nanoGL_Init's search order starts with libGLESv1_CM.so, which is the main OpenGL ES
library. If libGLESv1_CM.so cannot be found (this should not happen in any standard
Android device), then it attempts to load libGLESv2.so (OpenGL ES version 2). If both
fail, it bails out and returns an error. To load the library, NanoGL uses loadDriver, which
wraps the UNIX system call:

```
dlopen(name, RTLD_NOW | RTLD_LOCAL)
```

This system call loads a dynamic library from the OS search path and returns a pointer to the loaded library. With this pointer, we can then load symbols (functions) and other data structures from the library using the system call:

```
void * function = dlsym(library, "function_name")
```

This system call will load a function given by `function_name` from the library and store it in a pointer that can be used to call the function dynamically (on the fly). Finally, `nanoGL_Init` calls `CreateGlEsInterface` to create the OpenGL ES interface.

`CreateGlEsInterface` loops through two data structures, as shown in Listing 6–2. The first is a set of function pointers defined in the structure `GlESInterface`. This structure contains a function pointer for every API call in OpenGL ES. The second data structure is a set of API entries defined in `gl_entries.in`. For every function pointer in `GlESInterface` there must be an equivalent API entry in `gl_entries.in` in the same order. The order is absolutely crucial, because if it does not match, then horrible things will happen at runtime. At the end of the loop, the `GlESInterface` will point to all the OpenGL ES functions defined in the API. This allows NanoGL to work as a filter for OpenGL. Thus, whenever the Quake engine does a GL API call (`glBegin`, for example), NanoGL will filter the call through its interface, perform its magic, and send the result to the underlying OpenGL ES backend, effectively solving our immediate mode drawing dilemma.

Listing 6–2. *Data Structures Used to Initialize the NanoGL Interface*

```
/*
    // gl_entries.in
    GL_ENTRY(int,eglChooseConfig,int dpy, const int *attrib_list,
        int *configs, int config_size, int *num_config)
    GL_ENTRY(int,eglCopyBuffers,int dpy, int surface, void* target)
    GL_ENTRY(int,eglCreateContext,int dpy, int config,
        int share_list, const int *attrib_list)

// GL
    GL_ENTRY(void,glActiveTexture,unsigned int texture)
    GL_ENTRY(void,glAlphaFunc,unsigned int func, float ref)
    GL_ENTRY(void,glAlphaFuncx,unsigned int func, int ref)
    GL_ENTRY(void,glBindTexture,unsigned int target, unsigned int texture)
    // More GL functions here
*/
// glesinterface.h
struct GlESInterface
 {
    // entries must match gl_entries.in
    int (*eglChooseConfig) (int dpy, const int *attrib_list, int *configs
            , int config_size, int *num_config);
    int (*eglCopyBuffers) (int dpy, int surface, void* target);
    int (*eglCreateContext) (int dpy, int config, int share_list, const int
*attrib_list);

    void (*glActiveTexture) (unsigned int texture);
    void (*glAlphaFunc) (unsigned int func, float ref);
    void (*glAlphaFuncx) (unsigned int func, int ref);
```

```
    void (*glBindTexture) (unsigned int target, unsigned int texture);
    // More functions here
}
```

We will compile NanoGL as a static library within the Quake project so that it can be reused by other engines, such as Quake II, in Chapter 7. Now let's take a look at the changes required to get the engine going.

Quake for Android Architecture

NanoGL will allow us to reuse about 90 percent of the renderer with no changes and about 95 percent of the entire engine. Figure 6–1 shows the architecture of this app.

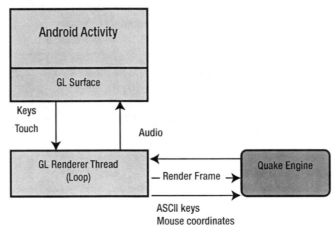

Figure 6–1. *Quake for Android architecture*

The silver boxes represent thin Java wrapper classes. The green box is the C engine, where most of the work will take place. In the following sections, we will look at how we can create a nimble Java OpenGL renderer for Quake. Next, we'll see how to handle audio independently of the format; then, how to provide support for keyboard and multi-touch events. But first, let's see how the rendering works.

Java OpenGL Renderer Architecture

Android provides the built-in classes GLSurfaceView and GLSurfaceView.Renderer, which we can extend for this implementation. These classes are very thin and their only job is to provide a simple interface between the device and the native library. Listing 6–3 shows the implementation.

> **TIP:** The full source for the renderer is available from the book source under ch06.Quake.

Listing 6–3. *Implementation of GLSurfaceView and Renderer for Quake*

```java
package com.opengl;
// ...
public class QuakeView extends GLSurfaceView implements Natives.EventListener {
  private static final String TAG = "QuakeView";

  {
    // Load native lob
    System.loadLibrary("quake");
  }

  boolean mGameLoaded = false;

  // private Context mContext;
  private String[] mArgs;

  public QuakeView(Context context) {
    super(context);
    init(context);
  }

  public QuakeView(Context context, AttributeSet attrs) {
    super(context, attrs);
    init(context);
  }

  private void init(Context context) {
    // We want events.
    setFocusable(true);
    setFocusableInTouchMode(true);
    requestFocus();

    Log.d(TAG, "QuakeView init");

    // Listen for JNI events
    Natives.setListener(this);
  }

  public void setRenderer(String[] args) {
    mArgs = args;

    Log.d(TAG, "Setting startup args & renderer");

    setRenderer(new QuakeRenderer());
  }


  /**
   * Renderer
   */
  public class QuakeRenderer implements GLSurfaceView.Renderer {

    @Override
    public void onDrawFrame(GL10 arg0) {
      if (mGameLoaded) {
        Natives.RenderFrame();
      }
```

```
        }

        @Override
        public void onSurfaceChanged(GL10 arg0, int width, int height) {
          Log.d(TAG, "onSurfaceChanged w=" + width + " h=" + height);

        }

        @Override
        public void onSurfaceCreated(GL10 arg0, EGLConfig arg1) {
          Log.d(TAG, "onSurfaceCreated");

          if (mArgs != null) {
            mGameLoaded = true;
            Natives.QuakeMain(mArgs);
          }
        }
      }

      /**
       * Native Callbacks
       */
      @Override
      public void OnInitVideo(int w, int h) {
        Log.d(TAG, "OnInitVideo. " + w + "x" + h + " Starting native audio.");

        // Native audio
        NativeAudio.start();
      }}
```

The class QuakeView from Listing 6–3 extends the built-in class GLSurfaceView, which provides a surface for rendering using OpenGL. QuakeView also includes the following classes:

- QuakeRenderer: This is an inner class that creates a simple OpenGL renderer, which can be used to call native functions on the C engine. This class provides the following events:

    - onDrawFrame: This event fires whenever the renderer draws a frame and it is used to perform OpenGL API calls. It has one argument: GL10, the interface to the OpenGL context. In a pure Java game, this context will be used to perform GL API calls; however, we are rendering everything in the native side, thus this parameter is not used.

    - onSurfaceChanged: This event fires whenever the surface changes; for example, when it is first created or when the orientation of the parent changes. It can fire many times throughout the lifetime of the application.

    - onSurfaceCreated: This event fires only once when the surface is first created. It receives a GL context (GL10) and the GL configuration (EGLConfig). It is useful to adjust the graphics configuration, such as pixel, format, depth buffer, and more.

- *Natives*: This is a user-defined interface class to all things native. It contains the definitions of the native methods to be called from Java, which are as follows:

  - `QuakeMain(String[] argv)`: This is the main entry point to the engine. It essentially calls the main C function with an array of string arguments.

  - `RenderFrame()`: This native function renders 1 frame of the game.

  - `keyPress(int key)`: This function sends an ASCII key pressed event to the engine.

  - `keyRelease(int key)`: This function sends an ASCII key-released event to the engine.

  - `mouseLook(int mouseX, int mouseY)`: This native function is used to send the XY delta coordinates of a touch event used to look around 3D space whenever a finger is dragged on screen.

  - `PaintAudio( ByteBuffer buf)`: This function is used to read a byte buffer from the native audio buffer of the engine. The buffer is then played from Java using the Android MediaTrack API.

- The Natives class also wraps a set of JNI-C callbacks that the engine uses to send information back to the thin Java wrappers (see Listing 6–4). These callbacks are as follows:

  - `OnInitVideo(int w, int h)`: This tells Java that the native video has been initialized. It is used to start the Java audio thread.

  - `OnSysError(String message)`: This method is called by the engine when a fatal system error occurs and the program needs to terminate.

Listing 6–4. *Java Class for Native Functions and C Callbacks*

```
package quake.jni;

import java.nio.ByteBuffer;
import android.util.Log;

public class Natives {
  public static final String TAG = "Natives";

  private static EventListener listener;

  public static interface EventListener {
    void OnInitVideo(int w, int h);
  }

  public static void setListener(EventListener l) {
    listener = l;
  }
```

```java
/**
 * Main Quake Sub
 * @param argv Engine args
 * @return
 */
public static native int QuakeMain(String[] argv);

/**
 * Render 1 frame
 *
 */
public static native int RenderFrame();

/**
 * Key press
 * @param key ascii code
 */
public static native int keyPress(int key);

/**
 * Key release
 */
public static native int keyRelease(int key);


/**
 * Forward movement using mouse coords
 * @param mouseX Delta X
 * @param mousey Delta Y
 */
public static native int mouseMove(int mouseX, int mouseY);


/**
 * Native audio painter. The native code will write audio bytes to the buffer.
 * Mostly PCM 16 stero 22500 (WAV)
 */
public static native int PaintAudio(ByteBuffer buf);


/**********************************************************
 * C - Callbacks
 **********************************************************/

/**
 * Fires on init graphics
 *
 * @param w  width of the image
 * @param h height
 */
private static void OnInitVideo(int w, int h) {
  if (listener != null)
    listener.OnInitVideo(w, h);
}

/**
 * Fires when the C lib calls SysError()
```

```
 * @param message
 */
private static void OnSysError(final String message) {
  Log.e(TAG, "Natives::OnSysError " + message);

  if (listener != null)
    listener.OnSysError(message);

  }
}
```

To listen for events from the native engine, QuakeView implements
Natives.EventListener and calls:

```
// Listen for JNI events
Natives.setListener(this);
```

An important step is to load the native library using the System class:

```
// Load native lib
System.loadLibrary("quake");
```

This will load the library libquake.so from the project folder libs/armeabi. This will take
care of the renderer, but we must also handle audio, keyboard, and touch events.

Handling Audio Independently of the Format

One of the most frustrating things when working with native code in Android is audio
handling. There are few options to work with outside the Java realm, making native
development very tough. In the early days, Google used the obscure Enhanced Audio
System (EAS) API to provide audio. I've never heard about it or seen any game engine
use it. Nevertheless, progress has been made and now new open APIs such as Open
Audio Library, or OpenAL, are supported. OpenAL is used by modern engines, but
unfortunately Quake does not use it.

Lucky for us, we can use a neat feature from JNI to access the memory address from a
Java ByteBuffer within C. This allows the native code to simply write audio bytes to that
memory address, which in turn will be played by the Java code using the Android
MediaTrack API.

> **TIP:** Using the MediaTrack API provides audio format independence. Whatever the format of your
> sound file, Android will detect it and call the right driver for it (as long as the format is supported
> by the platform). Plus it works in all versions of Android, thus giving you the widest range of
> device support.

The process works as follows:

1. Consider a class dubbed NativeAudio that drives the audio playback with a static method start. Within start, we create a Java thread that contains an instance of the Android MediaTrack API.

2. MediaTrack can be used to play audio by declaring an instance of an audio track with a set of user defined audio parameters. In this case, we wish to stream (hence AudioManager.STREAM_MUSIC) at a frequency of 22kHz, using 2 channels (STEREO) with a buffer size of 4 * (22050 / 5):

```
mTrack = new AudioTrack(
    android.media.AudioManager.STREAM_MUSIC,
    22050,
    AudioFormat.CHANNEL_CONFIGURATION_STEREO, // stereo
    AudioFormat.ENCODING_PCM_16BIT,  // 16 bit audio
    4 * (22050 / 5),                                          // Buffer size
    AudioTrack.MODE_STREAM);
```

3. When the thread starts, it will enter a loop continuously reading from the C engine using the native function Natives.PaintAudio(audioBuffer). The process will continue until the loop is told to stop using a boolean variable. In that case, the thread will terminate and the audio track will be disposed, as shown in Listing 6–5.

Listing 6–5. *Playing Native Audio Using Android's MediaTrack*

```
public class NativeAudio {

  public static void start() {

    mStarted = true;

    new Thread(new Runnable() {
      public void run() {
        // Android Audio API
        AudioTrack mTrack;

        mTrack = new AudioTrack(android.media.AudioManager.STREAM_MUSIC,
            22050,
            AudioFormat.CHANNEL_CONFIGURATION_STEREO, // stereo
            AudioFormat.ENCODING_PCM_16BIT, // 16 bit audio
            4 * (22050 / 5),                // Buffer size
            AudioTrack.MODE_STREAM);

        int audioSize = (2048 * 4);
        ByteBuffer audioBuffer = ByteBuffer.allocateDirect(audioSize);

        byte[] audioData = new byte[audioSize];


        Log.d(TAG, "Audio start.");

        mTrack.play();
```

```
      while (!mDone) {
        if (!mPaused) {
          Natives.PaintAudio(audioBuffer);

          audioBuffer.position(0);
          audioBuffer.get(audioData);

          // Write the byte array to the track
          mTrack.write(audioData, 0, audioData.length);
        } else {
          try {
            Thread.sleep(100);
          } catch (Exception e) {
          }
        }
      }
    }

    }
  }).start();
  }
}
```

> **TIP:** Quake encodes audio files in 16–bit WAV format at a frequency of 22 kHz.

Finally, whenever we wish to start the audio playback, we can simply call Nativeaudio.start(). At that point, the Java thread will fire and begin reading audio bytes from the C library. This is not an optimal solution (the most efficient one would be to write the audio directly from the native engine), but it works very well with no lag in sound whatsoever. The following are some things to carefully consider:

- The Java audio buffer must be a direct ByteBuffer. This is critical, as the code cannot use short or integer buffers. A direct byte buffer is required because the Java virtual machine will make a best effort to perform native I/O operations directly upon it. On the other hand, non-direct byte buffers copy the content to (or from) an intermediate buffer before (or after) each invocation of one of the underlying operating system's native I/O operations.

- The native engine should use a byte array of audio encoded in the same format (in this case 16–bit stereo at 22 kHz), which will be copied into the Java byte buffer and then played by the audio track.

- The NativeAudio class requires the companion JNI C function PaintAudio to copy the native byte buffer into the Java byte buffer, as shown in Listing 6–6.

Listing 6–6. *Companion PaintAudio JNI Function for NativeAudio*

```
// copy len bytes of native audio into stream
extern int paint_audio (void *unused, void * stream, int len);

JNIEXPORT jint JNICALL Java_quake_jni_Natives_PaintAudio
  ( JNIEnv* env, jobject thiz, jobject buf )
```

```
{
    void *stream;
    int len;

    stream = (*env)->GetDirectBufferAddress(env,  buf);
    len = (*env)->GetDirectBufferCapacity (env, buf);

    return paint_audio ( NULL, stream, len );
}
```

As we can see from Listing 6–6, PaintAudio must be declared as native in the Java class quake.jni.Natives.java. Things worth noting are the calls to GetDirectBufferAddress, which fetches and returns the starting address of the memory region referenced by the given direct java.nio.Buffer; and GetDirectBufferCapacity, which returns the capacity in bytes of the memory region referenced by the given direct buffer.

Now that we have a reference to the Java byte buffer and its size, we can call the native audio painter to fill it up.

Handling Keyboard Events

You can listen for key presses or releases in Android by simply overriding the methods onKeyDown and onKeyUp in a view or main activity class. The process can be summarized as follows (also see Listing 6–7):

- When a key is pressed or released, the events onKeyDown, onKeyUp will fire in the OpenGL view class QuakeView. It is important to note that Quake handles keys in ASCII format, but Android uses a different encoding format. Thus, we use the delegate class QuakeKeyEvents to translate them.

- The delegate QuakeEvents will translate the key into an ASCII code and invoke the native method keyPress or keyRelease, respectively. ASCII code will then be sent to the engine for consumption.

- The companion C implementations for keyPress and keyRelease named Java_quake_jni_Natives_keyPress and Java_quake_jni_Natives_keyRelease will push the ASCII key to the engine queue using Key_Event.

Listing 6–7. *Keyboard Java/C Handlers*

```
// In QuakeView.java

public boolean onKeyDown(final int keyCode, final KeyEvent event) {
    queueEvent(new Runnable() {
        public void run() {
            QuakeKeyEvents.onKeyDown(keyCode, event);
        }
    });
    return true;
}
```

```java
    public boolean onKeyUp(final int keyCode, final KeyEvent event) {

      queueEvent(new Runnable() {
        public void run() {
          QuakeKeyEvents.onKeyUp(keyCode, event);
        }
      });
      return true;
    }

// In QuakeEvents.java
  public static final int K_TAB = 9;
  public static final int K_ENTER = 13;
  public static final int K_ESCAPE = 27;
  public static final int K_SPACE = 32;

  // more ASCII keys...

  //key maps for motorola droid
  private static final int[] sKeyCodeToQuakeCode = {
        '$', K_ESCAPE, '$', '$',   K_ESCAPE, K_CTRL, '$', '0', //  0.. 7
        '1', '2', '3', '4',   '5', '6', '7', '8', //  8..15
        '9', '$', '$', K_UPARROW,   K_DOWNARROW
            , K_LEFTARROW, K_RIGHTARROW, K_ENTER, // 16..23
        '$', '$', '$', K_HOME,   '$', 'a', 'b', 'c', // 24..31

        'd', 'e', 'f', 'g',   'h', 'i', 'j', 'k',     // 32..39
        'l', 'm', 'n', 'o',   'p', 'q', 'r', 's',     // 40..47
        't', 'u', 'v', 'w',   'x', 'y', 'z', ',',     // 48..55
        '.', K_ALT, K_ALT, K_SHIFT,   K_SHIFT, K_TAB, ' ', '$', // 56..63
        '$', '$', K_ENTER, K_BACKSPACE, '`', '-', '=', '[', // 64..71
        ']', '\\', ';', '\'', '/', K_CTRL,  '#', '$', // 72..79
        K_CTRL, '$', K_ESCAPE, '$',  K_SPACE           // 80..84
  };

  public static boolean onKeyDown(int keyCode, KeyEvent event) {
    try {
      Natives.keyPress(keyCodeToQuakeCode(keyCode));
    } catch (UnsatisfiedLinkError e) {
      Log.d(TAG, e.toString());
    }

    return true;
  }

  public static boolean onKeyUp(int keyCode, KeyEvent event) {
    try {
      Natives.keyRelease(keyCodeToQuakeCode(keyCode));
    } catch (UnsatisfiedLinkError e) {
      Log.d(TAG, e.toString());
    }
  }
}

// In jni_quake.c
// engine key event processor
extern void Key_Event (int key, qboolean down);
```

```
JNIEXPORT jint JNICALL Java_quake_jni_Natives_keyPress
  (JNIEnv * env, jclass cls, jint key)
{
  Key_Event((int)key, 1);
  return key;
}

JNIEXPORT jint JNICALL Java_quake_jni_Natives_keyRelease
  (JNIEnv * env, jclass cls, jint key)
{
  Key_Event((int)key, 0);
  return key;
}
```

The translation of the Android keys to ASCII can be tricky; this is where hardware fragmentation issues come into play. As we can see in Listing 6–7, an array of integers (sKeyCodeToQuakeCode) is used for key translation, where the index of the array represents the Android key and the value is the ASCII code. This array works well in the Motorola Droid 1, but it will not be accurate in other devices, as each vendor builds keyboards with different layouts. Not event among the Motorola Droid versions 1, 2, and 3 are the layouts the same. This means you may have to adjust the array slightly, depending on what device keyboards you need to support. Hardware fragmentation is just a fact of life in open platforms. Next, we tackle touch handling.

Handling Touch Events

Touch events work in a similar way as key events. Listing 6–8 demonstrates how to cascade XY delta touch coordinates to the native engine to control the pitch and yaw of the character in 3D space.

Listing 6–8. *Translating XY Touch Coordinates into Pitch and Yaw*

```
// in QuakeView.java
  private float moveX = 0f;
  private float moveY = 0f;

  public boolean onTouchEvent(final MotionEvent e) {
    final int action = e.getAction();

    queueEvent(new Runnable() {
      public void run() {
        if (action == MotionEvent.ACTION_DOWN) {
          // QuakeKeyEvents.onKeyDown(KeyEvent.KEYCODE_ENTER, null);
          moveX = e.getX();
          moveY = e.getY();
        }
        else if (action == MotionEvent.ACTION_UP) {
          moveX = moveY = 0;
        }
        else if (action == MotionEvent.ACTION_MOVE) {
          final float dx = e.getX() - moveX;
          final float dy = e.getY() - moveY;

          final float DX = Math.abs(dx);
```

```
            final float DY = Math.abs(dy);

            if (DX < 30 && DY < 30) {
              return;
            }
            Natives.mouseMove((int) dx, (int) dy);
          }
        }
      });
      return true;
    }

// in Natives.java
public static native int mouseMove(int deltaX, int deltaY);

// in jni_quake.c
extern int    mouse_x, mouse_y;
JNIEXPORT jint JNICALL Java_quake_jni_Natives_mouseMove
  (JNIEnv * env, jclass cls, jint mx, jint my)
{
  // for pitch & yaw (look)
  mouse_x = (int)mx;
  mouse_y = (int)my;
/*
  for forward or side movement  use
  mouse_side = (int)mx;
  mouse_fwd = (int)my;
*/
}

// In gl_vidandroid.c (VIDEO DRIVER)
// Set PITCH & YAW
void IN_MouseLook (usercmd_t *cmd)
{
  if (!mouse_avail)
    return;

  if (m_filter.value)
  {
    mouse_x = (mouse_x + old_mouse_x) * 0.5;
    mouse_y = (mouse_y + old_mouse_y) * 0.5;
  }

  old_mouse_x = mouse_x;
  old_mouse_y = mouse_y;

  mouse_x *= sensitivity.value;
  mouse_y *= sensitivity.value;

// Set PITCH and YAW based on mouse XY delta coordinates
  cl.viewangles[YAW] -= m_yaw.value * mouse_x;

  V_StopPitchDrift ();

  cl.viewangles[PITCH] += m_pitch.value * mouse_y;

  if (cl.viewangles[PITCH] > 80)
```

```
        cl.viewangles[PITCH] = 80;

   if (cl.viewangles[PITCH] < -70)
       cl.viewangles[PITCH] = -70;

   mouse_x = mouse_y = 0;
}

// Character move
void IN_Move (usercmd_t *cmd)
{
   // to look
   IN_MouseLook(cmd);
   // to move
   //IN_MouseMove(cmd);
}
```

When the user drags a finger across the screen, the onTouchEvent on the GL view will fire. This event receives motion event information such as an action: ACTION_DOWN, ACTION_UP or ACTION_MOVE, depending on the type of motion. Because the native engine runs in a separate thread, onTouchEvent uses the built-in sub queueEvent to process the action safely into the game thread. When the finger goes down (ACTION_DOWN), the XY coordinates of the press are recorded. When the finger goes up (ACTION_UP) the XY coordinates are reset to 0. When the finger is dragged (ACTION_MOVE), the delta coordinates (DX, DY) are calculated, and if they exceed a threshold value (30 pixels in this case), they are sent to the engine by consumption using JNI. This requires the native method int mouseMove(int deltaX, int deltaY) in Natives.java and its C counterpart Java_quake_jni_Natives_mouseMove. The C implementation of mouseMove simply records the values of delta XY coordinates to be processed by the video driver. There is one important function in the video driver that processes movement: IN_Move. Within this function, we use a mouse handler, IN_MouseMove, to control the pitch and yaw of the character in 3D space. More details on this will be explained in the following sections.

Game Startup Activity

This is the final piece of the puzzle, the main entry point to the app: the game activity (see Listing 6–9). Its job is to do the following:

- Create an instance of the view QuakeView.

- Set a renderer with a set of string arguments that will be sent to the engine at startup.

- Set QuakeView as the content that will start the rendering process and begin the game!

Listing 6–9. *Main Startup Activity*

```
public class QuakeActivity extends Activity {

   QuakeView mQuakeView;
```

```
@Override
public void onCreate(Bundle savedInstanceState) {
  super.onCreate(savedInstanceState);

  // setContentView(R.layout.main);
  mQuakeView = new QuakeView(this);

  int w = getWindow().getWindowManager().getDefaultDisplay().getWidth();
  int h = getWindow().getWindowManager().getDefaultDisplay().getHeight();

  // Put the game file pak0.pak files under /sdcard/quake/base!
  final String baseDir = "/sdcard/quake";

  String args = "quake"
      + ",-width," + String.valueOf(w)
      + ",-height," + String.valueOf(h)
      + ",-basedir," + baseDir
      + ",-game,base"
      + ",+skill,0"
      + ",+crosshair,1"
      + ",+gl_ztrick,0";

  mQuakeView.setRenderer(args.split(","));

  setContentView(mQuakeView);

}

@Override
public boolean onKeyDown(int keyCode, KeyEvent event) {
  return mQuakeView.keyDown(keyCode, event);
}

@Override
public boolean onKeyUp(int keyCode, KeyEvent event) {
  return mQuakeView.keyUp(keyCode, event);
}
}
```

The array of arguments sent to the engine is critical; if any mistakes are made, the whole thing will fail. Listing 6–9 shows the most important, and includes the following:

- -width and -height: These two are important. They tell the engine the size of the video buffer and will differ by the device. The easiest way to get their values at runtime is to query the default display.

- -basedir: This is the default base directory that contains all the game files. In this case, you must upload your game files manually to /sdcard/quake. Note that the directory will have to also be created.

- -skill: Sets the game skill level. (0 = easy, 1 = normal, 2 = hard, 3 = nightmare)

- +crosshair: Displays a crosshair wherever you aim your weapon.

- +gl_ztrick: This is required because Quake uses a buffering method that avoids clearing the Z buffer, but some hardware platforms (like Android) don't like it. It is set to 0 to prevent the status bar and console from flashing every other frame.

This takes care of the thin Java wrappers for Quake. Now we need to modify the C engine slightly to make it work nicely with this Java code.

Changes Required to the Native Quake Engine

Thanks to NanoGL we can keep around 95 percent of the engine intact. If we do a line count of all the C code (including headers), we get close to 75,000 lines of code. Here we realize the amount of work we have saved—thank you again NanoGL (there are no words to describe how wonderful this tiny piece of software is). Nevertheless, there are still some cosmetic changes we need to make to the engine to make it play nicely with Android. The following is an overview of what is needed:

- *Video handler*: A video handler is usually required for all platforms where the engine is to be compiled. This is the most difficult and time-consuming change.

- *Movement handlers*: Custom handlers for pitch, yaw, forward, and side movement required to work with their JNI counterparts.

- *Audio handler*: A simple audio handler to configure the native audio buffer and copy its contents to the JNI audio buffer used by the Java MediaTrack API.

- *Game loop*: The main method of the engine needs to be modified slightly to work with the Android renderer thread.

Video Handler Changes

The video handler file is called gl_vidandroid.c and it is located in the project source under ch06.Quake/jni/Quake/android. It is a pretty big file, so I will explain the most important tasks it performs. Every OpenGL video handler must implement a set of standard functions that will be called at certain points on the engine execution, including the following:

- VID_Init: Initializes the video subsystem (see Listing 6–10). It has one argument: an array of bytes representing a 256–size color palette encoded as RGB color elements (1 byte per element, 768 in total). VID_Init performs the following tasks:

  - It loads video user parameters, such as the width and height of the screen (by calling COM_CheckParm).

  - It sets the values for the video data structure, including width, height, and others.

- It loads the NanoGL wrapper. This must be done before any calls to the OpenGL ES API are performed.

- It initializes the OpenGL pipeline.

- It adjusts the brightness. Quake is well known for having a very dark video display. VID_Init uses the user-defined gamma parameter to adjust the brightness of the display at startup.

- It creates the color palette used by the video renderer.

Listing 6–10. *Video Initialization*

```
void VID_Init(unsigned char *palette)
{
// Load user prams
  if ((i = COM_CheckParm("-width")) != 0)
    width = atoi(com_argv[i+1]);

  if ((i = COM_CheckParm("-height")) != 0)
    height = atoi(com_argv[i+1]);

// Set video size & others
  vid.width = vid.conwidth = width;
  vid.height = vid.conheight = height;
  ...

// Load NanoGL
  if ( !nanoGL_Init() ){
    Sys_Error("Failed to load NanoGL wrapper.");
  }

// Init GL
  gl_vendor = glGetString (GL_VENDOR);
  Con_Printf ("GL_VENDOR: %s\n", gl_vendor);
  ...

// Adjust Brightness
  Check_Gamma(palette);

// Create palette
  VID_SetPalette(palette);

}
```

- VID_SetPalette: Required to create a palette used to assign colors to textures and other graphical elements in the game. It must be a 256 RGB888 array of bytes.

- VID_Shutdown: Called whenever the video subsystem is shut down; for instance, when the user quits the game. It performs trivial cleanup tasks.

- GL_BeginRendering: Fires when the rendering starts for each frame of the game. This function needs to know the left and top XY coordinates of the screen, plus the width and height of the video.

```
void GL_BeginRendering (int *x, int *y, int *width, int *height)
{
  extern cvar_t gl_clear;

  *x = *y = 0;
  *width = scr_width;
  *height = scr_height;

}
```

- GL_EndRendering: Fires whenever the rendering of a frame of the game completes. A call to glFlush causes all issued GL commands to be executed as quickly as they are accepted by the OpenGL pipeline.

```
void GL_EndRendering (void)
{
  glFlush();
}
```

Brightness of the color palette can be adjusted by altering the values of its RGB pixels. Because Quake uses a 256 RGB888 palette, the brightness can be increased or decreased using the formula

$$P(i) = [(P(i) + 1)/256]^\wedge gamma * 255 + 0.5 ; P(i): [0,255]$$

Where P(i) represents a pixel in the palette and gamma is a user parameter read from the command line, whose range goes from 0 to 1. Note that P(i) must be clamped between 0 and 255, as shown in Listing 6–11.

Listing 6–11. *Brightness Control*

```
static void Check_Gamma (unsigned char *pal)
{
  float f, inf;
  unsigned char palette[768];
  int   i;

  if ((i = COM_CheckParm("-gamma")) == 0) {
    vid_gamma = 0.5; // default to 0.5
  } else
    vid_gamma = Q_atof(com_argv[i+1]);

  for (i=0 ; i<768 ; i++)
  {
    f = pow ( (pal[i]+1)/256.0 , vid_gamma );
    inf = f*255 + 0.5;
    if (inf < 0)
      inf = 0;
    if (inf > 255)
      inf = 255;
    palette[i] = inf;
  }
  // assign new values
  memcpy (pal, palette, sizeof(palette));
}
```

Handling Pitch and Yaw

In a first-person shooter game like Quake, pitch and yaw are commonly used to aim your weapon. In the PC world, this is usually done using the mouse to control the direction of a crosshair. On a touch device, on the other hand, we don't have such luxury but we can decide which sections of the screen control what. For example, on 3D space, if sweeping on the left half of the screen, we can move our character forwards or sideways. If sweeping on the right half, we could aim. It is all up to you. Listing 6–12 shows how we can control aiming by altering the yaw and pitch of the built-in client view angles data structure (cl.viewangles).

> **TIP:** Yaw (also known as heading) is the angular movement of the eye in the X axis. Pitch is the angular movement of the eye in the Y axis.

Listing 6–12. *Aim Control with Yaw and Pitch*

```
void IN_LookMove (usercmd_t *cmd)
{
  if (!mouse_avail)
    return;

  if (m_filter.value)
  {
    mouse_x = (mouse_x + old_mouse_x) * 0.5;
    mouse_y = (mouse_y + old_mouse_y) * 0.5;
  }
  old_mouse_x = mouse_x;
  old_mouse_y = mouse_y;

  mouse_x *= sensitivity.value;
  mouse_y *= sensitivity.value;

// set YAW
  cl.viewangles[YAW] -= m_yaw.value * mouse_x;

  V_StopPitchDrift ();

//  PITCH
  cl.viewangles[PITCH] += m_pitch.value * mouse_y;

  if (cl.viewangles[PITCH] > 80)
    cl.viewangles[PITCH] = 80;
  if (cl.viewangles[PITCH] < -70)
    cl.viewangles[PITCH] = -70;
  mouse_x = mouse_y = 0;
}
```

Note that the yaw and pitch are controlled by the mouse_x and mouse_y variables. These are delta increments in the XY axis sent through JNI by the QuakeView Java class. The center of the screen represents the origin (0,0). Down or left increments are negative, up or right increments are positive. The function V_StopPitchDrift prevents the pitch angle to reset to the origin whenever the movement stops (you release the finger). This is typical behavior of Quake in the desktop (if you aim with the mouse, as soon as you move it outside the game view, your aim will drift back to the origin).

Handling Forward and Side Movement

Forward and side movements are handled in similar way as pitch and yaw. Quake uses built-in data structures: cmd->sidemove to control side movements and cmd->forwardmove for forward movement (see Listing 6–13). These variables need to be increased or decreased by some increment. In our case, the increments are controlled by the variables: mouse_side and mouse_fwd. These two variables will be updated by JNI whenever you drag a finger on the screen. The companion JNI implementations are described in the previous section, "Handling Touch." Note that the both forward and side movements are multiplied by two Quake default values: m_side and m_forward. These are used to control the range of movement; also keep in mind that mouse_side and mouse_fwd are delta values in the XY direction where the origin (0,0) is defined at the point where the finger goes down. The delta values are then calculated by subtracting the XY coordinates of the pointer and then sent through JNI for consumption.

Listing 6–13. *Handling Forward and Side Movement*

```
// these will be updated by JNI
int mouse_side;
int mouse_fwd;

void IN_FwdSideMove (usercmd_t *cmd)
{
   cmd->sidemove += m_side.value * mouse_side;
   cmd->forwardmove -= m_forward.value * mouse_fwd;
}

void IN_Move (usercmd_t *cmd)
{
  IN_FwdSideMove (cmd);
  IN_LookMove (cmd)
}
```

Audio Handler Changes

To implement our own audio handler code for Android, we must take a look at the sound data structure defined in sound.h (see Listing 6–14). Quake uses a direct memory access (DMA) technique, where the most relevant values are as follows:

- channels: The number of audio channels: 1 for mono, 2 for stereo.
- samples: The size of the audio buffer.
- submission_chunk: This has something to do with how Quake mixed the audio buffer internally, but it is not relevant in our case.
- samplepos: This is the position or the current audio byte being played.

- samplebits: This is the audio resolution. Quake uses 16–bit WAV audio.

- speed: This is the audio frequency. It defaults to 22 kHz.

Note that there are also two sound-related variables: shm and sn. The first one is a pointer used to do all the behind-the-scenes work and it must point to sn, which is the real audio data structure. This is done on audio initialization, as seen in the "Fixing the Game Loop" section.

Listing 6–14. *Quake Audio Data Structure*

```
// In sound.h
// Internal Audio data structure
typedef struct
{
  qboolean    gamealive;
  qboolean    soundalive;
  qboolean    splitbuffer;
  int      channels;
  int      samples;          // mono samples in buffer
  int      submission_chunk;   // don't mix less than this #
  int      samplepos;         // in mono samples
  int      samplebits;
  int      speed;
  unsigned char *buffer;
} dma_t;

extern volatile dma_t *shm;
extern volatile dma_t sn;
```

With this information, we can easily implement a custom audio handler for Android. In Listing 6–15, we have the file snd_android.c, which implements the following functions:

- SNDDMA_Init: Required to initialize the audio handler. It defined the audio parameters described in Listing 6–14—audio resolution (16 bit), frequency (22kHz), number of channels (2 for stereo), the size of the samples (audio buffer)— and tells Quake that audio has been initialized successfully.

- SNDDMA_GetDMAPos: Tells Quake the current position in the audio buffer.

- paint_audio: Gets called by the JNI implementation of the Java class NativeAudio.PaintAudio, described in the "Handling Audio" section. The Java audio handler will use a thread and loop around calling NativeAudio.PaintAudio.

- NativeAudio.PaintAudio: Uses its JNI companion to call paint_audio to store audio bytes from the Quake audio buffer into the Java audio buffer, which will then be played using the Android MediaTrack API.

> **TIP:** snd_android.c is located in the book source under ch06.Quake/jni/Quake/android.

Listing 6–15. *Quake Audio Handler for Android*

```
// in snd_android.c
// This function is called from JNI to fill the audio buffer
// params: stream (Java audio buffer), len: stream size
int paint_audio (void *unused, void * stream, int len)
{
  if (!snd_inited)
    return 0;

  if (shm) {
    // make the quake au buffer point to stream
    shm->buffer = (unsigned char *)stream;
    shm->samplepos += len / (shm->samplebits / 4);

    // write sound bytes to stream
    S_PaintChannels (shm->samplepos);
    return len;
  }
  return 0;
}

// Audio Initializer
qboolean SNDDMA_Init(void)
{
  /* Most of the wav files are 16 bits, 22050 Hz, mono */
  /* Fill the audio DMA information block */
  shm = &sn;

  shm->samplebits = 16;

  // malloc max : 7 MB  => -12 MB !!
  shm->speed = 22050;
  shm->channels = 2;

  LOGD("SNDDMA_Init Speed %d channels %d", shm->speed, shm->channels);

  shm->samples = 2048 * shm->channels;
  shm->samplepos = 0;
  shm->submission_chunk = 1;
  shm->buffer = NULL;

  snd_inited = 1;

  return true;
}

// Get
int SNDDMA_GetDMAPos(void)
{
  return shm->samplepos;
}
```

Fixing the Game Loop

Thus far, we got custom video, movement, and audio handlers for Quake. The final piece is to modify the main Quake loop slightly to work nicely with Android. We must do this because the way GLSurfaceView.Renderer works. When Android creates a GLSurfaceView, you must set a renderer by implementing GLSurfaceView.Renderer. When this renderer kicks in, the following sequence of events will occur:

- OpenGL initialization will occur, including creating a GL context with drawing information such as pixel format, depth, stencil, buffers, and others.

- GLSurfaceView.Renderer.onSurfaceCreated will be called when the surface is created. This is where we must fire the Quake main function to start the game. Note that we must also send the plethora of arguments that Quake will expect from the command line.

- GLSurfaceView.Renderer.onSurfaceChanged will be called whenever the surface changes due to some event; for example, when the phone goes to sleep, wakes up, or receives a call, etc.

- GLSurfaceView.Renderer.onDrawFrame will fire for every interaction of the renderer thread. This is where we must perform all the OpenGL operations. When this method completes, the OpenGL buffers will be swapped and the frame will be rendered on screen.

Take a look at Quake's main function in Listing 6–16. It loops forever, rendering a frame at the end of each loop interaction. If we start main from onSurfaceCreated, then the Android thread will hang forever on the while loop. Therefore, we must comment this loop (as shown in Listing 6–17) to let onSurfaceCreated complete normally.

> **TIP:** sys_android.c can be found under ch06.Quake/jni/Quake/android in the book source.

Listing 6–16. *Changes to Quake's Main Game Loop*

```
// in sys_android.c Quake main function
int main (int c, char **v)
{
  double    time, oldtime, newtime;

  // Quake initialization…

// We don't need this loop in Android
#ifdef HAVE_RENDER_LOOP
    oldtime = Sys_FloatTime () - 0.1;

    while (1)
    {
        newtime = Sys_FloatTime ();
```

```
            time = newtime - oldtime;

            if (cls.state == ca_dedicated)
            {   // play vcrfiles at max speed
                if (time < sys_ticrate.value ) // Vladimir && (vcrFile == -1 || recording) )
                {
                    usleep(1);
                    continue;          // not time to run a server only tic yet
                }
                time = sys_ticrate.value;
            }

            if (time > sys_ticrate.value*2)
                oldtime = newtime;
            else
                oldtime += time;

            Host_Frame (time);

// graphic debugging aids
            if (sys_linerefresh.value)
                Sys_LineRefresh ();


    }
#endif
}
```

But we also need to implement onDrawFrame, which must perform all OpenGL operations before swapping buffers. To do this, we simply take the code we commented out from Quake's main function and put in its own function, called RenderFrame. This function essentially renders a single frame of the game and will be called by the Java class Natives.RenderFrame, described in the "Java OpenGL Renderer Architecture" section.

Listing 6–17. *Rendering a Single Frame in Quake*

```
// sys_android.c: This will be invoked from JNI on each renderer frame
// This code is taken from the main while loop
void RenderFrame()
{
  double    time, newtime;
  static double oldtime;

  // Init this var
  if (oldtime == 0.0 )
    oldtime = Sys_FloatTime () - 0.1;

// find time spent rendering last frame
  newtime = Sys_FloatTime ();
  time = newtime - oldtime;

  if (cls.state == ca_dedicated)
  {
    if (time < sys_ticrate.value )
    {
      usleep(1);
      return; // not time to run a server only tic yet
    }
```

```
      time = sys_ticrate.value;
  }

  if (time > sys_ticrate.value*2)
    oldtime = newtime;
  else
    oldtime += time;

  Host_Frame (time);

// graphic debugging aids
  if (sys_linerefresh.value)
    Sys_LineRefresh ();
}
```

The JNI-C companion that implements Natives.RenderFrame and calls RenderFrame is declared in the file jni_quake.c (under the ch06.Quake/jni/Quake/android in the book source).

```
extern void RenderFrame();

JNIEXPORT jint JNICALL Java_quake_jni_Natives_RenderFrame
  (JNIEnv * env, jclass cls)
{
  RenderFrame();
}
```

We have created the basic Android architecture for the Quake engine, plus done the required changes to the native engine. We now have all the pieces to get Quake up and running in our Android device. Let's look at how this happens.

Running on a Device

Before running on a device, the very first thing we need to do is compile the native library. To do this, we must create the compilation scripts: Application.mk and Android.mk.

Application.mk is tiny. It contains the name of the modules you wish to build and the path to Android.mk, which is the real compilation script. In this case, we want to compile two modules: NanoGL as a static library (so it can be reused in Chapter 7) and the Quake engine. NanoGL will compile into libNanoGL.a and Quake will compile into libquake.so, and will include libNanoGL.a.

```
APP_BUILD_SCRIPT := $(call my-dir)/Quake/Android.mk
APP_MODULES      := NanoGL quake
```

Android.mk is where all the meat lives. The first thing it does is compile the NanoGL static library, as follows:

```
LOCAL_MODULE    := NanoGL
DIR:= $(LOCAL_MODULE)
LOCAL_C_INCLUDES := jni/Quake/NanoGL/GL
LOCAL_SRC_FILES := $(DIR)/eglwrap.cpp  $(DIR)/nanogl.cpp $(DIR)/nanoWrap.cpp
include $(BUILD_STATIC_LIBRARY)
```

- LOCAL_MODULE: Specifies the module to compile

- LOCAL_C_INCLUDES: Specifies a list of directories where to look for header files.

- LOCAL_SRC_FILES: Specifies the source files to compile

- BUILD_STATIC_LIBRARY: Calls the Android build system to create libNanoGL.a

Next, Android.mk compiles the Quake engine, as shown in Listing 6–18.

Listing 6–18. *Android.mk fragment to Compile the Quake Engine*

```
LOCAL_MODULE := quake
LOCAL_CFLAGS := -O3 -DANDROID -DGLQUAKE -Wfatal-errors \
  -D_stricmp=strcasecmp -D_strnicmp=strncasecmp -Dstricmp=strcasecmp \
  -Dstrnicmp=strncasecmp

LOCAL_C_INCLUDES := jni/Quake/android jni/Quake/NanoGL
LOCAL_LDLIBS := -ldl -llog
LOCAL_STATIC_LIBRARIES := libNanoGL

RENDERER_SRC := gl_draw.c gl_mesh.c gl_model.c \
  gl_refrag.c gl_rlight.c gl_rmisc.c \
  gl_screen.c gl_rmain.c gl_rsurf.c \
  gl_warp.c \

SND_SRC := snd_dma.c snd_mem.c  snd_mix.c

ANDROID_SRC :=  android/jni_quake.c \
  android/snd_android.c \
  android/gl_vidandroid.c \
  android/sys_android.c \
LOCAL_SRC_FILES :=  \
  cl_demo.c \
  cl_input.c \
  cl_main.c \
  ... \
  net_udp.c \
  net_bsd.c \
  cd_null.c \
  crc.c net_vcr.c \
  $(RENDERER_SRC) $(SND_SRC) $(ANDROID_SRC)

include $(BUILD_SHARED_LIBRARY)
```

This time, the name of the module is quake. Note that the name must match the one defined in Application.mk. The following are the compilation options.

- LOCAL_CFLAGS: This variable defines the compiler options for the module. In this case, -03 tells the compiler to use optimization level 3 (which is heavy and produces fast code). –DANDROID is a flag for conditional compilation within the Android code. -DGLQUAKE is required by the engine to use the OpenGL renderer instead of the default software. -Wfatal-errors will abort compilation when any error occurs. -D_stricmp=strcasecmp and the rest of flags are substitutions of string comparison functions with their standard C counterparts.

Next, we see that the source is divided into the following:

- LOCAL_LDLIBS: Defines shared libraries to link against; in this case, the dynamic loader (ldl), and the log system (-llog).

- LOCAL_STATIC_LIBRARIES: This variable is important. Here, we tell the compiler to include the static library libNanoGL.a. Without this, compilation will fail.

- RENDERER_SRC: Defines the OpenGL renderer files.

- SND_SRC: Defines the sound subsystem files.

- ANDROID_SRC: Defines the Android-related files, including:

  - jni_quake.c: Contains the JNI implementations for all the native methods defined in Natives.java and NativeAudio.java.

  - snd_android.c: Implements the audio driver for Android. It works in conjunction with NativeAudio.java and jni_quake.c.

  - gl_vidandroid.c: Implements the video handler for Android.

  - sys_android.c: Implements changes to the main Quake loop to work along with the Android OpenGL renderer API.

- LOCAL_SRC_FILES: Defines the sources for the engine, including the sources defined in this list.

The following steps show how we compile Quake using Cygwin on a Windows system:

1. Copy the chapter source ch06.Quake into your local machine.

2. Open a Cygwin console and change to the project folder.

```
$ cd  /cygdive/c/temp/ch06.Quake
```

3. Compile the native library (see Figure 6–2).

```
$ ndk-build
```

```
/cygdrive/c/temp/Docs/Workspace/ch06.Quake                          _ □ X
Clean: stdc++ [armeabi]

Administrator@jonathanlaptop /cygdrive/c/temp/Docs/Workspace/ch06.Quake
$ ndk-build
Android NDK: WARNING: Unsupported source file extensions in /cygdrive/c/temp/Doc
s/Workspace/ch06.Quake/jni/Quake/Android.mk for module quake
Android NDK:     \
Compile thumb   : quake <= cl_demo.c
Compile thumb   : quake <= cl_input.c
Compile thumb   : quake <= cl_main.c
Compile thumb   : quake <= cl_parse.c
Compile thumb   : quake <= cl_tent.c
Compile thumb   : quake <= chase.c
Compile thumb   : quake <= cmd.c
Compile thumb   : quake <= common.c
Compile thumb   : quake <= console.c
Compile thumb   : quake <= cvar.c
Compile thumb   : quake <= gl_draw.c
Compile thumb   : quake <= gl_mesh.c
Compile thumb   : quake <= gl_model.c
Compile thumb   : quake <= gl_refrag.c
Compile thumb   : quake <= gl_rlight.c
Compile thumb   : quake <= gl_rmisc.c
Compile thumb   : quake <= gl_screen.c
Compile thumb   : quake <= host.c
Compile thumb   : quake <= host_cmd.c
Compile thumb   : quake <= keys.c
Compile thumb   : quake <= menu.c
Compile thumb   : quake <= mathlib.c
Compile thumb   : quake <= net_dgrm.c
Compile thumb   : quake <= net_loop.c
Compile thumb   : quake <= net_main.c
Compile thumb   : quake <= pr_cmds.c
Compile thumb   : quake <= pr_edict.c
Compile thumb   : quake <= pr_exec.c
Compile thumb   : quake <= r_part.c
Compile thumb   : quake <= sbar.c
Compile thumb   : quake <= sv_main.c
Compile thumb   : quake <= sv_phys.c
Compile thumb   : quake <= sv_move.c
Compile thumb   : quake <= sv_user.c
Compile thumb   : quake <= zone.c
Compile thumb   : quake <= view.c
Compile thumb   : quake <= wad.c
Compile thumb   : quake <= world.c
Compile thumb   : quake <= snd_dma.c
Compile thumb   : quake <= snd_mem.c
Compile thumb   : quake <= snd_mix.c
Compile thumb   : quake <= gl_rmain.c
Compile thumb   : quake <= gl_rsurf.c
Compile thumb   : quake <= gl_warp.c
Compile thumb   : quake <= jni_quake.c
Compile thumb   : quake <= snd_android.c
Compile thumb   : quake <= gl_vidandroid.c
Compile thumb   : quake <= sys_android.c
Compile thumb   : quake <= net_udp.c
Compile thumb   : quake <= net_bsd.c
Compile thumb   : quake <= cd_null.c
Compile thumb   : quake <= crc.c
Compile thumb   : quake <= net_vcr.c
Compile++ thumb : NanoGL <= eglwrap.cpp
Compile++ thumb : NanoGL <= nanogl.cpp
Compile++ thumb : NanoGL <= nanoWrap.cpp
StaticLibrary   : libstdc++.a
StaticLibrary   : libNanoGL.a
SharedLibrary   : libquake.so
Install         : libquake.so => libs/armeabi/libquake.so

$ _
```

Figure 6–2. *Compiling the Quake native library*

4. Connect your Android device to your laptop or start the emulator.

5. Copy the Quake shareware game file to the sdcard under
   /sdcard/quake/base. From a DOS prompt you can do this by typing:

```
C:\>adb shell mkdir -p /sdcard/quake/base
C:\>adb push /QUAKE_INSTALL/id0/pak0.pak /sdcard/quake/base
```

> **NOTE:** The Quake shareware game files are copyrighted by id Software and must be obtained from the company's web site.

6. Create a Run Configuration for the project. In Eclipse, click the main menu **Run ➤ Run Configuration**. In the Run Configuration wizard right-click **Android Application ➤ New**. Enter a name and select the ch06.Quake project, as shown in Figure 6–3.

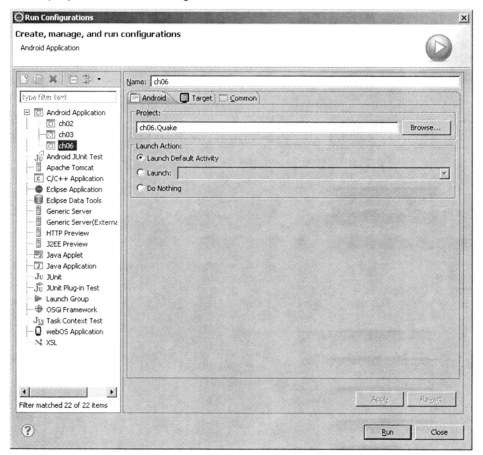

Figure 6–3. *Creating a Run Configuration*

7. Click Run and take a look at the Android log to see that everything goes smoothly (see Listing 6–19 and Figure 6–4).

Listing 6–19. *Android Log Output for Quake*

```
08-10 14:51:02.352: DEBUG/QuakeView(335): onSurfaceCreated
08-10 14:51:02.352: DEBUG/QJNI(335): Quake Main[0]=quake
08-10 14:51:02.352: DEBUG/QJNI(335): Quake Main[1]=-width
08-10 14:51:02.352: DEBUG/QJNI(335): Quake Main[2]=480
```

```
08-10 14:51:02.352: DEBUG/QJNI(335): Quake Main[3]=-height
08-10 14:51:02.352: DEBUG/QJNI(335): Quake Main[4]=800
08-10 14:51:02.352: DEBUG/QJNI(335): Quake Main[5]=-basedir
08-10 14:51:02.352: DEBUG/QJNI(335): Quake Main[6]=/sdcard/quake
08-10 14:51:02.363: DEBUG/QJNI(335): Quake Main[7]=-game
08-10 14:51:02.363: DEBUG/QJNI(335): Quake Main[8]=base
08-10 14:51:02.363: DEBUG/QJNI(335): Quake Main[9]=+skill
08-10 14:51:02.363: DEBUG/QJNI(335): Quake Main[10]=0
08-10 14:51:02.363: DEBUG/QJNI(335): Quake Main[11]=+showpause
08-10 14:51:02.363: DEBUG/QJNI(335): Quake Main[12]=0
08-10 14:51:02.363: DEBUG/QJNI(335): Quake Main[13]=+crosshair
08-10 14:51:02.363: DEBUG/QJNI(335): Quake Main[14]=1
08-10 14:51:02.363: DEBUG/QJNI(335): Quake Main[15]=+gl_ztrick
08-10 14:51:02.363: DEBUG/QJNI(335): Quake Main[16]=0
08-10 14:51:02.363: INFO/QJNI(335): Loading quake/jni/Natives
08-10 14:51:02.682: INFO/SYSLinux(335): Added packfile /sdcard/quake/base/pak0.pak (339
files)
08-10 14:51:02.703: INFO/SYSLinux(335): Playing registered version.
08-10 14:51:02.712: INFO/SYSLinux(335): PackFile: /sdcard/quake/base/pak0.pak : gfx.wad
08-10 14:51:02.824: INFO/SYSLinux(335): Console initialized.
08-10 14:51:02.892: INFO/SYSLinux(335): UDP Initialized
08-10 14:51:02.892: INFO/SYSLinux(335): TCP/IP address 127.0.0.1
08-10 14:51:02.913: INFO/SYSLinux(335): Exe: 10:28:40 Aug 10 2011
08-10 14:51:02.913: INFO/SYSLinux(335): 16.0 megabyte heap
08-10 14:51:02.948: INFO/SYSLinux(335): PackFile: /sdcard/quake/base/pak0.pak :
gfx/palette.lmp
08-10 14:51:02.981: INFO/SYSLinux(335): PackFile: /sdcard/quake/base/pak0.pak :
gfx/colormap.lmp
08-10 14:51:02.983: INFO/SYSLinux(335): Can't register variable in_mouse, allready
defined
08-10 14:51:02.983: INFO/SYSLinux(335): Can't register variable m_filter, allready
defined
08-10 14:51:02.983: DEBUG/QJNI(335): Initializing Signal Traps.
08-10 14:51:02.983: DEBUG/QJNI(335): Loading nano GL Wrapper
08-10 14:51:02.983: INFO/nanoGL(335): nanoGL: Init loading driver libGLESv1_CM.so
08-10 14:51:02.983: WARN/nanoGL(335): <eglChooseConfig> not found in libGLESv1_CM.so.
Trying libEGL.so.
08-10 14:51:02.993: WARN/nanoGL(335): <eglCopyBuffers> not found in libGLESv1_CM.so.
Trying libEGL.so.
08-10 14:51:02.993: WARN/nanoGL(335): <eglCreateContext> not found in libGLESv1_CM.so.
Trying libEGL.so.
libGLESv1_CM.so. Trying libEGL.so.
08-10 14:51:02.993: WARN/nanoGL(335): <eglDestroySurface> not found in libGLESv1_CM.so.
Trying libEGL.so.
08-10 14:51:03.002: WARN/nanoGL(335): <eglReleaseTexImage> not found in libGLESv1_CM.so.
Trying libEGL.so.
08-10 14:51:03.002: WARN/nanoGL(335): <eglSurfaceAttrib> not found in libGLESv1_CM.so.
Trying libEGL.so.
08-10 14:51:03.002: DEBUG/QuakeView(335): OnInitVideo. 480x480 Starting native audio.
08-10 14:51:03.012: INFO/SYSLinux(335): GL_VENDOR: Android
08-10 14:51:03.012: INFO/SYSLinux(335): GL_RENDERER: Android PixelFlinger 1.4
08-10 14:51:03.012: INFO/SYSLinux(335): GL_VERSION: OpenGL ES-CM 1.0
08-10 14:51:03.062: DEBUG/Audio(335): Audio start.
08-10 14:51:04.722: INFO/SYSLinux(335): Video mode 480x800 initialized.
08-10 14:51:04.793: INFO/SYSLinux(335): PackFile: /sdcard/quake/base/pak0.pak :
gfx/conback.lmp
08-10 14:51:04.993: INFO/SYSLinux(335): Sound Initialization
```

```
08-10 14:51:05.602: DEBUG/QSound(335): SNDDMA_Init Speed 22050 channels 2
08-10 14:51:05.602: INFO/SYSLinux(335): Sound sampling rate: 22050
08-10 14:51:06.633: WARN/AudioFlinger(34): write blocked for 726 msecs, 1 delayed
writes, thread 0xc658
08-10 14:51:06.942: INFO/SYSLinux(335): PackFile: /sdcard/quake/base/pak0.pak :
sound/ambience/water1.wav
08-10 14:51:07.033: INFO/SYSLinux(335): PackFile: /sdcard/quake/base/pak0.pak :
sound/ambience/wind2.wav
sound/weapons/ric2.wav
08-10 14:51:07.383: INFO/SYSLinux(335): PackFile: /sdcard/quake/base/pak0.pak :
sound/weapons/ric3.wav
08-10 14:51:07.428: INFO/SYSLinux(335): PackFile: /sdcard/quake/base/pak0.pak :
sound/weapons/r_exp3.wav
08-10 14:51:07.482: INFO/SYSLinux(335): ========Quake Initialized=========
08-10 14:51:07.494: DEBUG/SYSLinux(335): Linux Quake -- Version 1.300
08-10 14:51:08.253: INFO/SYSLinux(335): 3 demo(s) in loop
```

> **TIP:** If something goes wrong, make sure you have the folder /sdcard/quake/base in your
> device and that it contains the file pa0.pak. This file should be around 19 MB in size. The
> Android log will tell you if there is a failure of any kind.

Figure 6–4. *Quake for Android in action*

Summary

In this chapter, you learned how you can bring a powerful PC engine like Quake to Android with minimum effort. Some of the things this chapter delivered are:

- A slick way to deal with the PC OpenGL caveats, such as immediate mode drawing with almost no code changes to the original source. I showed this by bringing Quake to Android while keeping 98 percent of the original OpenGL renderer intact and 95 percent of the entire engine.

- Efficient ways to cascade keyboard and touch events from Java to the C engine for consumption, while preserving the original event processors.

- The implementation of these techniques with code samples and chapter source.

Porting a game like Quake to OpenGL ES would normally take countless hours—probably months of grueling work by a team of developers. In this chapter, I showed how one person using powerful tools can get this game going with less than 500 lines of new code.

Chapter **7**

3D Shooters for Quake II

This chapter builds upon the previous one to deliver the next great PC engine: Quake II. What makes this chapter unique is that, thanks to the wonderful reusability of Java and the power of the C language, we will be able to do the following:

- Reuse the thin Java wrappers to the Quake engine from Chapter 6 with no changes whatsoever.

- Keep 99 percent of the native engine intact with the help of NanoGL.

- Make tiny changes to the C code in the remaining 1 percent of the native engine in order to make it Android-friendly.

We'll start by learning how to add set nimble Java wrappers to get the engine running quickly in Android, including game startup, video rendering, and key and audio events. Next, we'll look at an efficient way of dealing with system errors (the ones that can crash you app). Then, the video handler changes required to the native engine. And finally, building the native code and running it in the emulator; as well as a performance test of the engine running on multiple devices at different resolutions.

Reviewing the Code

To get an idea of the amount of work we should save, let's take a look at the number of lines of C code for the engine.

```
$ find -name "*.[ch]" | xargs wc -l
  1058 ./client/adivtab.h
   181 ./client/anorms.h
    81 ./client/asm_i386.h
   123 ./client/block16.h
   124 ./client/block8.h
    26 ./client/cdaudio.h
   584 ./client/client.h
   650 ./client/cl_cin.c
```

```
 1543 ./client/cl_ents.c
 2298 ./client/cl_fx.c
...
173666 total

$ ref_gl> wc -l *.[ch]
  181 anorms.h
   37 anormtab.h
  416 gl_draw.c
 1590 gl_image.c
  729 gl_light.c
  458 gl_local.h
...
 1756 gl_rmain.c
  248 gl_rmisc.c
 1662 gl_rsurf.c
  662 gl_warp.c
  557 qgl.h
   51 warpsin.h
10692 total
```

In the first part, we have about 180,000 total lines of code (including header files); this includes almost 11,000 lines of code for the OpenGL renderer. I've estimated less than 2,000 lines of new code to make the engine Android-friendly. Thus, you will find that we will squeeze a tremendous amount of work—that would have taken a small team of developers several months to complete—into a project that a single guy can complete over a weekend.

Escaping the Shackles of the Java Heap

The Quake II engine is the perfect proof of concept for graphics rendering on a mobile device. Written around 1998, it has the same hardware requirements as a modern smartphone:

- 600 Mhz processor with a powerful GPU

- 80 MB RAM

- 40 MB of disk (for the shareware version), or 100 MB for retail

Believe or not, Quake II is so portable that some guys took the time to bring the game to pure Java 3D: the name of the project is Jake 2 (www.bytonic.de/html/jake2.html). There is even a port of Quake II by Google that runs on a web browser using WebGL. As a matter of fact, when Android was in its infancy, and the NDK didn't even exist, I took a couple of weeks to get Jake 2 to compile on Android's Jalvik VM. It was a lot of hard work just to find out that Java is simply not capable of handling any kind of powerful 3D game engine due to the constraints it imposes on the developer.

When thinking of a project like Jake 2, the key is the amount of RAM required to play the game: 80 MB. This is why there will never be a powerful 3D engine written in Java on Android. The Android Java VM only lets programs allocate a maximum of 16 MB of RAM—and it cannot be changed. As any Java developer knows, on the PC, the size of the heap (or RAM) can be changed at runtime with a simple command line argument. This is not possible in Android. I found this out the hard way when playing with Jake 2. All powerful 3D engines must be written in C/C++; there is simply no way around this.

> **NOTE:** Writing game engines in C/C++ allows the developer to use disk space and RAM in any way he or she chooses, limited only by what the hardware can provide. Java, on the other hand, will shackle you to 16 MB of RAM, from which you cannot escape.

Taming the Mighty Quake II Engine

To make the Quake II engine work seamlessly in Android, we will reuse most of the Java wrappers from Chapter 6. Plus, we'll have to implement custom video and audio handlers for this particular engine. All in all, most of the work will basically consist of the following:

- About 2,000 lines of new C code (for the video an audio handling).
- The Java code from Chapter 6, with tiny changes to make them fit Quake II.

If we dig around the source of both the Quake I and II engines, we realize there is a whole lot of common code between them. Nevertheless, Quake II has been greatly modularized (in comparison to Quake I), consisting of basically the following three separate components:

- *The client*: In Linux, this is the game executable, dubbed quake2.
- *The game library*: Quake II was designed to work with a plethora of mission packs, extensible mods, and so forth. By decoupling the game library into a separate component, mod developers can simply create new games by writing a new game library, leaving the other components intact.
- *The renderer*: Quake II supports two renderer types: software and hardware (using Open GL). In Linux, the renderers are called ref_soft.so for software, and ref_glx.so (for OpenGL under UNIX/Window). Note that there are multiple OpenGL renderer implementations, each with different names.

This great modularization works wonders on the desktop, where developers simply have to code a new game library and leave the other components intact. In Android (or any mobile platform for that matter), this can be a pain to develop, as the compiler tools are cumbersome (compared to the desktop), plus the way Android loads shared libraries is not the same as in the standard Linux OS. Lucky for us, Quake II can compile all three components as a standalone (hard linked) library. Thus in Android, to make things even easier, we will compile Quake II as a single, hard-linked library dubbed libquake2.so.

More details on doing so will be explained in the "Building Quake II with the NDK" section.

Code Reusability

Thanks to the great object-oriented and reusability features of Java, most of the classes from Chapter 6 can be reused without change. There are some tiny changes to the startup class, but besides that, the code is identical. Best of all, this code could be used in any type of native engine, not just Quake I and Quake II. To recap, Table 7–1 lists the Java classes and their tasks.

Table 7–1. *Java Classes and Tasks*

Package	Class Name	Description
com.opengl	QuakeActivity	This is the game startup class. It requires tiny changes mostly related to the game startup arguments.
com.opengl	QuakeKeyEvents	This class translates Android key event codes into ASCII codes understood by the Quake II engine. It will be reused without change.
com.opengl	QuakeView	This class extends the Android API GLSurfaceView to provide a surface for OpenGL rendering. It also contains the API GLSurfaceView.Renderer used to implement rendering calls into the native engine. It will be reused without change.
quake.audio	NativeAudio	This class implements a thread that reads the audio buffer from the native layer and sends it to the device hardware using the Android MediaTrack API. It will be reused without change.
quake.jni	Natives	This is the most important class. It declares the JNI native methods for communication between the Java and C code, plus it implements a set of callbacks that can be used from the C layer to send messages to the Java layer. This class will be reused without change.

Most of the native access methods reside in the class Natives.java; they are as follows:

■ native void QuakeMain(String[] argv): This method calls the Quake II main method. Its job is to convert the Java String arguments (argv) into a C array that can be fed into the engine. It also loads the Natives.java class to fire up callbacks when the native engine needs to send a message back to Java (for example, when a system/fatal error occurs and the application needs to terminate). This method requires no change to work with Quake II.

■ native void RenderFrame(): This native method renders a single frame of the game. We must do so to play nice with the Android OpenGL surface renderer, which uses a separate thread to render one frame at a time. This method requires no change to work with Quake II.

■ native int keyPress(int key) and keyRelease(int key): These two are used to push ASCII keys into the key processor. Note that the Android key codes will be translated into ASCII by the Java wrappers. These methods need to be updated to work with Quake II.

■ native void mouseLook(int mouseX, int mouseY): This method is used to look around 3D space when the player sweeps a finger across the screen. It receives delta coordinates for yaw (mouseX), and pitch (mouseY). This method requires no change.

■ native void mouseMove(int mouseX, int mouseY): This method is used to move the characters forward or sideways in 3D space. It receives delta coordinates in the XY axis. This method requires no change.

■ native void PaintAudio(ByteBuffer buf): This method reads a byte buffer of audio from the C engine into a Java buffer and writes it into the device audio hardware using Android's MediaTrack API. This method requires no change.

Game Startup

QuakeMain is the function that kicks things off. It starts the Quake II engine with a given array of arguments. The next fragment shows its declaration and Natives.java and C implementation in jni_quake.c.

> **NOTE:** The C implementations for all the native Java methods in Natives.java are located in the project source under ch07.QuakeII/jni/quake2-3.21/android/jni_quake.c.

```
// Java
package quake.jni;

public class Natives {
  ...
  public static native int QuakeMain(String[] argv);
  ...
}
```

```
// in jni_quake.c
JNIEXPORT jint JNICALL Java_quake_jni_Natives_QuakeMain
  (JNIEnv * env, jclass cls, jobjectArray jargv)
```

Note that the Java string arguments map into a jobjectArray in C, and they must be converted to the standard char *[] format. Fortunately, JNI provides utility functions to do this easily.

1. First, get the size of the array.

```
jsize clen = (*env)->GetArrayLength(env, jargv);
```

2. Next, allocate a C array of the same size.

```
char * args[(int)clen];
```

3. Then, loop through the size value, extracting a Java string from the array, and converting that Java string into a C string with the following.

```
int i;
jstring jrow;
for (i = 0; i < clen; i++)
{
    jrow = (jstring)(*env)->GetObjectArrayElement(env, jargv, i);
    const char *row  = (*env)->GetStringUTFChars(env, jrow, 0);
```

4. Then, simply allocate space for the corresponding C string using the malloc system call.

```
    args[i] = malloc( strlen(row) + 1);
    strcpy (args[i], row);
```

Make sure to release the Java string when done. Failing to do so will create a memory leak.

```
    // free java string jrow
    (*env)->ReleaseStringUTFChars(env, jrow, row);
}
```

5. Finally, invoke Quake II main sub with the arguments that we just created.

```
// Invoke Quake's main sub.
main (clen, args);
```

Rendering a Single Frame

Both the Java and C implementations for RenderFrame are the same as Chapter 6. In Natives.java we declared the native method RenderFrame(), which is implemented as shown in the following fragment:

```
extern void RenderFrame();

JNIEXPORT jint JNICALL Java_quake_jni_Natives_RenderFrame
  (JNIEnv * env, jclass cls)
{
```

```
    RenderFrame();
}
```

The C keyword extern void RenderFrame() tells the compiler that elsewhere exists a function called RenderFrame, which will be invoked within the JNI implementation. RenderFrame is a new function and needs to be created.

Listing 7–1 shows the Quake II main function from the project source at ch07.QuakeII/jni/quake2-3.21/android/sys_linux.c. We notice that it loops forever (by using a while (1) loop).

Listing 7–1. *Quake II Main Function*

```
int main (int argc, char **argv)
{
  int   time, oldtime, newtime;

  // go back to real user for config loads
  saved_euid = geteuid();
  seteuid(getuid());

  Qcommon_Init(argc, argv);

  nostdout = Cvar_Get("nostdout", "0", 0);
  if (!nostdout->value) {
    printf ("Linux Quake -- Version %0.3f\n", LINUX_VERSION);
  }
  oldtime = Sys_Milliseconds ();

// main render loop
  while (1) {
// find time spent rendering last frame
    do {
      newtime = Sys_Milliseconds ();
      time = newtime - oldtime;
    } while (time < 1);
    Qcommon_Frame (time);
    oldtime = newtime;
  }
}
```

This infinite loop does not work well with Android because Android's rendering thread already has a loop of its own. Calling an infinite loop within another loop will deadlock the rendering thread and make your application crash. Therefore, we must comment the infinite loop. We can also see that within the loop, one frame is rendered at a time using Qcommon_Frame(time). This is what we need; we can just extract what is inside this loop and put it in RenderFrame(). Thus, the code in Listing 7–1 becomes the code in Listing 7–2.

Listing 7–2. *Modified Quake II Main Function to Render a Single Frame*

```
void RenderFrame()
{
  int   time, newtime;
  static int oldtime;

  // Init this var
```

```
   if (oldtime == 0 )
     oldtime = Sys_Milliseconds ();

   do {
     newtime = Sys_Milliseconds ();
     time = newtime - oldtime;
   } while (time < 1);
   Qcommon_Frame (time);
   oldtime = newtime;
}

int main (int argc, char **argv)
{
// …
// main render loop?
#ifndef ANDROID
   while (1) {
// find time spent rendering last frame
     do {
       newtime = Sys_Milliseconds ();
       time = newtime - oldtime;
     } while (time < 1);
     Qcommon_Frame (time);
     oldtime = newtime;
   }
#endif
}
```

What we have done is simply extract whatever is inside the while loop and put it in RenderFrame() to render a single frame. Also notice that we use conditional compilation:

```
#ifndef ANDROID
   while (1) {

     …
   }
#endif
```

#ifndef ANDROID tells the compiler to include the enclosed code only if the flag ANDROID has not been defined at compilation time. This creates portability and allows the same code to work in multiple Linux flavors. Therefore, this tiny change allows the following sequence of events to occur seamlessly:

1. When the application starts, the main activity will start (Java).

2. The activity will create an OpenGL surface and start a separate rendering thread (Java).

3. When the surface is first created, the QuakeMain native method will be invoked only once, which will in turn call the Quake II main function (Java/C) passing game startup arguments.

4. The rendering thread will loop continuously, firing the render frame event—which will invoke the native function RenderFrame to draw a single frame of the game.

5. After the single frame rendering completes, Android will invoke the OpenGL swap buffers operation to display the graphics on the device and the process will resume back from step 4 until the user decides to terminate the program.

Now that we have the rendering smoothed, let's tackle key events.

Pumping Key Events

Keys are sent from the Java wrappers to the C engine via the native functions: keyPress and keyRelease declared in quake.jni.Natives.java. Both functions have as an argument the ASCII code of the key, which must be translated from the Android key format. The translation is identical to Chapter 6 under the "Handling Key Events" section, where we used an array of key mappings between Android codes and ASCII codes. The tricky part is dealing with all the different keyboard layouts of the dozens of keyboard-equipped phones out there. Nevertheless, the C implementations of keyPress and keyRelease need a tiny change to feed the key to the Quake II engine handler, as shown in Listing 7–3.

Listing 7–3. *Key Handlers for Quake II Java Wrappers*

```
// in jni_quake.c
JNIEXPORT jint JNICALL Java_quake_jni_Natives_keyPress
  (JNIEnv * env, jclass cls, jint key)
{
  Key_Event((int)key, 1);
  return key;
}

JNIEXPORT jint JNICALL Java_quake_jni_Natives_keyRelease
  (JNIEnv * env, jclass cls, jint key)
{
  Key_Event((int)key, 0);
  return key;
}
```

Listing 7–3 shows the parameter key, which must be an ASCII code—and I wish to stress this because failing to translate the key properly will make all kinds of weird things happen and cause you a lot of headaches—being fed to the Quake II key handler:

```
Key_Event((int)key, 1);
```

The first argument of Key_Event is the ASCII code, and the second is a Boolean variable where 1 means key pressed and 0 means key released.

Moving in 3D Space

When moving a Quake II character in 3D space, we have four choices: moving forwards, moving sideways, and the ability to look around by controlling the yaw (or angular movement in the X coordinate) or pitch (angular movement in the Y coordinate). To do so, there are two native methods in Natives.java:

```
mouseMove(int deltaX, int deltaY)
mouseLook(int deltaX, int deltaY)
```

mouseMove controls forward or sideways movement by feeding XY increments (or deltas) to the Quake II engine. mouseLook does the same thing with yaw and pitch increments. The C companions for mouseMove and mouseLook are identical to Quake I in Chapter 6; however, Quake II requires a movement handler that must be implemented. This handler is called IN_Move and it is shown in Listing 7–4.

Listing 7–4. *Moving in 3D Space*

```c
// jni_quake.c
// forwards/sideways deltas
extern int    mouse_side, mouse_fwd;

// Yaw/pitch deltas
extern int    mx, my;

JNIEXPORT jint JNICALL Java_quake_jni_Natives_mouseLook
  (JNIEnv * env, jclass cls, jint mousex, jint mousey)
{
  mx = (int)mousex;
  my = (int)mousey;
}

extern int    mouse_side, mouse_fwd;

JNIEXPORT jint JNICALL Java_quake_jni_Natives_mouseMove
  (JNIEnv * env, jclass cls, jint jx, jint jy)
{
  mouse_side = (int)jx;
  mouse_fwd = (int)jy;
}

// vid_so.c
int mouse_side = 0;
int mouse_fwd = 0;
int mx, my; // mouse look

void IN_Move (usercmd_t *cmd)
{
  old_mouse_x = mx;
  old_mouse_y = my;

  mx *= 3; //sensitivity
  my *= 3; //sensitivity

  // Look: yaw/pitch
  in_state.viewangles[YAW] -= m_yaw->value * mx;
  in_state.viewangles[PITCH] += m_pitch->value * my;
  mx = my = 0;

  // Move
  cmd->sidemove += m_side->value * mouse_side;
  cmd->forwardmove -= m_forward->value * mouse_fwd;

}
```

IN_Move is the Quake II input handler for movement. For forward or side movement, IN_Move provides the command structure usercmd_t *cmd, which can be used to control the character by consuming two delta values in the XY coordinates:

```
cmd->sidemove += m_side->value * DELTA_X;
cmd->forwardmove -= m_forward->value * DELTA_Y;
```

DELTA_X and DELTA_Y are the increments in the XY direction provided by Java when the user drags a finger on screen. m_side and m_forward are two internal constants used to control the sensitivity of the movement, and cmd->sidemove and cmd->forwardmove are the internal variables that contain the actual character position on 3D space. Note that to move forward in the Quake I/II 3D space coordinate system, the increments in the Y axis must be negative. This is the inverse of dragging a finger up the screen, which provides a positive increment.

To control yaw and pitch, on the other hand, we provide another set of increments in XY, but in this case we use the Quake II view angles data structure (in_state.viewangles):

```
in_state.viewangles[YAW] -= m_yaw->value * DELTA_X;
in_state.viewangles[PITCH] += m_pitch->value * DEALTA_Y;
```

By providing an increment in the X coordinate, we can control the yaw or side angular movement, thus making our character look sideways. An increment in the Y coordinate will result in pitch change or up/down angular movement. As before, m_yaw and m_pitch are two internal constants used to control sensitivity, and viewangles[YAW] and viewangles[PITCH] contain the actual angular values.

> **TIP:** It is up to you as a developer to decide how to control the forward/sideways or yaw/pitch Java and C handlers. For example, dragging a finger on the left half of the screen could trigger the side movement handlers, and dragging on the right half could trigger the look handlers.

Audio Handling

Audio handling in Quake II works the same way as in Chapter 6. In the Java class NativeAudio, declare a native method PaintAudio that receives a ByteBuffer as argument:

```
static native PaintAudio( ByteBuffer buf )
```

The Java ByteBuffer represents an array of audio bytes to be played using Android's MediaTrack API. Listing 7–5 shows the C implementation of this function; it simply gets the memory address of the Java buffer using GetDirectBufferAddress plus its size (with GetDirectBufferCapacity), then it calls the external function paint_audio to fill it up. paint_audio is the same as in Quake I and it is defined in snd_android.c; however, the audio initialization is slightly different.

> **NOTE:** jni_quake.c and snd_android.c can be found on the book source under
> ch07.QuakeII/jni/quake2-3.21/android.

Listing 7–5. *Java/C Audio Handlers*

```c
// jni_quake.c
extern int paint_audio (void *unused, void * stream, int len);

JNIEXPORT jint JNICALL Java_quake_jni_Natives_PaintAudio
 ( JNIEnv* env, jobject thiz, jobject buf )
{
  void *stream;
  int len;

  stream = (*env)->GetDirectBufferAddress(env,  buf);
  len = (*env)->GetDirectBufferCapacity (env, buf);

  paint_audio (NULL, stream, len );
  return 0;
}

// snd_android.c
qboolean SNDDMA_Init(void)
{
  // most of the wav files are 16 bits, 22050 Hz, stereo
  dma.samplebits = 16;
  dma.speed = 22050;
  dma.channels = 2;

  LOGD("SNDDMA_Init Speed %d channels %d", dma.speed, dma.channels);

  dmapos = 0;

  // Sample size
  dma.samples = 32768;
  dma.samplepos = 0;
  dma.submission_chunk = 1;

  dmasize = (dma.samples * (dma.samplebits/8));
  dma.buffer = calloc(1, dmasize);

  snd_inited = 1;
  return 1;
}
```

Audio initialization in Listing 7–5 consists of telling Quake II information about its format, such as:

- Resolution: 16 bit
- Frequency: 22 kHz
- Number of channels: 2 for stereo
- Buffer size

For this purpose, Quake II defines the audio data structure dma as:

```
// snd_loc.h
typedef struct
{
  int      channels;
  int      samples;          // mono samples in buffer
  int      submission_chunk; // don't mix less than this #
  int      samplepos;        // in mono samples
  int      samplebits;
  int      speed;
  byte     *buffer;
} dma_t;

extern  dma_t dma;
```

When Quake II starts, it will call SNDDMA_Init to initialize the audio, and the following sequence of events will take place to quick off the audio playback:

1. When the user starts the game, the Java native method QuakeMain will be invoked, which will translate the array of Java string arguments into a C array and pass them to the Quake II engine.

2. Quake II will start up, process the arguments, and at some point call SNDDMA_Init.

3. Once the audio and video are initialized, the C to Java callback jni_init_video will be called to send a message to the Java wrappers that video is ready. At this point, the Java code will start the audio thread declared in NativeAudio.java by invoking NativeAudio.start().

4. Audio playback will start.

The jni_init_video callback is explained in detail in the section on video handling.

What to Do When Fatal Errors Occur

The user needs to be notified when a fatal error such as a crash or missing resource occurs. For this purpose, we can use JNI to invoke a Java method such as:

OnSysError(final String message)

This method could pop up a dialog box to notify the user of the error, and then terminate the program. Listing 7–6 presents such an implementation.

Listing 7–6. *Handling Fatal Errors*

```
// sys_linux.c
void Sys_Error (char *error, ...)
{
  va_list     argptr;
  char        string[1024];

  CL_Shutdown ();
  Qcommon_Shutdown ();
```

```
    va_start (argptr,error);
    vsprintf (string,error,argptr);
    va_end (argptr);

    jni_sys_error(string);
}

// jni_quake.c
void jni_sys_error(const char * text) {
  JNIEnv *env;

  if ( !g_VM) {
    LOGE("jni_fatal No Java VM available. Aborting\n");
    exit (0);
  }

  (*g_VM)->AttachCurrentThread (g_VM, &env, NULL);

  // need a valid environment and class
  if ( !env || !jNativesCls) {
    return;
  }

  jmethodID mid = (*env)->GetStaticMethodID(env, jNativesCls
    , "OnSysError"
    , "(Ljava/lang/String;)V");

  // invoke Natives.OnSysError(text)
  if (mid) {
      (*env)->CallStaticVoidMethod(env, jNativesCls
          , mid
          , (*env)->NewStringUTF(env, text) );
  }
}
```

Whenever a fatal error occurs, Quake II will call Sys_Error with a description of the error. The client will be shut down and the arguments will be packed into a string and sent to the C to Java callback jni_sys_error:

```
    va_start (argptr,error);
    vsprintf (string,error,argptr);
    va_end (argptr);

    jni_sys_error(string);
```

jni_sys_error will then:

1. Attach to the current thread by calling AttachCurrentThread.

> **NOTE:** C functions that are not invoked from a JNI implementation performing JNI API calls must attach to the current thread by calling: (*g_VM)->AttachCurrentThread (g_VM, &env, NULL).

2. Load the static method OnSysError from the quake.jni.Natives Java class with the signature:

```
(Ljava/lang/String;)V
```

Ljava/lang/String; simply says there is one argument of type java.lang.String. The V tells the return type is of type void. It is critical to get the signature right otherwise GetStaticMethodID won't be able to find the

3. Invoke the method with the string argument. Note that C strings must be converted into Java string using NewStringUTF(env, C_CHAR_ARRAY).

Listing 7–7 shows the error handler in action. The JNI function QuakeMain starts printing the boot-up arguments and calling the engine main function. Quake II then initializes the audio and video, but fails to find a valid game file, so it bails out.

Listing 7–7. *Error Log Showing Missing Game Files*

```
DEBUG/QuakeActivity(841): Display Size:800,480
DEBUG/QuakeView(841): Setting startup args & renderer
INFO/ActivityManager(72): Displayed com.opengl.q2/com.opengl.QuakeActivity: +2s542ms
DEBUG/QuakeView(841): onSurfaceCreated
DEBUG/Q2JNI(841): Q2Main[0]=quake2
DEBUG/Q2JNI(841): Q2Main[1]=+set
DEBUG/Q2JNI(841): Q2Main[2]=basedir
DEBUG/Q2JNI(841): Q2Main[3]=/sdcard/quake2
DEBUG/Q2JNI(841): Q2Main[4]=+set
DEBUG/Q2JNI(841): Q2Main[5]=skill
DEBUG/Q2JNI(841): Q2Main[6]=0
DEBUG/Q2JNI(841): Q2Main[7]=+set
DEBUG/Q2JNI(841): Q2Main[8]=nocdaudio
DEBUG/Q2JNI(841): Q2Main[9]=1
DEBUG/Q2JNI(841): Q2Main[10]=+set
DEBUG/Q2JNI(841): Q2Main[11]=cd_nocd
DEBUG/Q2JNI(841): Q2Main[12]=1
DEBUG/Q2JNI(841): Q2Main[13]=+set
DEBUG/Q2JNI(841): Q2Main[14]=s_initsound
DEBUG/Q2JNI(841): Q2Main[15]=1
DEBUG/Q2JNI(841): Q2Main[16]=+set
DEBUG/Q2JNI(841): Q2Main[17]=vid_ref
DEBUG/Q2JNI(841): Q2Main[18]=glx
DEBUG/Q2JNI(841): Q2Main[19]=+set
DEBUG/Q2JNI(841): Q2Main[20]=gl_mode
DEBUG/Q2JNI(841): Q2Main[21]=4
DEBUG/Q2JNI(841): couldn't exec default.cfg
DEBUG/Q2JNI(841): couldn't exec config.cfg
DEBUG/Q2JNI(841): basedir is write protected.
DEBUG/Q2JNI(841): Console initialized.
DEBUG/Q2JNI(841): ------- sound initialization -------
DEBUG/QSound(841): SNDDMA_Init Speed 22050 channels 2
DEBUG/Q2JNI(841): sound sampling rate: 22050
DEBUG/Q2JNI(841): ------------------------------------
DEBUG/Q2JNI(841): ref_gl version: GL 0.01
DEBUG/Q2JNI(841): SDL audio device shut down.
ERROR/Natives(841): Natives::OnSysError Couldn't load pics/colormap.pcx
ERROR/QuakeView(841): Couldn't load pics/colormap.pcx
```

Sys_Error gets invoked, which in turn calls jni_sys_error, which sends the message back to the Java QuakeView class that terminates the program. Of course, you should pop up a message box to the user telling him about the error before terminating the program.

```
ERROR/Natives(841): Natives::OnSysError Couldn't load pics/colormap.pcx
ERROR/QuakeView(841): Couldn't load pics/colormap.pcx
```

OpenGL Immediate Mode Issues

Before we start digging into the video handlers, I'd like to stress the tremendous amount of work saved in this project by reusing NanoGL to deal with the immediate mode headaches of OpenGL. As shown at the beginning of this chapter, Quake II's OpenGL renderer is about 11,000 lines of very difficult C code. All this code would have been translated into OpenGL ES and taken months of pro bono work by a team of many developers. Now all that work is reduced to a few weekend hours by one dude. Keep this wonderful software tool in mind when you decide to bring other projects to your mobile device, as NanoGL can be reused without change by any mobile program.

Video Handlers

Video handlers are probably the most laborious part of this project. Any Quake II video handler must implement six handler functions. Of the lot, only the following three will require actual implementations, the rest will be just empty declarations:

- GLimp_Init(void *hinstance, void *hWnd): This function is used to initialize the OpenGL renderer. The arguments hinstance and hWnd are Windows-only variables and do not apply in the Android/Linux world.

- GLimp_SetMode(int *pwidth, int *pheight, int mode, qboolean fullscreen): This function is used to set the video mode of the game, including the width and, height of the screen. The argument fullscreen does not apply in our case.

- GLimp_EndFrame (): This function gets called after the rendering of each frame completes. It is meant to tell the OpenGL ES pipeline it is time to draw.

The following video functions are called from various points of the drawing cycle and must be declared, but don't apply to our project, thus will be empty:

- GLimp_Shutdown( ): Called when the OpenGL renderer is shut down. It can fire many times during the life cycle of the game.

- GLimp_BeginFrame(float camera_separation): Called before each frame of the game is drawn.

- GLimp_AppActivate(qboolean active): Called once when the application is activated.

Video Initialization

During video initialization, we load the NanoGL handlers and tell the engine the renderer is ready to perform OpenGL calls, as shown in Listing 7–8.

Listing 7–8. *Video Initialization*

```
// gl_glx.c
static qboolean gl_initialized = false;

int GLimp_Init( void *hinstance, void *wndproc )
{
  if ( ! gl_initialized ) {
    //  init NanoGL
    if ( ! nanoGL_Init() ) {
      return false;
    }
    gl_initialized = true;
  }
  return true;
}
```

Because Quake II allows switching screen resolutions and renderers on the fly, GLimp_Init may fire more than once during the game life cycle; thus we must make sure initialization occurs only once.

Setting the Video Mode and Size

The Quake II OpenGL renderer video resolution is calculated from the command line by sending the arguments:

```
+ set gl_mode MODE_NUMBER
```

Where MODE-NUMBER maps to an array of screen resolutions (see Listing 7–9). For example, gl_mode 3 tells the engine to use a 569 × 320 video resolution. If the video mode is not specified at startup, the default value is 3.

Listing 7–9. *Setting the Video Mode*

```
// vid_so.c
typedef struct vidmode_s
{
  const char *description;
  int        width, height;
  int        mode;
} vidmode_t;

vidmode_t vid_modes[] =
{
#ifdef ANDROID
  { "Mode 0: 256x256",    256, 256,   0 },
  { "Mode 1: 320x320",    320, 320,   1 },
  { "Mode 2: 480x320",    480, 320,   2 },
  { "Mode 3: 569x320",    569, 320,   3 },
```

```
    { "Mode 4: 800x480",    800, 480,    4 },
#else
   ...
#endif
};

// gl_glx.c
int GLimp_SetMode( int *pwidth, int *pheight, int mode, qboolean fullscreen )
{

  if ( !ri.Vid_GetModeInfo( &width, &height, mode ) )
  {
    ri.Con_Printf( PRINT_ALL, " invalid mode\n" );
    return rserr_invalid_mode;
  }

  ri.Con_Printf( PRINT_ALL, " %d %d\n", width, height );

  *pwidth = width;
  *pheight = height;

  // let the sound and input subsystems know about the new window
  ri.Vid_NewWindow (width, height);

  return rserr_ok;
}

// vid_so.c
qboolean VID_GetModeInfo( int *width, int *height, int mode )
{
  if ( mode < 0 || mode >= VID_NUM_MODES )
    return false;

  *width  = vid_modes[mode].width;
  *height = vid_modes[mode].height;

  return true;
}

/**
* VID_NewWindow
*/
void VID_NewWindow ( int width, int height)
{
  viddef.width  = width;
  viddef.height = height;

  //tell java  about it
  jni_init_video (width, height);
}
```

For Android, we have defined a set of resolutions that include all possible sizes for the different types of Android devices out there:

```
#ifdef ANDROID
    { "Mode 0: 256x256",    256, 256,    0 },
    { "Mode 1: 320x320",    320, 320,    1 },
    { "Mode 2: 480x320",    480, 320,    2 },
```

```
{ "Mode 3: 569x320",   569, 320,   3 },
{ "Mode 4: 800x480",   800, 480,   4 },
...
#endif
```

When the Quake II engine starts up, GLimp_SetMode will be invoked. Here, we must get the screen resolution by calling

```
ri.Vid_GetModeInfo( &width, &height, mode )
```

where width and height are references that will store the size of the screen, and mode is the gl_mode argument sent in the command line. Note that ri.Vid_GetModeInfo is nothing more than a function pointer that references the real Vid_GetModeInfo function declared in vid_so.c:

```
ri.Vid_GetModeInfo = Vid_GetModeInfo
```

This is done because, as we mentioned at the beginning of the chapter, Quake II has been greatly modularized, and in the default configuration—where the client, game, and renderer are compiled in separate libraries—functions can be called across libraries. This makes the code very complex, but the benefits are well worth it: very easy to maintain and enhance. Vid_GetModeInfo simply uses the value of mode to look up the video modes table (vid_modes) and obtain the size of the screen:

```
*width  = vid_modes[mode].width;
*height = vid_modes[mode].height;
```

Once the screen size is received, GLimp_SetMode sends the information back to the parent and tells the other subsystems that a new window has been created:

```
*pwidth = width;
*pheight = height;
// let the sound and input subsystems know about the new window
ri.Vid_NewWindow (width, height);
```

In Android, VID_NewWindow, will update the video definition with the screen values and call the C to Java callback jni_init_video:

```
viddef.width  = width;
viddef.height = height;

//tell java  about it
jni_init_video (width, height);
```

jni_init_video will, in turn, invoke the Java static method OnInitVideo declared in quake.jni.Natives.java with the width and height of the screen:

```
// jni_quake.c
  jmethodID mid = (*env)->GetStaticMethodID(env, jNativesCls
      , "OnInitVideo"
      , "(II)V");

  if (mid) {
      (*env)->CallStaticVoidMethod(env, jNativesCls, mid, width, height);
  }
```

Note that the jni_init_video implementation is the same as Quake I in Chapter 6. Finally, OnInitVideo will call the listener OnInitVideo (QuakeView in this case), which will start the Java audio thread and start audio playback. Thus, the video initialization call stack can be summarized as follows:

- GLimp_SetMode (width, height, mode) – C

- Vid_GetModeInfo (width, height, mode) – C

- Vid_NewWindow (width, height) -C

- jni_init_video (width, height) – C/JNI

- OnInitVideo (width, height) – Java

- QuakeView (width, height) – Java

- NativeAudio.start() – Java

What to Do When the Rendering Completes

This is the last step in the rendering cycle. GLimp_EndFrame will fire after each frame of the game is rendered. Here we issue a qglFlush call, which causes all issued OpenGL commands to be executed as quickly as they are accepted by the actual rendering pipeline:

```
// gl_glx.c
void GLimp_EndFrame (void)
{
  qglFlush();
}
```

Now we are ready to build the engine and start laying Quake II in our mobile device.

Building Quake II with the NDK

The final step is to get the native code compiled into libquake2.so before we can start testing in our device. In the project source (under ch07.QuakeII/jni), we have three files that drive the compilation process: Application.mk, Android.mk, and hardlinkedq2gl.mk. Application.mk defines what modules are to be compiled. In our case, quake2 (as libquake2.so), and NanoGL (from Chapter 6), which will be compiled as a static library and embedded within libquake2.so:

```
# Application.mk
APP_BUILD_SCRIPT := $(call my-dir)/Android.mk
APP_MODULES      := quake2 NanoGL
```

Android.mk simply includes the real compilation script hardlinkedq2gl.mk. This is done because of a really annoying Android peculiarity: if you need to update the compilation script Android.mk (if you missed a compiler option, for example), then the compilation process will start from the beginning all over again. This can drive you crazy when you try to compile libraries with dozens and dozens of source files—especially in slow systems.

```
# Android.mk
include $(call my-dir)/hardlinkedq2gl.mk
```

> **TIP:** By including another script within Android.mk, the compilation process will resume from the last file whenever updates are performed to the included script.

In hardlinkedq2gl.mk, we build NanoGL as a static library first. Note that the source code lives in Chapter 6.

```
# hardlinkedq2gl.mk
LOCAL_PATH := $(call my-dir)

include $(CLEAR_VARS)

DIR:= ../../ch06.Quake/jni/Quake/NanoGL

LOCAL_MODULE     := NanoGL
LOCAL_C_INCLUDES := ../ch06.Quake/jni/Quake/NanoGL/GL
LOCAL_SRC_FILES := $(DIR)/eglwrap.cpp $(DIR)/nanogl.cpp \
        $(DIR)/nanoWrap.cpp

include $(BUILD_STATIC_LIBRARY)
```

Next, we build Quake II as a shared library (libquake2.so, see Listing 7–10). Note the following compiler options:

- -DANDROID: It tells the compiler to use the custom Android code declared throughout the engine.

- -DGLQUAKE: It tells the compiler to build the OpenGL renderer

- -DLIBQUAKE2: It tells the compiler to use custom Quake II code.

- -Dstricmp=strcasecmp: It replaces all occurrences of stricmp with strcasecmp for string comparison. Some Linux C-library implementations don't include stricmp.

- -DREF_HARD_LINKED: This is a critical option. It tells the compiler to pack the renderer and client modules as a single monolithic file. This makes the build/debug/run process much simpler in mobile platforms.

- -DGAME_HARD_LINKED: Another critical option. It tells the compiler to include the game module in the pack.

Listing 7–10. *Quake II Android Compilation Script*

```
# hardlinkedq2gl.mk
BUILDDIR:=quake2-3.21

include $(CLEAR_VARS)

LOCAL_MODULE := quake2

COMMON_CFLAGS :=-DANDROID -DGLQUAKE -DLIBQUAKE2 -Dstricmp=strcasecmp
```

```
LOCAL_CFLAGS := $(COMMON_CFLAGS) -DREF_HARD_LINKED -DGAME_HARD_LINKED
LOCAL_C_INCLUDES := $(COMMON_C_INCLUDES) ../ch06.Quake/jni/Quake/NanoGL
LOCAL_LDLIBS := -llog -ldl
LOCAL_STATIC_LIBRARIES := libNanoGL

# Q2 client
QUAKE2_OBJS := \
  $(BUILDDIR)/client/cl_cin.c \
  $(BUILDDIR)/client/cl_ents.c \
  $(BUILDDIR)/client/cl_fx.c \
  $(BUILDDIR)/client/cl_input.c \
  $(BUILDDIR)/android/vid_so.c \

  ....
  $(BUILDDIR)/android/sys_linux.c \

# Game
CGAME_SRC := \
  $(BUILDDIR)/game/q_shared.c \
  $(BUILDDIR)/game/g_ai.c \
  $(BUILDDIR)/game/p_client.c \

  ...
  $(BUILDDIR)/game/p_trail.c \
  $(BUILDDIR)/game/p_view.c \
  $(BUILDDIR)/game/p_weapon.c \

# OpenGL renderer
REF_FILES := \
  $(BUILDDIR)/ref_gl/gl_draw.c \
  $(BUILDDIR)/ref_gl/gl_image.c \
  $(BUILDDIR)/ref_gl/gl_light.c \
  $(BUILDDIR)/ref_gl/gl_mesh.c \
  $(BUILDDIR)/ref_gl/gl_model.c \
  $(BUILDDIR)/ref_gl/gl_rmain.c \
  $(BUILDDIR)/ref_gl/gl_rmisc.c \
  $(BUILDDIR)/ref_gl/gl_rsurf.c \
  $(BUILDDIR)/ref_gl/gl_warp.c \
  $(BUILDDIR)/linux/qgl_linux.c \
  $(BUILDDIR)/android/gl_glx.c \

LOCAL_SRC_FILES := $(QUAKE2_OBJS) $(CGAME_SRC) $(REF_FILES)

include $(BUILD_SHARED_LIBRARY)
```

To run the compilation process in Windows using Cygwin, start the Cygwin console, change to the folder containing the chapter source (see Figure 7–1), and invoke the Android build script ndk-build:

```
$ cd ch07.QuakeII
$ ndk-build
```

```
/cygdrive/c/temp/Docs/Workspace/ch07.QuakeII

Administrator@jonathanlaptop /cygdrive/c/temp/Docs/Workspace/ch07.QuakeII
$ ndk-build
Compile thumb  : quake2 <= cl_cin.c
Compile thumb  : quake2 <= cl_ents.c
Compile thumb  : quake2 <= cl_fx.c
Compile thumb  : quake2 <= cl_input.c
Compile thumb  : quake2 <= cl_inv.c
Compile thumb  : quake2 <= cl_main.c
Compile thumb  : quake2 <= cl_newfx.c
Compile thumb  : quake2 <= cl_parse.c
Compile thumb  : quake2 <= cl_pred.c
Compile thumb  : quake2 <= cl_tent.c
Compile thumb  : quake2 <= cl_scrn.c
Compile thumb  : quake2 <= cl_view.c
Compile thumb  : quake2 <= console.c
Compile thumb  : quake2 <= keys.c
Compile thumb  : quake2 <= menu.c
Compile thumb  : quake2 <= snd_dma.c
Compile thumb  : quake2 <= snd_mem.c
Compile thumb  : quake2 <= snd_mix.c
Compile thumb  : quake2 <= qmenu.c
Compile thumb  : quake2 <= m_flash.c
Compile thumb  : quake2 <= cmd.c
Compile thumb  : quake2 <= cmodel.c
Compile thumb  : quake2 <= common.c
Compile thumb  : quake2 <= crc.c
Compile thumb  : quake2 <= cvar.c
Compile thumb  : quake2 <= files.c
Compile thumb  : quake2 <= md4.c
Compile thumb  : quake2 <= net_chan.c
Compile thumb  : quake2 <= sv_ccmds.c
Compile thumb  : quake2 <= sv_ents.c
Compile thumb  : quake2 <= sv_game.c
Compile thumb  : quake2 <= sv_init.c
Compile thumb  : quake2 <= sv_main.c
Compile thumb  : quake2 <= sv_send.c
Compile thumb  : quake2 <= sv_user.c
Compile thumb  : quake2 <= sv_world.c
Compile thumb  : quake2 <= cd_linux.c
Compile thumb  : quake2 <= q_shlinux.c
Compile thumb  : quake2 <= vid_menu.c
Compile thumb  : quake2 <= glob.c
Compile thumb  : quake2 <= net_udp.c
Compile thumb  : quake2 <= pmove.c
Compile thumb  : quake2 <= jni_quake.c
Compile thumb  : quake2 <= snd_android.c
Compile thumb  : quake2 <= vid_so.c
Compile thumb  : quake2 <= gl_rmisc.c
Compile thumb  : quake2 <= gl_rsurf.c
Compile thumb  : quake2 <= gl_warp.c
Compile thumb  : quake2 <= qgl_linux.c
Compile thumb  : quake2 <= gl_glx.c
StaticLibrary  : libstdc++.a
StaticLibrary  : libNanoGL.a
SharedLibrary  : libquake2.so
Install        : libquake2.so => libs/armeabi/libquake2.so

Administrator@jonathanlaptop /cygdrive/c/temp/Docs/Workspace/ch07.QuakeII
$ _
```

Figure 7–1. *Compiling Quake II with the NDK*

The native library `libquake2.so` will be created under the Java project `ch07.QuakeII/libs/armeabi/libquake2.so`. Thus when the Java app starts, the `QuakeView` class will invoke

```
System.load("quake2")
```

This will load the native library and provide access to the JNI methods and the C to Java callbacks used by the Java code. Now let's play some Quake II.

Running on the Device or Emulator

With the native library compiled and ready for use, we can now run the game in the emulator; but first, connect your device/tablet or run an emulator, then create a run configuration in Eclipse, as shown in Figure 7–2.

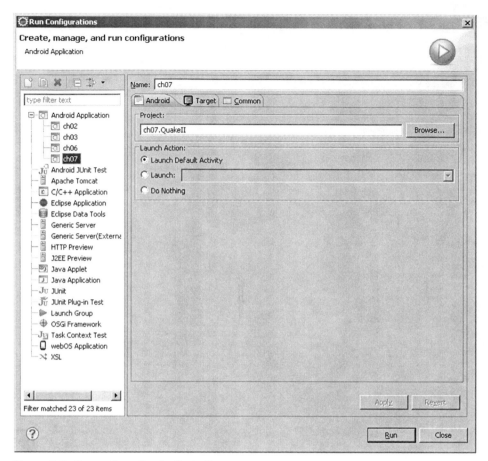

Figure 7–2. *Run configuration for Quake II*

Before running the game, make sure you put the Quake II game files in your device SDCard under

```
/sdcard/quake2/baseq2
```

Run the game and look at the Android log carefully. It should look something like Listing 7–11.

Listing 7–11. *Quake II Run Log File*

```
DEBUG/QuakeActivity(569): Display Size:800,480
DEBUG/QuakeView(569): Setting startup args & renderer
INFO/ActivityManager(72): Displayed com.opengl.q2/com.opengl.QuakeActivity: +3s469ms
DEBUG/QuakeView(569): onSurfaceCreated
DEBUG/Q2JNI(569): Q2Main[0]=quake2
DEBUG/Q2JNI(569): Q2Main[1]=+set
DEBUG/Q2JNI(569): Q2Main[2]=basedir
DEBUG/Q2JNI(569): Q2Main[3]=/sdcard/quake2
DEBUG/Q2JNI(569): Q2Main[4]=+set
DEBUG/Q2JNI(569): Q2Main[5]=skill
DEBUG/Q2JNI(569): Q2Main[6]=0
```

```
DEBUG/Q2JNI(569): Q2Main[7]=+set
DEBUG/Q2JNI(569): Q2Main[8]=nocdaudio
DEBUG/Q2JNI(569): Q2Main[9]=1
DEBUG/Q2JNI(569): Q2Main[10]=+set
DEBUG/Q2JNI(569): Q2Main[11]=cd_nocd
DEBUG/Q2JNI(569): Q2Main[12]=1
DEBUG/Q2JNI(569): Q2Main[13]=+set
DEBUG/Q2JNI(569): Q2Main[14]=s_initsound
DEBUG/Q2JNI(569): Q2Main[15]=1
DEBUG/Q2JNI(569): Q2Main[16]=+set
DEBUG/Q2JNI(569): Q2Main[17]=vid_ref
DEBUG/Q2JNI(569): Q2Main[18]=glx
DEBUG/Q2JNI(569): Q2Main[19]=+set
DEBUG/Q2JNI(569): Q2Main[20]=gl_mode
DEBUG/Q2JNI(569): Q2Main[21]=4
DEBUG/Q2JNI(569): Added packfile /sdcard/quake2/baseq2/pak0.pak (1106 files)
DEBUG/Q2JNI(569): execing default.cfg
DEBUG/Q2JNI(569): couldn't exec config.cfg
DEBUG/Q2JNI(569): basedir is write protected.
DEBUG/Q2JNI(569): Console initialized.
DEBUG/Q2JNI(569): ------- sound initialization -------
DEBUG/QSound(569): SNDDMA_Init Speed 22050 channels 2
DEBUG/Q2JNI(569): sound sampling rate: 22050
DEBUG/Q2JNI(569): ------------------------------------
DEBUG/Q2JNI(569): ref_gl version: GL 0.01
DEBUG/Q2JNI(569): QGL_Init:
INFO/nanoGL(569): nanoGL: Init loading driver libGLESv1_CM.so
WARN/nanoGL(569): <eglChooseConfig> not found in libGLESv1_CM.so. Trying libEGL.so.
WARN/nanoGL(569): <eglCopyBuffers> not found in libGLESv1_CM.so. Trying libEGL.so.
WARN/nanoGL(569): <eglCreateContext> not found in libGLESv1_CM.so. Trying libEGL.so.
WARN/nanoGL(569): <eglCreatePbufferSurface> not found in libGLESv1_CM.so. Trying
libEGL.so.
…
WARN/nanoGL(569): <eglBindTexImage> not found in libGLESv1_CM.so. Trying libEGL.so.
WARN/nanoGL(569): <eglReleaseTexImage> not found in libGLESv1_CM.so. Trying libEGL.so.
WARN/nanoGL(569): <eglSurfaceAttrib> not found in libGLESv1_CM.so. Trying libEGL.so.
DEBUG/Q2JNI(569): Initializing OpenGL display
DEBUG/Q2JNI(569): ...setting fullscreen mode 4:
DEBUG/Q2JNI(569):   800 480
DEBUG/QuakeView(569): OnInitVideo. 800x480 Starting native audio.
DEBUG/Q2JNI(569): GL_VENDOR: Google Inc
DEBUG/Q2JNI(569): GL_RENDERER: Android Pixel Flinger 1.0
DEBUG/Q2JNI(569): GL_VERSION: OpenGL ES-CM 1.0
DEBUG/Q2JNI(569): ...disabling CDS
DEBUG/Q2JNI(569): ...GL_EXT_compiled_vertex_array not found
DEBUG/Q2JNI(569): ...GL_EXT_point_parameters not found
DEBUG/Q2JNI(569): ...GL_EXT_shared_texture_palette not found
DEBUG/Q2JNI(569): ...GL_ARB_multitexture not found
DEBUG/Q2JNI(569): ...GL_SGIS_multitexture not found
DEBUG/Audio(569): Audio start.
DEBUG/Q2JNI(569): ------------------------------------
DEBUG/Q2JNI(569): ------- Server Initialization -------
DEBUG/Q2JNI(569): 0 entities inhibited
DEBUG/Q2JNI(569): 0 teams with 0 entities
DEBUG/Q2JNI(569): ------------------------------------
DEBUG/Q2JNI(569): ====== Quake2 Initialized ======
DEBUG/QuakeView(569): onSurfaceChanged w=800 h=404
```

```
DEBUG/Q2JNI(569): 0.0.0.0:0: client_connect
DEBUG/Q2JNI(569): -----------------------------------
DEBUG/Q2JNI(569): Installation
DEBUG/Q2JNI(569): Map: demo2
DEBUG/Q2JNI(569): pics
DEBUG/Q2JNI(569): maps/demo2.bsp
DEBUG/Q2JNI(569): models/weapons/v_blast/tris.md2
DEBUG/Q2JNI(569): models/objects/gibs/sm_meat/tris.md2
DEBUG/Q2JNI(569): models/objects/gibs/arm/tris.md2
DEBUG/Q2JNI(569): models/objects/debris3/tris.md2
DEBUG/Q2JNI(569): models/objects/barrels/tris.md2
DEBUG/Q2JNI(569): models/monsters/tank/tris.md2
DEBUG/Q2JNI(569): models/weapons/v_shotg/tris.md2
DEBUG/Q2JNI(569): images
```

As soon as the game starts up, you should be able to the game in action (see Figure 7–3).

Figure 7–3. *Quake II running at a 800 × 480 pixel resolution*

If any errors occur, they will be displayed in the Eclipse Android log view. Take a look at the "What to Do When Fatal Errors Occur" section for details.

Quake II Performance on Multiple Devices

To bring the proceedings to a close, I have created a little performance test of the Quake II engine in multiple generation devices (see Figure 7–4).

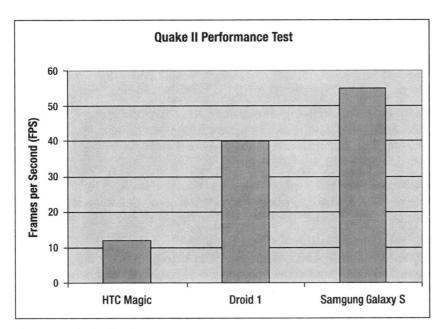

Figure 7–4. *Quake II performance test*

I have used three different devices for this test:

■ *HTC Magic*: This is a first-generation device with a 480 MHz processor, 150 MB of RAM, and 8 GB SDCard, and a Qualcomm GPU.

■ *Motorola Droid 1*: The quintessential Android device from Motorola, with a 600 MHz processor, 250 MB of RAM, 16 GB of SDCard, and the superb PowerVR GPU.

■ Samsung Galaxy S: A powerful, third-generation device from Samsung. It has a powerful 1 GHz processor, 250 MB of RAM, plenty of SDCard space, and a very powerful GPU.

The graph in Figure 7–4 shows the number of frames per second (FPS) of the game using the OpenGL renderer running on each device. As we can see, first-generation devices such as the HTC Magic (at 12 FPS) are simply not capable of running a powerful sucker like Quake II. The Motorola Droid 1, on the other hand, is more than capable of running the game at around 40 FPS. I am pretty sure this is possible thanks to the amazing PowerVR GPU that's inside—same as the iPhone. Finally, the Samsung Galaxy S, a really powerful device, blasts at around 55 FPS. This test clearly shows that Quake II performs astonishingly in second-generation or later Androids.

Summary

This is it. You have learned how engines such as Quake I, II, and Doom can be brought to your smartphone in record time by making use of the best that Android can offer:

- *Code reusability*: By combing the raw power of C/C++ with the elegant object-oriented features of Java, you can have your games up and running in no time. This is particularly useful if you are building for other platforms, such as iOS, RIM, or Palm.

- *JNI*: The Java Native Interface is what makes all of this possible. It let's you break free of the memory and performance constraints of the Java language, thus reducing development time and costs.

- *Powerful APIS for game development*: This includes hardware-accelerated graphics with OpenGL, audio handling independent of the format, keyboard handling, and single/multi-touch capabilities; plus Bluetooth for external controller support.

My goal in this book has been to show you that even though Java is the primary development language for Android, hybrid Java/C development is the only way to develop powerful games. I have done this by featuring three powerful engines that can be run in a mobile device: Doom and Quake I and II.

The Green Robot has taken off with a vengeance, and I hope my book is just what you need to quickly get up and running to build cutting-edge games. To all Android developers out there, the future of the platform is in your hands.

Deployment and Compilation Tips

In this appendix, we explore tips to deploy your application, compilation tips, and other time-saving goodies. Specifically, this appendix includes tips for the following:

- Signing your application manually. This is helpful if you use an automated build system to build and sign your apps. Keep in mind that applications must be signed before they can be distributed.

- Creating a key store for signature of your application package. This is required to sign your app either manually or using the workbench.

- Signing your application using the workbench. This will show you how to sign your app visually.

- A JNI cheat sheet for the most important tips you should remember when building hybrid games that use both Java and C/C++.

Let's get started!

Signing Your Application

Before your application can be installed in any Android device, it must be signed using a Java key store. This section describes the steps you must follow to accomplish this task. You can find more details in the Android Developer's Guide.

> **NOTE:** Android developers, more information about signing your applications is available at
> http://developer.android.com/guide/publishing/app-signing.html#setup.

Creating a Key Store

A key store is a password-protected file that contains public/private key pairs used for JAR signatures. You can create a key store with the following command:

```
$ keytool -genkey -v -keystore my-release-key.keystore -alias alias_name -keyalg RSA
  -validity 10000 -storepass <password1> -keypass <password2>
```

Table A–1 lists the possible arguments for the keytool command.

Table A–1. *Arguments for the keytool Command*

Argument	Description
-genkey	Generate a public and private key pair.
-v	Use verbose output.
-keystore	Specify the name of the key store.
-alias <alias_name>	Add an alias for the key pair.
-validity <valdays>	Specify the validity period in days.
-storepass <password>	Add a password for the key store.
-keypass <password>	Add a password for the key.

> **TIP:** When you run your applications in the emulator, the Eclipse workbench automatically signs the application using a debug key store. This key store can be found in %USERPROFILE%\debug.keystore (in Windows) and $HOME/.android/debug.keystore (in Linux). The debug key store password is "android", and the key alias and password are androiddebugkey/android.

Signing the Application

You have two choices when signing your application: manually using the Java SDK jarsigner command or visually using the Eclipse IDE.

> **NOTE:** Sometimes it may de desirable to sign your app manually, especially if you have an automated build system with no human interaction. Listing A–1 shows the batch commands required to sign your app manually.

Listing A–1. *Windows Batch Script to Sign the Wolf3D Application Package (APK)*

```
@echo off
set JAVA_HOME=c:\Program Files\Java\jdk1.6.0_07
set PKG=c:\tmp\APK\Wolf3D.apk

rem To sign
"%JAVA_HOME%\bin\jarsigner" -verbose -keystore ar-release-key.keystore %PKG%
android_radio

rem To verify that your .apk is signed, you can use a command like this
"%JAVA_HOME%\bin\jarsigner" -verbose -verify %PKG%
```

Listing A–1 uses the Java SDK jarsigner command and the key store created in the previous section to sign the packed application as follows:

```
jarsigner -verbose -keystore ar-release-key.keystore Wolfd3D.apk android_radio
```

The arguments are as follows:

- verbose displays information about the files being signed.

- keystore defines the location of the Java key store created in the previous section.

- Wolfd3D.apk is the application package to sign.

- android_radio is the alias that represents the public/private key pair used for signature.

> **CAUTION:** The keytool and jarsigner commands are part of the Java SDK, not the JRE. You will have to install a Java SDK and set up the paths in your system to be able to create a key store and sign your applications with jarsigner.

With the Android SDK 1.5 or later, signing your package is much easier, provided you already have a key store; you don't need the jarsigner command in this instance. To sign your package with the Eclipse workbench, follow these steps:

1. Right-click the project to be signed and select Android **Tools** ➤ **Export Signed Application Package** (see Figure A–1).

2. In the "Keystore selection" dialog shown in Figure A–2, select "Use existing keystore," and navigate to the key store created previously. Type the password for the key store.

3. Select the alias that represents the key pair to be used for signature and enter the corresponding password (see Figure A–3).

4. Enter the destination of the package, as shown in Figure A–4. Click Finish.

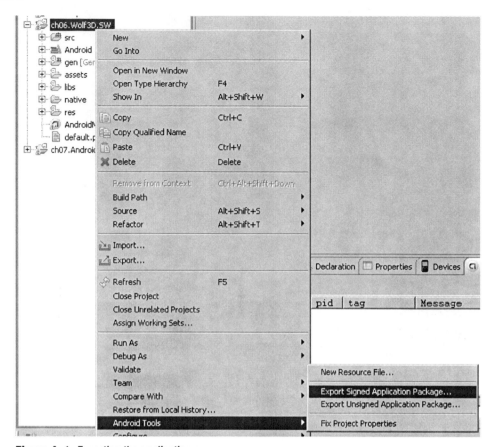

Figure A–1. *Exporting the application menu*

Figure A–2. *The "Keystore selection" dialog*

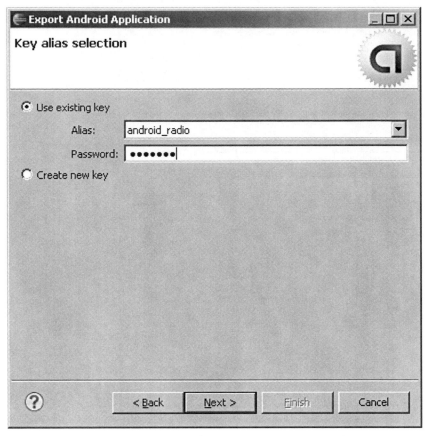

Figure A–3. *The "Key alias selection" dialog*

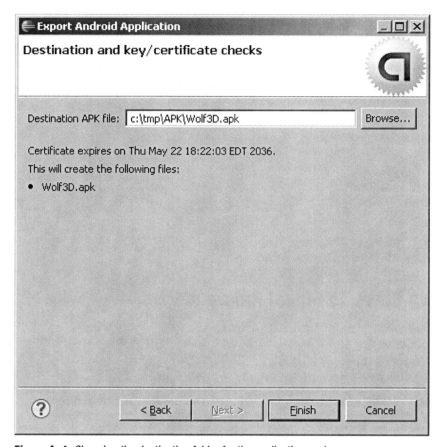

Figure A–4. *Choosing the destination folder for the application package*

JNI Cheat Sheet

Here you'll find a very helpful JNI cheat sheet that you can use when working on any type of JNI/C–related project. This section is divided in two basic communication pipelines:

■ *Native calls within Java code*: These are used to invoke any C function within Java code.

■ *C to Java callbacks*: These are useful to tell Java about events that occur on the native side, such as audio/video initialization, and so forth.

JNI Method Syntax

When implementing native methods, the syntax on the C implementation must be

```
JNIEXPORT <RETURNTYPE> JNICALL Java_<PACKAGE>_<CLASS>_<METHOD>
  (JNIEnv * env, jclass cls, <ARGUMENTS>)
```

Note that any periods used in the Java names must be replaced with underscore characters. Thus the Java native method:

```
package native;
class Natives {
  public static native void GameMain(String[] args);
}
```

must be declared in C as:

```
JNIEXPORT void JNICALL Java_native_Natives_GameMain
  (JNIEnv * env, jclass cls, jobjectArray jargv)
```

Loading a Java Class as Global Reference

If you must keep a reference to a Java class (to invoke callbacks when certain events occur, for example), always use a global reference, as follows:

```
jclass clazz    = (*env)->FindClass(env, "quake/jni/Natives");
jclass globalCls = (jclass)(*env)->NewGlobalRef(env, clazz);
```

Here we have loaded the Java class quake.jni.Natives and created a global reference for it. This reference can be used anywhere to invoke C to Java callbacks. You must use a global reference to prevent the JVM garbage collector from removing the class from memory. The fact is that we do not know at which point the JVM will decide to get rid of the class. This is why you need a global reference.

Converting a Java Array to a C array

This can be really helpful if you are sending startup arguments to the native side. Java string arrays cannot simply be used within C, they must be converted. For example:

■ To get the length of the Java array jarray:

```
(*env)->GetArrayLength(env, jarray);
```

■ To extract a Java string from the Java array jarray at position i:

```
jstring jrow = (jstring)(*env)->GetObjectArrayElement(env, jarray, i);
```

■ To convert the string jrow into a C string:

```
const char *row  = (*env)->GetStringUTFChars(env, jrow, 0);
```

Invoking Java Within C (Callbacks)

Callbacks are usually invoked from a different place than JNI functions (a game loop running in a separate thread, for example). Therefore, it is imperative that you attach to the current thread before doing any JNI API calls (if you don't, terrible things will happen).

```
(*g_VM)->AttachCurrentThread (g_VM, &env, NULL)
```

- To load the Java static method OnInitVideo, which has two integer arguments, width and height:

```
jmethodID mid = (*env)->GetStaticMethodID(env, jNativesCls, "OnInitVideo", "(II)V");
```

- To invoke the previous method using the global reference to the class previously loaded with two arguments:

```
(*env)->CallStaticVoidMethod(env, jNativesCls, mid, width, height);
```

Final Thoughts

I hope that you have enjoyed *Pro Android 4 Games*. I wrote this book to show you the things that can be done with Java and C, two powerful languages. I have shown how one person can bring a complex PC game to Android with little effort in record time using these two great languages. I'd like to finish up with the things I liked and disliked about writing software for Android as opposed to other mobile platforms, such as the iPhone OS. You may not agree with my statements, but they could be useful in your game development endeavors.

The following are the limitations in Android that I have come across while writing the games for this book:

- *Lack of an open audio library*: I consider this to be a serious limitation. Audio is critical in gaming, and most vendors nowadays try to use open APIs such Open Audio Library (AL) or the standard Linux sound devices. Up to version 2.0, Android used the SoniVox Enhanced Audio System (EAS). Although I am happy to report that in version 3 and later, Android supports the Open Audio Library (Open AL) capable of handling audio independent of the format.

- *Lack of streaming audio*: This is another serious issue. I found the lack of streaming audio to be the most frustrating thing about Android. I don't mind learning the EAS audio API, but the darn thing doesn't even support audio streaming. Audio streaming is critical and used extensively by Wolfenstein 3D and Doom in Chapters 6 and 7. To overcome this shortcoming, I was forced to cascade audio events to the Java layers, put the soundtracks in external files, and have the MediaPlayer handle them. In Android, you are boxed in by the MediaPlayer. Although with the SDK 1.5 or later, Google has added support for basic audio streaming with the class AudioTrack (which I found to be poorly documented); plus I have heard that Google is planning support for OpenAL (audio library)—this would be a good move. Low-level audio and video streaming is now available in Android 4 (Ice Cream Sandwich). See the Developer's Guide at `http://developer.android.com/sdk/android-4.0-highlights.html#DeveloperApis` for more information.

- *Not the best support for native development out there*: Nevertheless, I am happy to see that Google has realized that critical native development support for Android is essential for it to become a competitor in the mobile gaming arena. With the release of the Android NDK 1.6, things have improved greatly, but Android still lags behind the iPhone OS in this field.

- *Fragmented OpenGL ES 1.x/2.0 implementation*: As of SDK version 1.5, the Android implemented OpenGL ES 1.x. The iPhone OS has supported OpenGL ES 2.0 for a long time. I am happy to report that in versions 2.0 and later, Android fully implements OpenGL ES 2.0 for graphics acceleration. OpenGL ES 2.0 is not supported in all versions, however, creating fragmentation at the hardware level.

On the other hand, Android has some great features that make it a serious contender as a mobile development platform:

- *Open source*: An army of developers is out there ready to build code for this open platform, and new devices are popping up all the time.

- *Built on Linux*: I love Linux and I am always ready to support development in this beautiful OS. It is a masterpiece of software engineering.

- *Multitasking*: Whether multitasking is an advantage is in the eye of the beholder; so I am not sure where to put this one. There are those who say that multitasking is great for social networking applications because you can have multiple background processes feeding you information; but detractors claim that it hogs the CPU resources and diminishes battery life. I have to go with the detractors on this one.

- *Support for input from mice, joysticks, and gamepads*: Support for tablets is added in Android 3.1; for phones in 4.0.

All in all, with the release of the NDK, Android may become a serious contender with the iPhone OS for gaming. Android has a way to go to catch up, but the platform development seems to run at a tremendous pace. Android vs. the iPhone OS—I can't wait to see who wins. At the moment, my heart is with Android.

Index

■A

Aim control, 219
AL (Audio Library), 269
Android activity, 21, 43–44, 46, 64, 81
Android class, 48
Android interface, 131
Android method, 141
Android toolbar, 11
Android Virtual Devices (AVDs), 10–14,
    16
APK (Application Package), 263
applications
    architecture of, 23–34
        main activity file, 25–26
        native interface, 26–27
        native library, 27–34
    signing, 261–263
        key store, 262
        manually or visually, 262–263
    testing on device, 35–37
architecture, game
    for Doom, 151
    for Quake, 202–216
        game startup activity, 214–216
        handling audio independently of
            format, 207–210
        handling keyboard events,
            210–212
        handling touch events, 212–214
        Java OpenGL renderer
            architecture, 202–207
attaching, to shaders, 119
audio, handling, 38–43
    for Doom, 164–165
    for Quake, 207–210
Audio Library (AL), 269

AudioManager class, 161, 164
AVDs (Android Virtual Devices), 10–14,
    16

■B

Bluetooth controllers, Zeemote joystick,
    53–58
BluetoothAdapter.getDefaultAdapter( )
    method, 58

■C

C arrays
    converting Java arrays to, 268
    converting Java string arrays into, 32
C/C++ event handling, Java wrappers
        for, 38–48
    cascading video events, 43–48
    handling audio, 38–43
C language
    defining variable-arguments
        functions in, 33–34
    invoking Java language within, 269
C to Java callbacks, for Doom, 167,
        174–180
    fatal errors, 180
    graphics initialization, 174–175
    sound and music callbacks,
        176–177
    video buffer callback, 176
Call method, 29
callback listener, for Doom, 165–166
callbacks, 269
cascading video events, 43–48
    key events, 46

renderers
    mixed or hybrid, 44
    Pure Hardware, 44–45
    Pure Software, 43–44
    touch events, 47–48
cbb.asIntBuffer( ) method, 79
cbb.order.ByteOrder.nativeOrder( )
    method, 79
cheat sheets, JNI, 267–269
    converting Java array to C array, 268
    invoking Java language within C
        language, 269
    loading Java class as global
        reference, 268
    method syntax, 268
chooseConfig( ) method, 131
Compilation file, 34
compiling, 19–34
    Android project with native support,
        21–22
    application architecture, 23–34
        main activity file, 25–26
        native interface, 26–27
        native library, 27–34
    icosahedron project, 143
    with NDK
        Doom for Android, 187–189
        Quake II, 252–255
ConfigChooser class, 128
config.getButtonCount( ) method, 57
config.getJoystickCount( ) method, 57
connect( ) method, 56
ContextFactory class, 128
ContextFactory( ) method, 128
controllerUi.startConnectionProcess( )
    method, 56
CreateGlEsInterface( ) method, 200
creating AVDs, 11–14
Cube class, 75, 77–79
cube file, native, 93
Cube( ) method, 76, 78, 86
cube renderers, native, 87–93
    drawing frames, 89–90
    Java callback, 91–92
    native interface function, 92–93
    scene initialization, 87

Cube_draw( ) method, 88–91, 94
CubeRenderer class, 74–77
CubeRenderer.drawFrame( ) method,
    87, 89
CubeRenderer.surfaceCreated( )
    method, 87
Cygwin tool, 10

D

development, native, 19–58
    Bluetooth controllers, Zeemote
        joystick, 53–58
    compiling code, 19–34
        Android project with native
            support, 21–22
        application architecture, 23–34
    Java wrappers for C/C++ event
        handling, 38–48
        of audio, 38–43
        cascading video events, 43–48
    multitouch schemes, 48–53
        MultiTouchGesture class, 48–50
        MultiTouchScreen class, 50–51
        TestActivity class, 52–53
    Open GL API, 80–98
        main activity, 82–84
        native cube file, 93
        native cube renderer, 87–93
        native interface class, 84–85
        sample, 85–87, 94–98
    shared library, compiling, 34–35
    testing app on device, 35–37
devices
    configuring, 15–16
    power of, 60–61
    testing applications on, 35–37
Displayed activity, 97–98
doNativeDraw( ) method, 86
Doom for Android, 145–192
    C to Java callbacks, 167, 174–180
        fatal errors, 180
        graphics initialization, 174–175
        sound and music callbacks,
            176–177
        video buffer callback, 176

changes to game, 181–187
  commenting SDL occurrences,
    182–183
  inserting fatal error callback, 182
  renaming main, 181–182
  sound system changes, 183
  video buffer changes, 184–187
compiling with NDK, 187–189
game architecture for, 151
handling audio independently of
    format, 164–165
and Java/C combo, 146–147
Java main activity, 151–163
  audio request handlers, 161
  creation handler, 152
  fatal error handler, 160–161
  game layout, 152–155
  graphics initialization handler,
    159
  image update handler, 159–160
  key and touch event handlers,
    157–158
  menu and selection handlers,
    155–156
  message updates, 160
  navigation controls, 162–163
native interface class, 165–167
  callback listener, 165–166
  native methods, 166
native method implementations,
    170–180
  key and motion events, 173
  native game loop, 171
overview, 149
testing in emulator, 189–191
draw( ) method, 66, 78
drawFrame( ) method, 75, 86–87,
    89–90, 93
drawing, zooming and, 107–111

▪E

EAS (Enhanced Audio System), 269
Eclipse platform, configuring, 2–9
e.getAction( ) method, 50, 139, 212

e.getPointerCount( ) method, 50–51,
    139
e.getX( ) method, 212
e.getY( ) method, 212
EGL (Embedded OpenGL), 72
eglChooseConfig( ) method, 121
EGLContext class, 80
EGLContext.getEGL( ) method, 80
egl.eglGetError( ) method, 129
EglHelper( ) method, 73
Embedded OpenGL (EGL), 72
Embedded System (ES), 60
emulators
  overview, 189–191
  running in Quake II, 255–258
Enhanced Audio System (EAS), 269
environments, 1–17
  AVDs, 10–14
  devices, configuring, 15–16
  Eclipse platform, configuring, 2–9
  NDK, installing, 9–10
  SDK, downloading and installing, 2
  setting up machine, 1–2
e.printStackTrace( ) method, 25, 68, 82
ES (Embedded System), 60
ES interface, 201
e.toString( ) method, 40, 157–158, 161,
    163, 168, 211
event.getAction( ) method, 47, 158
event.getButtonID( ) method, 57
event.getController( ) method, 56–57
event.getCurrentLevel( ) method, 56
event.getMaximumLevel( ) method, 56
event.getMinimumLevel( ) method, 56
event.getWarningLevel( ) method, 56
evt.getAction( ) method, 162–164
ex.printStackTrace( ) method, 73

▪F

fatal errors, handling for Quake II,
    245–248
FPS (frames per second), 45
Fragment Shader Language (FSL),
    115–117
fragment shaders, 114

frames, drawing, 89–90
frames per second (FPS), 45
FSL (Fragment Shader Language),
    115–117

G

game architecture
    for Doom, 151
    for Quake, 202–216
        game startup activity, 214–216
        handling audio independently of
            format, 207–210
        handling keyboard events,
            210–212
        handling touch events, 212–214
        Java OpenGL renderer
            architecture, 202–207
Game file, 149, 156
game layout, for Doom, 152–155
GameFileDownloader class, 151
G_CheckDemoStatus( ) method, 182
geometry shaders, 115
getConfigSpec( ) method, 75–76
geteuid( ) method, 239
getEvent( ) method, 73
getHolder( ) method, 68–69, 71
getSurfaceHolder( ) method, 69
getWindow( ) method, 52, 152, 215
getWindowManager( ) method, 52, 127,
    215
glClear( ) method, 76, 89–90
glCreateProgram( ) method, 118,
    135–136
glEnableClientState( ) method, 89
GLES interface, 197
glFlush( ) method, 218
gl.glLoadIdentity( ) method, 74, 76–77,
    89
glLoadIdentity( ) method, 74, 89–90
global references, loading Java classes
    as, 268
gl*Pointer( ) method, 78
GLSL (OpenGL ES 2.0 Shading
    Language), 115
GLSwapBuffers( ) method, 84–85, 87

GLThread class, 71–74
GLThread.surfaceCreated( ) method, 68
GLThread.surfaceDestroyed( ) method,
    69
gl_unimplemented( ) method, 197
GPU (Graphics Processing Unit), 43, 60
g.reset( ) method, 51
guardedRun( ) method, 71–73

H

handling audio, 38–43
    for Doom, 164–165
    for Quake, 207–210
hybrid renderers, 44
hybrid scaling, with Open GL API,
    99–111
    drawing into texture, 103–106
    initializing surface, 102
    reasons for, 99–102
    when image is not power of two,
        106–111

I

I (integer), 31
icosahedron project, 121–139
    activity, 127
    compiling, 143
    configuration chooser, 131–133
    manifest, 126–127
    pinching to zoom, 139–142
    project shaders, 134
    scene initialization, 135–137
    scene rendering, 137–138
    setting rotation speed, 138–139
    shape defined, 121–123
    surface renderer, 130–131
    surface view, 128–129
    swiping to change rotation speed,
        139–142
images, hybrid scaling when not power
    of two, 106–111
ImageView.getLayoutParams( ) method,
    159

immediate mode drawing, OpenGL ES
vs. OpenGL, 195–196
init( ) method, 69
InitGLStructs( ) method, 197, 199
init_scene( ) method, 87, 93
integer (I), 31
I_ShutdownGraphics( ) method, 182
isRunning( ) method, 40–41
item.getItemId( ) method, 156

■ J

jargon, for Quake, 193–194
Java activity, 21, 47, 58, 82
Java arrays
    converting string of into C array, 32
    converting to C array, 268
    getting size of, 33
Java/C combo, and Doom for Android,
146–147
Java callbacks, 91–92
Java class, 20, 27, 40, 61, 92, 180, 221,
236, 247, 268
Java heap, and Quake II, 234–235
Java language
    invoking static void method, 33
    invoking within C language, 269
    Open GL API in, 61–79
        Cube class, 77–79
        CubeRenderer class, 74–77
        example project, 62–66
        GLThread class, 71–74
        Java main activity, 67–68
        Surface View class, 68–71
Java main activity, for Doom, 151–163
    audio request handlers, 161
    creation handler, 152
    fatal error handler, 160–161
    game layout, 152–155
    graphics initialization handler, 159
    image update handler, 159–160
    key and touch event handlers,
        157–158
    menu and selection handlers,
        155–156
    message updates, 160

navigation controls, 162–163
Java method, 19, 23, 33, 46, 89, 103,
169, 176, 237, 245
Java Native Interface. See JNI
Java Virtual Machine (JVM), 30
Java wrappers, for C/C++ event
    handling, 38–48
    of audio, 38–43
    cascading video events, 43–48
JavaGLActivity.onCreate( ) method, 67
JIT (Just in Time), 38
JNI class, 43, 176
JNI (Java Native Interface), cheat sheet,
267–269
    converting Java array to C array, 268
    invoking Java language within C
        language, 269
    loading Java class as global
        reference, 268
    method syntax, 268
JNI method, 92, 178, 255
jni.Natives.LibMain( ) method, 33
jni.Natives.OnMessage( ) method, 37
Just in Time (JIT), 38
JVM (Java Virtual Machine), 30

■ K

key events, 46
key stores, 262

■ L

libraries
    compiling shared, 34–35
    native, 27–34
listener.GLSwapBuffers( ) method, 85
loading, shaders, 118–119

■ M

MAC (message authentication code), 54
main activity
    files, 25–26
    Java, 67–68
    Open GL API, 82–84

main( ) method, 31, 181
mEglHelper.finish( ) method, 73–74
mEglHelper.swap( ) method, 74, 87
message authentication code (MAC), 54
method syntax, JNI, 268
mGLSurfaceView.onPause( ) method,
    68, 83
mGLSurfaceView.onResume( ) method,
    68, 83
mGLThread.onPause( ) method, 70
mGLThread.onResume( ) method, 70
mGLThread.requestExitAndWait( )
    method, 71
mGLThread.start( ) method, 70–71, 86
mGLThread.surfaceCreated( ) method,
    70
mGLThread.surfaceDestroyed( )
    method, 70
mixed renderers, 44
MotionEvent type, 141
mRenderer.getConfigSpec( ) method,
    73
mTrack.play( ) method, 40, 208
multitouch schemes, 48–53
    MultiTouchGesture class, 48–50
    MultiTouchScreen class, 50–51
    TestActivity class, 52–53
MultiTouchGesture class, 48–50
MultiTouchGesture.eGestureType type,
    49
MultiTouchScreen class, 50–52
mView.getLayoutParams( ) method, 159
MyApp( ) method, 20

N

NanoGL, for Quake, 197–202
NanoGL interface, 200
nanoGL_Destroy( ) method, 199–200
nanoGL_Init( ) method, 199–200, 217,
    249
Native activity, 83
native cube file, 93
native cube renderers, 87–93
    drawing frames, 89–90
    Java callback, 91–92

native interface function, 92–93
scene initialization, 87
native development, 19–58
    Bluetooth controllers, Zeemote
        joystick, 53–58
    compiling code, 19–34
        Android project with native
            support, 21–22
        application architecture, 23–34
    Java wrappers for C/C++ event
        handling, 38–48
        of audio, 38–43
        cascading video events, 43–48
    multitouch schemes, 48–53
        MultiTouchGesture class, 48–50
        MultiTouchScreen class, 50–51
        TestActivity class, 52–53
    Open GL API, 80–98
        main activity, 82–84
        native cube file, 93
        native cube renderer, 87–93
        native interface class, 84–85
        sample, 85–87, 94–98
    shared library, compiling, 34–35
    testing app on device, 35–37
Native Development Kit (NDK),
    installing, 9–10
native interface class
    for Doom, 165–167
        callback listener, 165–166
        native methods, 166
    overview, 84–85
native interface function, 92–93
native interfaces, 26–27
native libraries, 27–34
    defining variable-arguments function
        in C language, 33–34
    invoking Java static void method, 33
    Java arrays
        converting string of into C array,
            32
        getting size of, 33
Native method, 169
NativeAudio class, 209
NativeAudio.start( ) method, 204, 209,
    245, 252

NativeRender( ) method, 84–85
Natives class, 28, 30, 33, 91, 170–171, 205
Natives.EventListener interface, 158
Natives.java class, 237
Natives.NativeRender( ) method, 86
Natives.OnMessage method, 33
Natives.RenderFrame( ) method, 203
navigation controls, for Doom, 162–163
NDK, compiling with, Doom for Android, 187–189
NDK (Native Development Kit), installing, 9–10

O

OnCloseAudio( ) method, 40, 42
onCreate( ) method, 72, 152
onDestroy( ) method, 72
onDetachedFromWindow( ) method, 70–71
OnImageUpdate( ) method, 172
OnLockAudio( ) method, 40–41
onPause( ) method, 68, 70, 83
onResume( ) method, 68, 70, 83
OnUnLockAudio( ) method, 41
Open GL API
    hybrid scaling with, 99–111
        drawing into texture, 103–106
        initializing surface, 102
        reasons for, 99–102
        when image is not power of two, 106–111
    in Java language, 61–79
        Cube class, 77–79
        CubeRenderer class, 74–77
        example project, 62–66
        GLThread class, 71–74
        Java main activity, 67–68
        Surface View class, 68–71
    native development, 80–98
        main activity, 82–84
        native cube file, 93
        native cube renderer, 87–93
        native interface class, 84–85
        sample, 85–87, 94–98

power of devices, 60–61
OpenGL ES
    vs. OpenGL, 195–196
        floating point issues, 196
        immediate mode drawing, 195–196
OpenGL ES 1.x, vs. OpenGL ES 2.0, 120–121
OpenGL ES 2.0, 113–120
    fragment shaders, 114
    FSL, 115–117
    geometry shaders, 115
    GLSL, 115
    icosahedron project, 121–139
        activity, 127
        compiling, 143
        configuration chooser, 131–133
        manifest, 126–127
        pinching to zoom, 139–142
        project shaders, 134
        scene initialization, 135–137
        scene rendering, 137–138
        setting rotation speed, 138–139
        shape defined, 121–123
        surface renderer, 130–131
        surface view, 128–129
        swiping to change rotation speed, 139–142
    vs. OpenGL ES 1.x, 120–121
    shaders, 114–120
        attaching to shader, 119
        creating program, 117–118
        getting link status, 119
        linking shader program, 119
        loading shader, 118–119
        program validation and status, 120
        using program, 120
    vertex shaders, 114
    VSL, 115
OpenGL ES 2.0 Shading Language (GLSL), 115
OpenGL immediate mode, and Quake II, 248
OpenGL interface, 200
opengl.jni.Natives.NativeRender( ) method, 92

P

performance, of Quake II, 258–259
pinching to zoom, icosahedron project,
    139–142
PixelFormat class, 69
preloadSounds( ) method, 164
projects, icosahedron, 121–139
    activity, 127
    compiling, 143
    configuration chooser, 131–133
    manifest, 126–127
    pinching to zoom, 139–142
    project shaders, 134
    scene initialization, 135–137
    scene rendering, 137–138
    setting rotation speed, 138–139
    shape defined, 121–123
    surface renderer, 130–131
    surface view, 128–129
    swiping to change rotation speed,
        139–142
Pure Hardware renderers, 44–45
Pure Software renderer, 43–44

Q

qglFlush( ) method, 252
Quake for Android, 193–232
    changes to game, 216–225
        audio handler changes, 220–221
        fixing game loop, 223–225
        handling forward and side
            movement, 220
        handling pitch and yaw, 219–220
        video handler changes, 216–218
    game architecture, 202–216
        game startup activity, 214–216
        handling audio independently of
            format, 207–210
        handling keyboard events,
            210–212
        handling touch events, 212–214
        Java OpenGL renderer
            architecture, 202–207
    jargon for, 193–194

NanoGL for, 197–202
OpenGL vs. OpenGL ES, 195–196
    floating point issues, 196
    immediate mode drawing,
        195–196
    running on device, 225–229
Quake II for Android, 233–260
    code reusability, 236–245
        audio handling, 243–245
        game startup, 237–238
        handling key events, 241
        moving in 3D space, 241–243
        rendering single frame, 238–241
    compiling with NDK, 252–255
    handling fatal errors, 245–248
    and Java heap needed, 234–235
    OpenGL immediate mode issues,
        248
    performance of, 258–259
    running on device or emulator,
        255–258
    video handlers, 248–252
        setting video mode and size,
            249–252
        video initialization, 249
        when rendering completes, 252
QuakeRenderer( ) method, 203
QuakeView class, 248, 255

R

Renderer interface, 63–64, 67, 74
renderers
    mixed or hybrid, 44
    Pure Hardware, 44–45
    Pure Software, 43–44
RenderFrame( ) method, 205–206,
    224–225, 237–240
requestFocus( ) method, 203
reset( ) method, 49
r.run( ) method, 73
run( ) method, 40, 46, 72, 129, 160–161,
    208, 210–212
Runnable( ) method, 40, 46, 129,
    160–161, 208, 210–212

running
on device, Quake II, 255–258
in emulator, Quake II, 255–258
Quake for Android, 225–229

▉ S

scaling, hybrid, 99–111
drawing into texture, 103–106
initializing surface, 102
reasons for, 99–102
when image is not power of two,
106–111
scenes, initializing, 87
SD Card, 13
SDKs (Software Development Kits),
downloading and installing, 2
sEglSemaphore.acquire( ) method,
71–72
sEglSemaphore.release( ) method, 71,
73
seteuid.getuid( ) method, 239
setGameUI( ) method, 152
setRenderer( ) method, 71
setupPanControls( ) method, 152, 163
shaders, 114–120
attaching to, 119
creating program, 117–118
getting link status, 119
linking program, 119
loading, 118–119
program validation and status, 120
using program, 120
ShadersActivity class, 139
ShadersView object, 127
Software Development Kits (SDKs),
downloading and installing, 2
start( ) method, 208–209
static void method, Java language,
invoking, 33
stop( ) method, 39, 41–42
string arrays, Java, converting into C
array, 32
super( ) method, 72
super.onDetachedFromWindow( )
method, 70

super.onPause( ) method, 68, 83
super.onResume( ) method, 68, 83
Surface View class, 68–71
surfaceCreated( ) method, 69
SurfaceHolder.addCallback( ) method,
68
surfaces, initializing, 102
swapBuffers( ) method, 74
SysError( ) method, 206
System class, 207
System.currentTimeMillis( ) method, 130

▉ T

TestActivity class, 52–53
testing in emulator, Doom for Android,
189–191
textures, drawing into, 103–106
touch events, 47–48
t.start( ) method, 41

▉ U

UI (user interface), 192
USB driver, 15–16
user interface (UI), 192

▉ V

variable-arguments functions, defining
in C language, 33–34
vbb.asIntBuffer( ) method, 79
vbb.order.ByteOrder.nativeOrder( )
method, 78
Vertex Shader Language (VSL), 115
vertex shaders, 114
video, cascading events, 43–48
key events, 46
renderers, 43–45
touch events, 47–48
video handlers, for Quake II, 248–252
setting video mode and size,
249–252
video initialization, 249
when rendering completes, 252

View.OnTouchListener( ) method,
162–163
ViewRenderer( ) method, 128–129
VSL (Vertex Shader Language), 115

W

wait( ) method, 73

X, Y

XML file, 126

Z

zee.connect( ) method, 58
Zeemote class, 58
Zeemote joystick, 53–58
zooming, and drawing, 107–111

CPSIA information can be obtained at www.ICGtesting.com
Printed in the USA
LVOW090604110412

277098LV00003BA/53/P